A Pioneer
in Yokohama

*A Dutchman's Adventures
in the New Treaty Port*

C. T. ASSENDELFT DE CONINGH

A Pioneer
in Yokohama

*A Dutchman's Adventures
in the New Treaty Port*

From *Ontmoetingen ter Zee en te Land*

Edited and Translated,
with an Introduction, by
MARTHA CHAIKLIN

Hackett Publishing Company, Inc.
Indianapolis/Cambridge

Copyright © 2012 by Hackett Publishing Company, Inc.

15 14 13 12   1 2 3 4 5 6 7

For further information, please address
Hackett Publishing Company, Inc.
P.O. Box 44937
Indianapolis, Indiana 46244-0937

www.hackettpublishing.com

Interior design by Elizabeth L. Wilson
Composition by Innodata-Isogen, Inc.
Printed at Data Reproductions Corporation

Library of Congress Cataloging-in-Publication Data

Assendelft de Coningh, C. T. van (Cornelis Theodoor), 1821–1890.
  [Ontmoetingen ter zee en te land. Volume 2. English]
  A pioneer in Yokohama : a Dutchman's adventures in the new treaty port ;
from Ontmoetingen ter zee en te land / C.T. Assendelft de Coningh ; edited and
translated, with an introduction, by Martha Chaiklin.
       p. cm.
  Translation of 2nd volume of memoir entitled Ontmoetingen ter zee en te
land [Adventures at sea and on land], published in 1879 by W.C. De Graaff,
Haarlem, Netherlands.
  Includes bibliographical references and index.
  ISBN 978-1-60384-836-7 (paper) — ISBN 978-1-60384-837-4 (cloth)
  1. Assendelft de Coningh, C. T. van (Cornelis Theodoor), 1821–1890. 2.
Dutch—Japan—Yokohama-shi—Biography. 3. Merchants—Japan—Yokohama-
shi—Biography. 4. Yokohama-shi (Japan)—Biography. 5. Yokohama-shi
(Japan)—Description and travel. 6. Yokohama-shi (Japan)—History—19th
century. 7. Yokohama-shi (Japan)—Social life and customs—19th century. 8.
Netherlands—Relations—Japan. 9. Japan—Relations—Netherlands. I. Chaiklin,
Martha, 1960– II. Title.
  DS897.Y69D82713 2012
  952'.1364031092—dc23
  [B]   2012020501

∞

CONTENTS

A NOTE ON THE TRANSLATION AND ACKNOWLEDGMENTS

Although the author of this work had literary aspirations, its value to twenty-first century readers is historical. C. T. Assendelft de Coningh offers a unique account of a time period that is as fascinating as it is poorly documented. For this reason, I have kept the translation fairly literal. Place names and Japanese words are transcribed as in the original manuscript. Edo, the original name for Tokyo, is thus variously transcribed as Jeddo or Jedo. De Coningh, like many Dutch people, had a wide knowledge of other languages that he inserts frequently into the text; to turn all of the foreign phrases in his manuscript into English would alter his voice. English words in De Coningh's original manuscript are here shown in quotes. Likewise, De Coningh's footnotes are denoted with an asterisk, while mine are numbered.

I would like to take this opportunity to thank the many friends and some total strangers whose expertise I called on to untangle this idiosyncratic text:

First must be Marten Brienen because he called dibs on first. Simon J. Bytheway reassured me several times that this was a worthwhile project. In addition to Marten, many people answered my very odd questions out of pure altruism. These included John Lundstrom, Rudger van Dijk, Isabel van Daalen, Tim Couch, and Jeff Crowell. Other people assisted in various ways, including Margarita Winkel, James Hommes, Christopher Neander, and Tarik Allen. Some of the research was conducted with financial assistance from the Fulbright Foundation and the University of Pittsburgh. If I've forgotten to thank anyone for their help with this project, I hope they will believe I've done so only as a result of my poor record keeping and not because I'm ungrateful. I am also indebted to Rick Todhunter, Christina Kowalewski, and everyone at Hackett Publishing Company for giving this project a home. Finally I wish to thank my parents, Harris and Sharon, my sons, Samuel and David, and my friends Laura Mitchell and Kerry Ward. You are my rocks in the typhoon of life.

Despite all this help, all the mistakes are mine and mine alone.

C. T. Assendelft de Coningh, ca. 1850. Courtesy of Reinoud van Assendelft de Coningh.

INTRODUCTION

Threatened by the activities of Western missionaries, the Japanese military bureaucracy known as the Tokugawa Shogunate expelled all Westerners, save for the Dutch, from the country by 1639. The shogunate—formed in 1603 after more than a century of civil war fought along quasi-feudal lines—chose to impose this isolationism as a defense against a perceived conflict of loyalties engendered by conversions to Catholicism. To the Shogun, such demands for alliance with Rome conflicted with the oaths of allegiance Japanese warlords were required to make to the shogunate, and so threatened to undermine Japanese sovereignty and stability. Moreover, the conversion of various Japanese leaders to Christianity seemed to endanger the Shoguns' hard-won political unity.

In the 215 years that followed, Japan remained "closed" to any overtures made by Western countries. But the Japanese tolerated employees of the Dutch East India Company because the Company was a secular institution more interested in making a profit than in spreading religious doctrine. Moreover, the Company had made a number of concessions to the Shogunate in order to establish a monopoly on direct trade with Japan. They agreed to reside only on Deshima (or as De Coningh spells it, Decima), a small artificial island in the harbor at Nagasaki; restrict the number of traders working in Japan; prohibit the presence of women and churches; and submit to the confiscation of any religious materials while in port. Even with their monopoly secured, however, the once promising Dutch trade with Japan eventually shrank to a mere trickle of money and goods.

Then, in 1850, the United States government—inspired by the doctrine of Manifest Destiny, effectively banned from China, and desiring trade (especially whaling) and trans-Pacific sea routes—decided to "open" Japan. Through gunboat diplomacy, Commodore Mathew Perry was able to extract from the shogunate a simple supply treaty, the Treaty of Kanagawa in 1854; American Consul Townsend Harris then negotiated the treaties that opened Japanese ports to free trade in 1859. Because the Dutch political stance was staunchly free market, their official representatives were actively employed as middlemen in negotiating terms between the Japanese and Americans, thus giving them a unique perspective on one of the most important events in world history. A unique middleman of a different sort, merchant and sea captain Cornelis Theodoor Assendelft de Coningh witnessed life in Japan both before and immediately after the "opening" and left us a vivid, detailed, and lively account of his time there.

VAN ASSENDELFT DE CONINGH.

The Assendelft de Coningh coat of arms. The black eagle was from the De Coningh Family, the silver horse from the Assendelfts. Other maternal lineage was represented by the red star on gold ground (Van Carlingen) and crown over two salmon (Storm). This combined arms dates from the mid-eighteenth century. A. A. Vorsterman van Oijen, *Stam- en wapenboek van aanzienlijke Nederlandsche familiën, met genealogische en heraldische aanteekeningen*, Part 1, plate 20. Image courtesy of Walter Andreas Groen.

Who was C. T. Assendelft de Coningh?

Cornelis Theodoor Assendelft de Coningh—"Cees" to his friends—was born in Arnhem, a city located in the East Netherlands, on March 5, 1821. He was probably named after his paternal grandmother, Cornelia Theodora van der Houven. Though most of the men in his family were merchants connected to both the Dutch East and West India Companies since at least the early eighteenth century, his father Arie served in the *garde d'honneur* of Napoleon's army, an elite cavalry troop that fought at the Battle of Leipzig. After Napoleon's defeat, Arie volunteered for the Dutch army. Cornelis described his father as a "scholarly and overall extremely enlightened man, who was at least a quarter-century ahead of his time." Through assiduous parental tutoring both Cornelis and his brother Dirk advanced rapidly in school and passed the examinations required to join the Royal Netherlands Naval College (Koninklijk Instituut voor de Marine) at Medemblik, a prestigious institution located in northwestern Holland. (Founded in 1827 by King Willem I, the college is still in operation today.) Cornelis wanted to join the navy and Dirk wanted to be an engineer.[1]

As the time for their departure for school approached, Arie was visited by H. C. van der Houven, then the president of the Netherlands Trading Society (Nederlandsche Handel Maatschappij, or NHM). Though the society—a hybrid organization that had emerged from the ashes of the Dutch East India Company in 1824—was a publicly traded company, the largest shareholder was the king of the Netherlands. (The NHM later went through a number of changes, including a move into finance, and survives today as ABN AMRO Bank.) De Coningh described van der Houven as a venerable man, with powdered hair and striking eyes, who had a great influence upon his father. Van der Houven offered to place the young Cornelis under "our best Captain, Lanberg," on a ship to Batavia. "You know," he said, "that it is sometimes rather raw on board, but the beginning is always difficult." Arie "was not one to spare his children some raw treatment," and thus at age fifteen De Coningh's career was decided—a career he pursued for the rest of his life, spanning some thirty years and twenty voyages.[2] De Coningh's time in the NHM was filled with adventure, right to the very end; on his final voyage in their employ in 1851, he and his crew saved 676 sailors from the Danish supply brig *Thorwaldsen* who were stranded on an island somewhere between Batavia (Djakarta) and India. He subsequently received medals from both the South Holland Society and the government of Denmark in honor of these efforts.[3]

1. C. T. Assendelft de Coningh, *Ontmoetingen ter zee en te land.* vol. 1 (Haarlem: W. C. de Graaff, 1879), 4.

2. Ibid., 4–5.

3. AdeC 135 and 136.

In 1852 De Coningh established himself as a shipping agent in Amsterdam.[4] It was probably at this time that he made the connections with J. P. Carst and Murk Lels who were to become his first partners in Japan; he also wrote his first and most successful book, *Mijn verblijf in Japan* [*My Sojourn in Japan*], published in 1856. In 1859, De Coningh went to Japan again, this time as a private merchant, and his recollections of this later trip are related in the second part of the narrative that follows this Introduction. He left Japan in 1861, settling in the Netherlands for good in 1862. In this same year he was named a member of the Royal Netherlands Institute for Southeast Asian and Caribbean Studies (Koninklijk Instituut voor de Taal-, Land- en Volkenkunde van Nederlandsch-Indie, or KITLV), a research organization still located in Leiden. His further efforts to promote understanding between his own people and those of distant lands earned him membership in the Dutch–South African Association (Nederlansche Zuid Afrikaansche Vereeniging), which appears to have been devoted to the exchange of scholarly information and the support of Afrikaaner students. This interest in African matters must have been born during his years at sea because prior to the opening of the Suez Canal in 1869, ships leaving Europe almost inevitably stopped at the Cape. The De Coningh family archives show that he maintained at least one relationship there, as is evidenced by a letter to S. J. Du Toit in Pretoria, to whom he'd written in order to obtain positions for some brothers from Haarlem.[5]

De Coningh married Maria Elisabeth Steendijk (1832–1862) in 1854, and had three children with her. Although younger than De Coningh, Maria died in 1862. In 1868 he remarried to Wilhemina Johanna Vlek, who was seventeen years his junior, having three more children with her. In 1871 his family moved to Haarlem, where he remained until his death on February 28, 1890.[6] If not for his writings, these brief biographical details would comprise most of what we know about C. T. Assendelft de Coningh.

4. F. Smit Klein, *Levensbericht van C. Th. Assendelft de Coningh* (Leiden: E. J. Brill, 1891), 4.

5. AdeC 138.

6. Information on De Coningh's marriages and progeny from G. M. van Aalst, *Archief van de familie van Assendelft de Coningh 1645–1959* (Rijksarchief: The Hague, 1975), 13.

De Coningh in Japan

The Dutch relationship with Japan began in 1600 with the arrival of the *Liefde*, the sole survivor of a fleet of five that had departed from the Netherlands, in Usuki Bay. Regular trade commenced when the Dutch East India Company, founded in 1602 through the union of several smaller companies, established a factory in the port of Hirado in 1609. Although Portuguese and Spanish traders had preceded the Dutch, followed closely by the English, by 1639 the Dutch were the only Western nation with whom the Japanese would maintain trading relations. The English East India Company left in 1623 after an unprofitable decade. Suspicious of Christianity and its implications for conquest, the Shogunate expelled Spanish traders in 1624. The Portuguese were expelled for similar reasons in 1639. In a series of edicts, now known as the *sakoku*, or "closed country" edicts, the Japanese rulers also prohibited their own people from going abroad. By 1641, Dutch traders were required to live on a fan-shaped artificial island, only about 1,850 feet in circumference, that had originally been constructed to house the now-banned Portuguese. Thereafter, most interaction between the Dutch merchants and Japanese officials occurred through the offices of hereditary families of interpreters. Yoshio Sakunojō and Nakayama Sakusaburō, who appear in this book, both came from this kind of family. As is evident in De Coningh's description, this practice resulted in interpreters of very uneven talent.

After the Portuguese were expelled, the port of Nagasaki was placed under the direct control of the shogunate. This could be done with a minimum of fuss because the port had been granted to the Portuguese by the local *daimyo* and therefore did not belong to any particular domain. For most of the seventeenth century, trade between the Dutch and Japanese flourished, and was profitable for both sides. In the early eighteenth century, faced with fiscal difficulties, the shogunate restricted exports of precious and base metals; this decision hurt Dutch profits, and the Dutch East India Company's trade with Japan entered a period of slow decline. This decline was hastened when Napoleon's troops occupied the Netherlands from 1795 to 1813, and the East India Company went bankrupt. The Dutch merchants stranded on Deshima survived by occasionally chartering American, Danish, and Norwegian ships for the purposes of trade. Following a brief period of private trade by factory employees, the Dutch factory came under the control of the Nederlandsche Handel Maatschappij—De Coningh's employer. Although these changes signified radical changes in the political landscape of Europe, and in how

Japanese trade was handled on the European side, the trade system within Japan continued under more or less the same conditions, as if nothing had changed for the Dutch stationed there.

De Coningh traveled to Japan three times in his life: first as a sailor, then as a ship's captain, and finally as a merchant. On his first visit, under Captain Landberg on the *Elshout* in 1845, De Coningh was just a helmsman. As the Japanese—tired of rowdy sailors and wanting to limit contact with the rest of the world—had, a hundred years prior to his visit, ruled that only the captains of visiting ships could disembark, De Coningh was required to stay on the ship. He later wrote of having to satisfy himself with looking at the luxuriant banks of the bay in the hope that he would be able to return again to this beautiful land in more favorable circumstances.[7]

De Coningh was captain on his next visit in 1851, and was able to spend a total of about three months on the island. Aged only 30 at the time, this rapid promotion in ranks reflected his natural abilities as a seaman—and, probably, how well-connected his family was. This trip proved rich fodder for his literary aspirations, providing the material for his first book, *Mijn verblijf in Japan*, and the first chapter of this book. His ship, *Joän*, carried a cargo primarily of sugar and sappanwood (used for red dye); the return cargo was mostly copper and camphor. Soon after the events of this second voyage, Japan entered a period of radical change. The Treaty of Kanagawa exacted by Commodore Perry—an expedition one Japanese writer called the "White Disaster"[8]—only provided for the treatment of castaways and the refueling and resupplying of passing ships; it did not permit American ships to remain in Japanese ports, nor did it permit any legal trade between the two countries. The treaties that allowed free trade in restricted ports were first hammered out by Townsend Harris in 1856 and then renegotiated in 1858; these were soon followed by Japanese treaties with the rest of the so-called "Five Powers"—Russia, Great Britain, France, and the Netherlands. Initially, the ports of Nagasaki, Kanagawa, and Hakodate were opened to trade, while Niigata and Hyogo were opened soon after. Though Niigata never really developed as an important port, Hyogo (Kobe) quickly developed into a vibrant treaty port, second only to Yokohama, following its opening in 1868.

7. C. T. Assendelft de Coningh, *Mijn verblijf in Japan* (Amsterdam: Gebroeders Kraay, 1856), 1–2.

8. Okakura Kakuzo, *The Awakening of Japan* (New York: The Century Company, 1904), chap. 5.

Frontispiece from C. T. Assendelft de Coningh's first book, *Mijn verblijf in Japan*, 1856.

These unique "treaty ports" that opened in the latter half of the nineteenth century represented an attempt to balance East Asia's need for isolation and the West's increasingly aggressive imperialism, and were opened in Asia only under threat of force from the West. They were "environments, which were neither part of the internal Japanese trading system nor under total control of the Western Treaty Powers."[9] This system, inherited from China, had two provisions that were especially hateful to the Japanese: extraterritoriality and the loss of tariff control. Thus the treaty ports, with their large populations of non-Japanese residents, remained an essentially Western milieu. In Japan, treaty ports did not last into the next century—the treaties were revised in 1899— although they lasted until the Second World War in China.

After more than two hundred years of restricted contact with the outside world, submission to Western gunboat diplomacy exacerbated existing tensions between some members of the military class—known as *shishi*, or "righteous men"—and the shogunate. The *shishi* sought to restore the emperor as the center of government, and expel the so-called barbarians. With only a shallow understanding of the Japanese political system, the foreigners living in Yokohama referred to these men as *rōnin*, a term that actually refers to a masterless samurai. The presence of *shishi* dramatically shaped the lives of those in Yokohama.

In 1859, just after the treaties went into effect, De Coningh arrived in the newly opened port of Yokohama on his final journey to Japan. According to the treaties, Kanagawa was to have become the "treaty port," but the Japanese authorities moved the site of the free-trade harbor to Yokohama, building customs houses and residences there. The Japanese preferred Yokohama because, as the map shows, it was isolated from the mainland by a river, rather like Deshima. Kanagawa was also very close to the Tokaidō, a main road leading to the shogunal capital of Edo (Tokyo). It was feared that placing the foreigners too close to Edo might cause conflict, a fear that was borne out in what became known as the "Richardson Affair" or "Namamugi Incident" in 1862, after De Coningh's departure. (An Englishman, Charles Richardson, refused to halt in front of the train of the Satsuma *daimyo* and was slain by the guards in the retinue.) Moreover, Yokohama was a geographically better location for the intrepid Westerners, who could be protected from radical *shishi* there by both warships and shogunal forces.

William Gragg was a marine on the U.S.S. *Mississippi,* a sidewheel steamer anchored in the harbor in June 1859, just before the ports opened. He wrote that, "we found that fifty to seventy fine new buildings

9. Yuki Allyson Honjo, *Japan's Early Experience of Contract Management in the Treaty Ports* (London: Japan Library, 2003), 29.

had been erected in Kanagawa and at Yokohama, such as dwellings and stores, in anticipation of the opening of the ports for trade. . . ."[10] While the Western consular officials objected to this change of venue and remained in Kanagawa, the majority of merchants preferred Yokohama because Kanagawa had shoals and sand banks that were unsafe and required ships to anchor far out. Yokohama was simply a better harbor. The impasse was broken when Dr. George Hall, of the American firm Walsh & Co., preemptively procured what became known as Bund No. 2, and the firms Jardine Matheson and Dent & Co. followed immediately thereafter.[11]

Jardine Matheson (rep. William Keswick[12]), Dent & Co. (rep. Edward Clarke), Sassoon (rep. C. T. Elmstone), Walsh & Co. (rep. Richard Walsh), and Augustine Heard (rep. T. H. King) were major trading firms in Japan whose representatives are mentioned in this text. These companies played a significant role in the economic life of treaty ports all over East Asia. The first three were British (or Anglo-Persian in the case of Sassoon), the latter two were American. Broadly speaking, these firms sold opium and manufactured goods like textiles in China and purchased silk and tea to bring to the West. Trade was competitive and risky. Smaller merchants rose and fell rapidly. Even the large Dent and Augustine Heard companies closed down after about a decade. But Walsh & Co. lasted through the turn of the century, while Jardine Matheson and Sassoon still exist today. The vicissitudes of De Coningh's business ventures in Japan are no exception to this harshly competitive environment.

Not much is known about De Coningh's business in Japan beyond the hints given in his narrative. We know from this text that his firm exported silk, the most significant export out of Yokohama in the nineteenth century, and that he dabbled in gold. Though De Coningh makes light of his involvement in the gold trade, there is some evidence that he was more actively involved in this trade than he suggests. A shipment recorded by the *Hellespont* on December 3, 1859, shows De Coningh & Co. receiving a shipment of two thousand coins (one hundred more

10. William Gragg, *A Cruise in the U.S. Steam Frigate Mississippi: Wm. C. Nicholson, Captain, to China and Japan* (Boston: Damrell and Moore, 1860), 67.

11. Joseph Heco, *The Narrative of a Japanese* (San Francisco: American Japanese Publishing Association, n.d.), vol. 1, 216–17. Some sources, but none contemporary, say Keswick was first, perhaps because Jardine Matheson was at No. 1. Walsh, however, always took No. 2 in all treaty ports.

12. William Keswick (1834–1912) went on to head Jardine Matheson.

xviii   Introduction

even than the diplomat he criticizes, Dirk de Graeff van Polesbroek). As each coin was valued at $3.50, this was quite a significant amount.[13]

As to what he imported, there are references in the book to medicine and red Moroccan leather in his warehouse. A "market report" authored by De Coningh dated October 1, 1859, or less than a month after his arrival, recommended goods similar to the days of the NHM, including various kinds of textiles such as duffel and flannel, saffron, medicines, sugar in loaves, mirrors, and especially gin. For export he recommended food to be resold in China, as well as copper and gold coins.[14] Advertisements in the *Japan Herald*, Yokohama's first newspaper, show that in 1861 De Coningh's firm sold coal and oil casks, and in 1862 pianos and champagne as well.[15] Subsequently, De Coningh partnered with J. P. Carst (d. 1866)[16] and Murk Lels (1823–1891) and opened a branch in Nagasaki,[17] but this partnership apparently did not last. Carst & Lels continued into the next decade in Yokohama, but De Coningh went his own way as De Coningh & Co. As De Coningh himself did not return to Japan, it is unclear who oversaw his business in Japan. In 1868, De Coningh went into partnership with Augustus Scipion Vernede (1836–1877).[18] Some of the problems De Coningh and Vernede encountered are evident in a lawsuit brought against De Coningh & Co. in 1868 by a certain W. Heije. (At issue were guns that Heije had consigned to the former De Coningh & Co. in 1864. Mr. Heije thought he had been unjustly compensated and accused De Coningh and his partner of negligence. He lost both his case and the appeal, however, and was forced

13. John McMaster, "The Japanese Gold Rush of 1859," *The Journal of Asian Studies* 19, no. 3 (May 1960): 282.

14. "Marktberigt van de Coning, Carst & Lels, te Kanagawa (bij Jeddo) Japan, van October 1859," *De Economist*, vol. 9 (1860): 85–88.

15. *Japan Herald,* nos. 1–5, 1861.

16. The Carsts had a family plot in Yokohama and several members are buried there. From the names in the plot, it might be surmised that J. P. stood for Jan Pieter.

17. Mentioned in a letter to A. J. Bauduin, the Dutch consul on Deshima, in a letter to his sister on July 10, 1862, in the context of his task of disposing of the estate of N. C. Sieburgh, an employee of De Coningh, Carst & Lels. Quoted in Joshua Fogel, *Articulating the Sinosphere: Sino-Japanese Relations in Space and Time* (Cambridge, MA: Harvard University Press, 2009), 61.

18. According to a newspaper announcement, the new company was formed after the dissolution of De Coningh's partnership with Jan Coenraad Schoot and Jan Willem Fredrik Roose Haverkamp, all of Amsterdam. *Algemene Handelsblad*, No. 11068 June 27, 1867, 6.

to pay court costs.)[19] The partnership of De Coningh, Vernede & Co. is noted as being active in Yokohama and Hyogo (Kobe) in 1869, the latter of which had just opened to foreign residence in 1868.[20] This firm was in business at least until 1870 but was also short-lived. The *Japan Gazette Hong List and Directory* for 1874 shows only A. Vernede as resident on the Bluff in Yokohama, but there is no trace of the firm.

When De Coningh first moved to Yokohama, that city was in its earliest—and roughest—stages of becoming a Western settlement. Few other Westerners had arrived,[21] the amenities of city life were virtually unknown, and residents had no means by which to contact the rest of the world. In addition to a stark sense of isolation, early foreign merchants like De Coningh suffered through a period of significant political unrest in Japan. As the assassinations and fires described in *A Pioneer in Yokohama* show, the merchants had good reason to be concerned. As far as we can tell, De Coningh has not dramatized the fears of the early settlers for literary effect. In fact, he sent a letter to the Minister of Colonies in March of 1860 urgently requesting a warship for protection. Unfortunately this letter was not even forwarded to the Ministry of Foreign Affairs until seven months later, in October.[22]

Events in China soon distracted Western governments, making life even harder for the early emigrants to Japan. De Coningh's writings make apparent how much the events in China affected life in Yokohama. The treaty port system, already established in China in 1842, was taking hold all along that country's coast, increasing pressure on, and competition between, the Western powers. Meanwhile, the Taiping Rebellion was in full bloom, and the Arrow War (also called the Second Anglo-Chinese War or the Second Opium War, which lasted from 1856 to 1860) diverted all the Western gunships from Japan, leaving the settlers there unprotected. Yet the fact that Japan could provide many of the same goods as China—at greater profit, and with far less competition—made the emigrants' presence there all the more valuable. Supplies were sought

19. B. J. Lindtelo De Geer and Mr. van Benval Fauve, *Regtsgeleerd bijblad, behoorende nieuwe bijblagen* (Amsterdam: Johannes Müller, 1868), 18: 500–3.

20. Karl von Scherzer, *Fachmännische Berichte über österreich-ungarische Expedition nach Siam, China und Japan, 1868–1871* (Stuttgart: Julius van Maier, 1872), 269, 372.

21. Records for New Year's Day of 1860 list eighteen British, fifteen Americans, ten Dutch, and one French, although this does not include the foreigners in Kanagawa. Kato Yuzo, ed., *Yokohama Past and Present* (Yokohama: Yokohama City University, 1990), 28.

22. BUZA 3142.

from Japan for both foodstuffs and horses, which adversely affected the cost of living in Yokohama. After the Convention of Peking was signed in 1860, the treaty powers could better enforce their position in Japan.

The final pages of De Coningh's book allude to events that clearly affected him and his business interests in Japan, even though they occurred after he'd left. In the two years following De Coningh's departure, friction had increased on all fronts: within the shogunate, between the shogunate and the Imperial House, and between the Japanese and the Westerners. These tensions finally came to a head in 1863 in Shimonoseki, a city in the Chōshū domain (today it is Yamaguchi Prefecture) that stood along the Shimonoseki Straits, a narrow channel between Honshu—the main island of Japan—and the southern island Kyushu. Chōshū had been relegated to the lower, secondary class of *daimyo* known as *tozama* because its rulers had sided against the founder of the Tokugawa Shogunate in 1600 and were subsequently barred from positions of power. Chōshū then allied itself with the radical emperor Kōmei (reigned 1846–1867). Both Kōmei and the Chōshū leaders were anti-foreign, believing that Western presence should be barred from Japan again. In 1863 Kōmei was persuaded to sign an order expelling the "barbarians," against the wishes of the shogunate. Mōri Takachika, *daimyo* of Chōshū, then decided to enforce this order on his own. In the summer of 1863, the Chōshū military fired upon an American merchant vessel, a Dutch corvette, and a French dispatch boat. The Americans and French retaliated, destroying the gun batteries, but as soon as the warships departed, the batteries were rebuilt, even stronger than before. When the treaty brought by the allied Westerners was refused and the U.S.S. *Monitor* was fired upon on July 11th, the Western powers resolved to jointly attack the recalcitrant Chōshū warriors. On September 4th, fourteen ships—seven British, two French, two American, and three Dutch—attacked the rebels, and after two days of vigorous fighting, the Westerners occupied all of the gun batteries. A treaty was signed by the local Japanese officials on September 13 prohibiting the construction of any further gun batteries and requiring both the cessation of hostilities and free passage for foreign ships; the treaty also required that the rebels pay an unspecified indemnity.[23] This indemnity was set at a total of three million dollars, a sum divided between the Americans, British, French, and Dutch. It is interesting to note that in the Convention of

---

23. See Ernest Satow, *A Diplomat in Japan* (London: Oxford University Press, 1968), 95–133.

Shimonoseki signed on October 22, 1864, the allied powers offered to forgo the indemnity if a port were opened on the Inland Sea, which the Japanese refused.[24]

De Coningh the writer

Much of what we know about C. T. Assendelft de Coningh comes from his own writings. His family archive—held by the National Archive in The Hague—contains only a few of his letters, most of which are largely concerned with such pedestrian matters as finding his son a position in the NHM. Sadly, the archive contains no diaries or notes on which his longer works are clearly based, or letters or business records from his time in Japan, except for a lease agreement with Takaradaya Mohei in Yokohama from 1860.[25] Although De Coningh was inducted into the Society of Dutch Literature (Maatschappij der Nederlandse Letterkunde) in 1860, there are probably many other Dutch writers who are more deserving—from a purely literary standpoint—of translation. Nevertheless, he is a direct and engaging writer, with enough wit to make even his political ranting enjoyable. Moreover, De Coningh offers a unique view of a time and place for which we have few other accounts. Although he appeared to have had limited formal education, his writings show him to be extraordinarily well-read. It was no small task to track down all the references he makes in his book to other works. He provides a depth of detail and emotion that brings his tale to life.

Like *A Pioneer in Yokohama*, most of his other published works fall into the category of travel and adventure autobiography—characterized by such well-known books as *Two Years Before the Mast: A Sailing Life* (1840) by Richard Henry Dana and James Bradley Finley's *My Life Among the Indians or Personal Reminiscences and Historical Incidents* (1860)—that became so popular in the second half of the nineteenth century. Though the books in this genre share some characteristics with travel writing, the focus is always on the individual rather than scrutiny of "the other." Thus, in *A Pioneer*, De Coningh focuses on his life as an adventurer, a pioneer; he does not scrutinize the exotic aspects of his environment. One might even feel that the Japanese are given short shrift in this book. Those seeking greater anthropological detail can turn to his first book, *Mijn*

---

24. The convention is reproduced in full in J. H. Gubbins, *The Progress of Japan, 1853–1871* (New York: AMS Press, 1971), 296–98.

25. AdeC 137.

verblijf in Japan, a more conventional travelogue in which De Coningh gives much more detail on Japan as he experienced it in Nagasaki.

Conversely, the breadth of De Coningh's interaction with the foreign community, which tended to segregate itself along nationality and class lines, is unusual. The diplomats typically did not fraternize with the merchants much, and the English and Americans fraternized very little with the non-English-speaking nationalities, which they outnumbered by far. Even the American merchant and diarist Francis Hall, who arrived in Japan just two months after De Coningh—when the foreign population was well under a hundred—never mentions interacting with De Coningh once during the two years in which his stay in the country overlapped De Coningh's.[26] Perhaps because there were so few Dutchmen, and because De Coningh, like most educated Dutch, was multi-lingual, he seems to have crossed many of the foreigners' social and cultural boundaries.

Though his writing is focused on his own experiences, De Coningh also shows himself to be an especially good listener. Thus he relates not only his own actions and feelings, but also the stories of others. From him we learn why the interpreter needs gin, and the story of Jan Spuyter's uncle's adventures along the Barbary Coast. As a result, we have a peek into history from the "bottom up," of sailors and servants, rather than the usual "top-down" history of diplomats and military officers.

Travel writing of the nineteenth century has generally been negatively associated with imperialism. Though the treaty ports resulted from the rise of imperialism, De Coningh's writings reveal him as a Liberal, a humanist, and possibly a Freemason.[27] One important aspect of Dutch liberalism was an emphasis on open markets and free trade. If one subscribes to the Marxist-Leninist view that imperialism is the natural outgrowth of capitalism, than one could view this as an expression of an imperialist worldview. Nevertheless, De Coningh's most pointed remarks are directed at his own government, while he calls the Japanese—with the

26. Hall does mention the firm of De Coningh & Co. once, on February 16, 1861. After a rash of thefts, the firm set a watchman on the yard, which led to the capture of the thief who then gave up the names of his associates. F. G. Notehelfer, ed., *Japan through American Eyes* (Princeton, NJ: Princeton University Press, 1992), 304–5.

27. In this book De Coningh seems to allude to taking part in the final farewell, a Freemason practice, for the slain Dutch captains De Vos and Dekker. In *Mijn verblijf in Japan*, De Coningh discusses how his *History of Freemasonry* was confiscated because it had a cross on the title page.

exception of the *loonings* (Japanese *rōnin*) —"civilized." He shows little of the racism and anti-Semitism that is often encountered in writings of this period.

The construction of *A Pioneer in Yokohama* may seem a little odd, as if the pieces don't quite fit together. This is due, in part, to the fact that it comprised the second part of a two-volume memoir entitled *Ontmoetingen ter zee en te land* [Adventures at Sea and on Land]. The first volume consists of short sections on De Coningh's youth and his entry into the merchant marine, his early voyages to Indonesia, and even a vignette (surprisingly modern in tone) of life in Indonesia.[28] The second volume is translated in its entirety here. Therefore, if viewed as a larger collection of memoirs, *Pioneer* does not seem as disjointed.

Moreover, there are some indications that *Ontmoetingen* was not edited as thoroughly as De Coningh's first book. For example, *Mijn verblijf* is broken into chapters, featuring the detailed index-like chapter headings common in the nineteenth century. There are a few such breaks in Volume 1 of *Ontmoetingen*—but *A Pioneer in Yokohama* has no chapter breaks at all. The chapter breaks in this translation have been added to help the reader. Moreover, *Ontmoetingen* was not published in the publishing centers of Amsterdam or The Hague (*Mijn verblijf* was published in Amsterdam), but rather in Haarlem, where De Coningh lived. The publisher, W. C. de Graaff, appears to have been a bookseller who sometimes published books, which might explain its poor distribution. Coincidentally perhaps, De Graaff also published works by J. van Vloten (1818–1883), the historian De Coningh mentions in the last chapter.

The first section of *A Pioneer in Yokohama* might seem almost superfluous in light of the fact that De Coningh had already published an entire book about his visit to Japan in 1851. In the absence of any author's notes, one can only speculate as to motivation. It seems, however, that the first part of *Ontmoetingen* was a literary device intended as a counterpoint to the rest of the book. In this first section Japan is portrayed as idyllic and peaceful; upon his return in 1859, Japan is in turmoil. De Coningh uses this stark contrast to emphasize the discomfort of the early days in Yokohama. At the same time he represents what he perceived to be the

28. One of these, "Per Landmail," about a trip on a mail steamer from Southampton to Singapore, had been previously published in the 1860 *Jaarboekje Hollands*. This annual publication was edited by J. van Lennep, who also served as the president of the Maatschappij der Nederlandse Letterkunde and published several other De Coningh adventure stories between 1858 and 1862.

true, civilized nature of the Japanese, as opposed to the violent terrorists who threatened him during his stay in Yokohama. The first section might also have served to highlight what De Coningh perceived as the comfort of the upper-level Dutch diplomats on Deshima at the expense of not only others in Japan but the Dutch position in Japanese affairs. Moreover, since De Coningh was no longer in the employ of the NHM when the second book was published, he could be more openly barbed in his descriptions of Society employees.

De Coningh's highly readable style may make his book seem more like fiction than history. But everything that can be verified has been found to be accurate, or within the realm of slight human error. As such, his writings introduced the public to Japan and gave them a taste of exotic Japan. He continued this role even after his death, when "two large old vases, a variety of wood and ivory netsuke and a number of interesting photographs of the land and people" were contributed by his widow to an exhibit on Japan at the now defunct Museum van Kunstnijverheid [Museum of Industrial Arts] in Utrecht in 1890.[29]

As Yokohama grew, the rough days described by De Coningh were but a memory. Yokohama soon became a place with paved streets, a racecourse, and social clubs. Only seven years after De Coningh's departure, the Tokugawa Shogunate fell and was replaced by what eventually evolved into a parliamentary-style government. The number of foreign travelers increased, and as a result, so did the number of travel books about Japan. It was no longer the wild frontier town De Coningh experienced, but a rapidly expanding international port. Today Yokohama has nearly merged with Tokyo to form one megalopolis, but Yokohama retains ghostly vestiges of the frontier built by men like C. T. Assendelft de Coningh.

A brief note on currency

The currency issues of Tokugawa Japan, even before the advent of Western imperialism, were numerous and complex. The economy operated on a tri-metallic standard of gold, silver, and copper, from which coins were minted. The purity, and therefore the value, of these coins fluctuated. Paper money was used in some areas, and as copper veins began to give out, even lead and brass were used for small coins.

---

29. EvS. "Tentoonstelling van Japansche kunstvoorwerpen in Museum van Kunstnijverheid," in *Tijdschrift van Nijverheid* (1890): 107–10.

As a result, money changers were required to keep track of value. In the nineteenth century, the shogunal government, which had an effective monopoly on bullion supplies, created revenue by debasing the currency. There were many different kinds of coin in circulation, of which De Coningh mentions two: the gold ovular *koban* and the rectangular silver *ichibu* (what De Coningh calls *kobang* and *itzeboe*, respectively).

In the mid-nineteenth century, the Mexican silver dollar was used as a sort of international currency because of its relatively uniform size and purity (at about 0.8 ounces per coin). These Mexican dollars could therefore be used anywhere for their value as silver specie (27.073 grams at 0.9028 fineness). The exchange rate for debased Japanese coins to the known value of the Mexican silver dollars was the source of intensive negotiation, in which the value of gold to silver was set artificially high in Japan at 1:5, when in Europe it was 1:15. Though this exchange rate is usually referred to as a "gold rush," profits in copper were equally, if not more, significant. Because the shogunate had required trade to occur in Japanese currency and capped the amount that could be exchanged per day, the merchants in Yokohama resorted to subterfuge, requesting excessive amounts under such fictitious names as "Mr. Doodledoo," "Mr. Smell-bad," and "Mr. Balls."[30] The egress of currency was halted on November 14, 1859, when the shogunate accused the Western powers of acting in bad faith and halted currency trade. Speculation in coins and the issue of debased currency by the shogunate resulted in the inflation De Coningh describes, and it was rampant for the rest of the decade.

De Coningh often converts currency into guilders for his Dutch readers. This denomination was used in the Netherlands from the seventeenth century until the adoption of the euro in 2002. It was abbreviated with an *f* from the word *florin*, which although derived from the Italian word *florin*, was used interchangeably with guilder in the nineteenth century.

A briefer note on Japanese government officials

In 1603, Tokugawa Ieyasu was named shogun of Japan. Though the emperor still resided in Kyoto and had a few powers and rights, the true

---

30. Rutherford Alcock, "The Stoppage of Trade by the Japanese Authorities," *House of Commons Papers*, vol. 69, 1860.

power was largely held by the head of a hereditary military establishment, the shogun. In contemporary Dutch, this position was referred to as the *keizer*, a term normally translated as "emperor."

The shogunate was, however, essentially a bureaucracy. The shogun was advised by a group of councilors and had a staff of officials, called *bugyō*, to supervise most of the administrative work. Though the term "governor" is often used by non-Japanese speakers to refer to anyone holding the position of *bugyō*, the English term does not accurately convey the duties of the Japanese administrator. There was, for example, a finance *bugyō*; "minister" or "secretary" might be more accurate.

A third position De Coningh mentions is that of *metsuke*. This is often translated as "spy," but there was very little that was covert about their activities. *Metsuke* were more like employees of an internal affairs department charged with ensuring that all government employees were doing their jobs correctly. In Dutch these men were called *dwarskijkers*, which suggests "one who looks across."

De Coningh also refers to the *banjoosten* on Deshima. There is a difference of opinion as to exactly which position this corrupted Dutch word refers to, but it was a position in the local government. The most likely position was the *bantō* or *bangashira*. They were also in charge of security and the formalities of trade.

SOURCES CONSULTED

ARCHIVES CONSULTED

Archives in the Nationaal Archief in the Netherlands are identified by the following abbreviations in the notes:
Buitenlandse Zaken (BUZA)
Familie Assendelft de Coningh (AdeC)
Nederlandse Factorij Japan (NFJ)

PRINTED SOURCES

Aalst, G. M. van. *Archief van de familie van Assendelft de Coningh 1645–1959.* The Hague: Algemeen Rijksarchief, 1975.

Alcock, Rutherford. *The Capital of the Tycoon—A Narrative of a Three Years' Residence in Japan.* 2 vols. London: Longman, Green, Longman, Roberts & Green, 1863. Reprint, St. Clair Shores, MI: Scholarly Press, n.d.

————. "The Stoppage of Trade by the Japanese Authorities." *House of Commons Papers,* vol. 69, 1860.

Assendelft de Coningh, C. T. *Mijn verblijf in Japan.* Amsterdam: Gebroeders Kraay, 1856.

————. *Ontmoetingen ter zee en te land.* 2 vols. Haarlem: W. C. de Graaff, 1879.

Black, John R. *Young Japan: Yokohama and Yedo 1858–1879.* 2 vols. Oxford: Oxford University Press, 1968.

Blum, Paul C., trans. "Father Mounicou's *Bakumatsu* Diary, 1856–64." *The Transactions of the Asiatic Society of Japan,* 3rd series, no. 13 (December 1976): 5–103.

Brooke, George M., ed. *John M. Brooke's Pacific Cruise and Japanese Adventure, 1858–1860.* Honolulu: University of Hawaii Press, 1986.

Chaiklin, Martha. "Monopolists to Middlemen: Dutch Liberalism and American Imperialism in the Opening of Japan." *Journal of World History* 21, no. 2 (June 2010): 249–69.

De Geer, B. J. Lindtelo, and Mr. Van Benval Fauve, *Regtsgeleerd bijblad, behoorende nieuwe bijblagen.* Amsterdam: Johannes Müller, 1868.

De Graeff van Polsbroek, Dirk. *Journaal van jonkheer Dirk de Graeff van Polsbroek*. Edited and with introduction by Herman J. Moeshart. Assen: Van Gorcum, 1987.

De Wolff, A. J. J. *Herinneringen uit Japan*. Brussels, 1890.

Dennys, N. B. *The Treaty Ports of China and Japan*. London: 1867. Reprint, San Francisco: China Materials Center, 1977.

Doeff, *Hendrik. Herinneringen uit Japan*. Haarlem: François Bohn, 1833.

———. *Recollections of Japan*. Translated by Annick M. Doeff. Trafford: Bloomington, IN, 2003.

EvS. "Tentoonstelling van Japansche kunstvoorwerpen in Museum van Kunstnijverheid." *Tijdschrift van Nijverheid* (1890): 107–10.

Fogel, Joshua. *Articulating the Sinosphere: Sino-Japanese Relations in Space and Time*. Cambridge, MA: Harvard University Press, 2009.

Fonblanque, Edward Barrington de. *Niphon and Pe-Che-Li; or, Two Years in Japan and North Eastern China*. London: Saunders, Otley and Co., 1862.

Frost, Peter. *The Bakumatsu Currency Crisis*. Harvard East Asian Monographs, 36. Cambridge, MA: Harvard University Press, 1970.

Gragg, William. *A Cruise in the U.S. Steam Frigate Mississippi: Wm. C. Nicholson, Captain, to China and Japan*. Boston: Damrell and Moore, 1860.

Gubbins, J. H. *The Progress of Japan, 1853–1871*. New York: AMS Press, 1971.

Hammersmith, Jack L. *Spoilsmen in a "Flowery Fairyland": The Development of the U.S. Legation in Japan, 1859–1906*. Kent, OH: Kent State University Press, 1998.

Heco, Joseph. *The Narrative of a Japanese*. Yokohama: 1895. Reprint, San Francisco: American Japanese Publishing Association, n.d.

Heusken, Henry. *Japan Journal, 1855–1861*. Translated and edited by Jeanette C. van der Corput and Robert A. Wilson. New Brunswick, NJ: Rutgers University Press, 1964.

Honjo, Yuki Allyson. *Japan's Early Experience of Contract Management in the Treaty Ports*. London: Japan Library, 2003.

Johnston, James D. *China and Japan: Being a narrative of the cruise of the U.S. steam-frigate Powhatan, in the years 1857, '58, '59, and '60. Including an account of the Japanese embassy to the United States*. Philadelphia: C. Desilver; Baltimore: Cushings & Bailey, 1861.

Kato Yuzo. *Yokohama Past and Present*. Yokohama: Yokohama City University, 1990.

Klein, F. Smit. *Levensbericht van C. Th. Assendelft de Coningh*. Leiden: E. J. Brill, 1891.

Lensen, George Alexander. *The Russian Push Toward Japan: Russo-Japanese Relations, 1697–1875*. Princeton, NJ: Princeton University Press, 1959.

"Marktberigt van de Coning, Carst & Lels, te Kanagawa (bij Jeddo) Japan, van October 1859." *De Economist* 9 (1860): 85–88.

McCabe, Patricia. *Gaijin Bochi: The Foreigners' Cemetery, Yokohama, Japan*. London: British Association for Cemeteries in South Asia, 1994.

McMaster, John. "The Japanese Gold Rush of 1859." *The Journal of Asian Studies* 19, no. 3 (May 1960): 273–87.

Medzini, Meron. *French Policy in Japan During the Closing Years of the Tokugawa Regime*. Cambridge, MA: Harvard University Press, 1971.

Meijlan, G. F. *Japan*. Amsterdam: J. Westerman & Zoon, 1830.

———. *Geschiedkundig overzigt van den handel der europezen op Japan*. Batavia: Ter lands drukkerij, 1833.

Molhuysen, P. C., and P. J. Blok, eds. *Nieuw Nederlandsch biografisch woordenboek*. Leiden: A. W. Sijthoff, 1911–1937.

Moss, Michael. *Seizure of Mr. Moss and His Treatment by the Consul General*. London: William Ridgeway, 1863.

Murphy, Kevin C. *The American Merchant Experience in the 19th Century*. London and New York: Routledge Curzon, 2003.

Notehelfer, F. G, ed. *Japan through American Eyes: The Journal of Francis Hall, Kanagawa and Yokohama 1859–1866*. Princeton, NJ: Princeton University Press, 1992.

Overmeer Fisscher, J. F. van. *Bijdrage tot de kennis van het Japansche rijk*. Amsterdam: J. Müller & comp., 1833.

Paske-Smith, M. *Western Barbarians in Japan and Formosa*. Kobe: J. L. Thompson, 1930.

Paul, Huibert. "De Coningh on Deshima: *Mijn verblijf in Japan*, 1856." *Monumenta Nipponica* 32, no. 3 (Autumn 1977): 347–64.

Satow, Ernest. *A Diplomat in Japan*. London: Oxford University Press, 1968.

Sawa, Mamoru. *Yokohama gaikokujin kyoryūchi hoterushi*. Tokyo: Hakutō shobō, 2001.

Scherzer, Karl von. *Fachmännische Berichte über österreich-ungarische Expedition nach Siam, China und Japan, 1868–1871.* Stuttgart: Julius van Maier, 1872.

Smith, George. *Ten Weeks in Japan.* London: Green, Longman and Roberts, 1861.

Van Daalen, Isabel Tanaka. "Rangaku oranda tsūji keizu (II)—Nakayama ke." *Nichiran gakkai kaishi* Vol. 27, no. 1, special section.

Yokohama Archives of History, ed. *Yokohama gaikokujin kyoryūchi.* Yokohama: Yūrindō, 1998.

Yokohama Kaikō Shiryō Fukyu Kyōkai, ed. *Yokohama mono no hajimeko.* Yokohama: Kaiko Shiryōkan, 1988.

Yokohama Shiyakusho, ed. *Yokohamashi shiko.* Kyoto: Rinsen shobo 11 v, 1931. Reprint 1985 2 (seiji 2 hen).

Yoshihara Kenichirō. *Edo no zeni to shomin no kurashi.* Tokyo: Dōseisha, 2003.

CHRONOLOGY OF EVENTS
MENTIONED IN THIS BOOK

1851

July 6	*Joän* departs Batavia
August 7	*Joän* arrives in Nagasaki harbor
November 10	*Joän* departs Nagasaki
December 5	*Joän* arrives in Batavia

1859

May	*Argonaut* leaves Amsterdam
Early July	*Argonaut* departs Batavia
July 4	Treaty ports in Japan are opened
August 23	*Fenimore Cooper* is beached (typhoon)
August 25	Deadly attack on Russian sailors
September 4	*Argonaut* arrives in Yokohama; Robert Weir accidentally shot by James L. Brooke
September 19	Robert Weir dies from gunshot wound
October 3	U.S.S. *Powhatan* arrives in Kanagawa
October 12	*Powhatan* departs for Shanghai
November 5	Assassination of Chinese servant of José Loureiro
November 14	End of "Gold Rush"; Shogunate effectively halts currency exchange
November 28	Night of earthquake

1860

January 3	Fire in Yokohama
January 4	Organization of Yokohama Volunteers (unverified)
February 25	Deadly attack on Dutch Captains De Vos and Dekker
February 29	Funerals of De Vos and Dekker
March 5	Gun scare from the H.M.S. *Camilla*
March 24	Assassination of Ii Naosuke

September 2   The *Camilla* departs Hakodate
September 9   Typhoon; Probable date of the *Camilla*'s capsize

1861

January 14   Fire in Yokohama
January 16   Assassination of Henry Heusken

1864

September 5   Battle of Shimonoseki

A Pioneer
in Yokohama

Chapter 1

"Blow favorably O Winds, flow smoothly O Sea!" I said to myself, after the poet[1] when, in the first light of early morning in July 1859, we lifted anchor on the *Argonaut* in the roadstead[2] of Batavia. Presently a fresh land-wind transported the ship northward with swollen sails.

"What awaits us in far Japan—the land of our destination, the land of secrets and enigmas?" I asked myself as the bright morning light permitted me a last, slowly sinking glimpse of the forest of masts of anchored ships, the last beacon of European civilization. "What will we find? Success or disappointment, welcome or resistance, peace or conflict, affluence or misery, life or death?" I was gripped with apprehension, being completely unsure how the least-known and fiercest people of the East, who had been isolated for centuries, would receive the peaceful pioneers forced upon them by the might of the West.

The wind had blown fairly favorably for about thirty days, and the sea had flowed tolerably smoothly, when, on a bright and clear evening, the peak of Ohoshima,[3] a high volcanic island at the entrance to the bay of Edo, on the western horizon of the waters of the Pacific Ocean, unfurled before us. Under small sails[4] we headed for land during the night, and by the first morning light the east coast of Japan, like a wall of green forest, lay a short distance from us. Far, very far inland, the eternally snowy top of Fuzi-Jamma[5] jutted high over everything, shining like a silver crest against the blue heavens, having already received the first daylight long before even a few rays of sun lit the earth below.

O beautiful land! It was on that fine September morning that I saw thine east coast for the first time. For centuries thou had long been hidden there. Only now and then could an explorer behold your

1. This is from the poem "De Oostindievaart" ["The East India Voyage"] by Barthold Henrik Lulofs (1787–1849).
2. A sheltered offshore anchorage for large ships.
3. Ōshima. Last erupted 1990.
4. The *Argonaut* was probably square-rigged with several masts, each containing various kinds of sails. Small sails were used in light wind or calm weather.
5. Mt. Fuji.

exterior adornment, but never could he tread under the shadow of your luxuriant trees, never could he set foot on your green hills or in your peaceful villages, never could he stand among your forests of blooming camellias.

How often since have I felt, when admiring your magnificent vistas from the peaks of your lushly verdant mountains, that your outward appearance does not belie what is within.

The world is adorned with two jewels that stand out from among the many splendors it has given man and the riches of the kingdom of creation that cover our earth. Though both continually move us to reverent admiration, the full glory of their beauty is revealed to the human eye at completely different times. Much as a woman's beauty is enhanced by the sparkling lights of the ballroom, so a ray of sunlight makes the blinding shimmer of a diamond flicker tenfold; whoever has the good fortune to admire a beautiful woman during the day is doubly entranced when he sees her again at night, in festive garb, under blazing lights reflected by mirrors. Then his admiration is amplified to intoxicating rapture. But a beautiful land that rises from among the waves must be seen from the sea, early in the morning; then it is doubly beautiful, with its ranges of green mountains and hills, forests, flowers and fields, all bathed in the foam of the boiling sea, just as the first glow of the morning sun conjures golden streaks across the land, illuminating, like so many pearls, the millions of drops of the driven surf.

That is how the coast of Japan appeared as we approached it; we sailed into the Bay of Jeddo[6] shortly thereafter.

Before we go any further, it is necessary to say a few words of introduction about what Japan was like before some ports in this land were opened to a few nations.[7] One might otherwise think, in view of the things I will relate later, that it was a land of savages and barbarians.

People know that Japan was closed to the entire outside world until 1859, and that only eight or ten Netherlanders were allowed to stay on Decima, a small, artificially built island right next to the city of Nagasaki.[8] One ship was sent to Japan from Batavia annually, with a cargo of goods for which copper bars were received in return; it was a sort of

6. Tokyo Bay. The name of the city was changed from Edo in 1868. *Edo* is variously transcribed as *Jedo* or *Jeddo* in De Coningh's text.
7. The first ports opened were Kanagawa (Yokohama), Nagasaki, and Hakodate.
8. De Coningh has ignored the Chinese and Koreans, who also had official trading relationships.

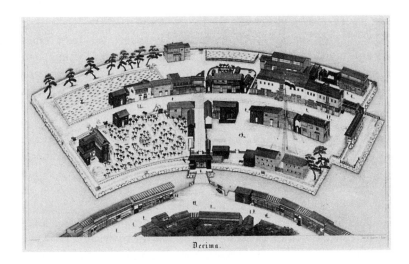

Map of Deshima from J. H. H. Levyssohn, *Bladen over Japan* (1852).
Levyssohn left the year before De Coningh arrived, but this is probably the
most contemporaneous illustration. Collection of the Royal Netherlands
Institute of Southeast Asian and Caribbean Studies.

courtesy barter trade between the Dutch East Indian Government and
Japan.[9] This old relationship, which dated from 250 years before, was
maintained, especially on the Japanese side, not out of the desire for
profit, but in order to find out, if indirectly, what was happening in
the rest of the world. Their friendship, therefore, was not without great
importance both from a political as well as from a scientific point of
view; for through the arrival of the annual ship, the Japanese could
come to know of any danger threatening from the outside world,
and because of their thirst for knowledge, they were enlightened on
the advances of science in a variety of fields through the books and
instruments we brought. What little profit we made, in the last fifty
years, when the trade was cut back to one ship, was no longer worth
mentioning. Yet in the seventeenth and the first half of the eighteenth
centuries, when the East India Company was allowed to trade with four
or five more ships a year for the Japan trade, they were thereby able to
earn millions. In the last years of the closing, the Japan trade yielded

9. This only describes conditions of the nineteenth century. The number of ships, the
content of cargo, and the conditions of trade underwent considerable change through
the early modern period.

possibly a ton of gold per year for the government of the Netherlands Indies; it was thus not much return for the trouble. But the business was continued because an establishment already sat on Decima, and, if trade was a privilege to be bestowed, it seemed better to be the only ones to have entrance to the secret empire than not, under whatever restricted conditions.

For the most part, the resident personnel on Decima during this time consisted, as a rule, of the *Opperhoofd*,[10] four assistants and a doctor. The first, as his official title denotes, was entrusted with the highest authority and supervision over the few personnel—and then, in the final period, over the insignificant barter trade. The position of "*Opperhoofd* of the Netherlands trade in Japan," as the full title read, was usually assigned to a senior official from Java who had earned a few years' rest at high salary before retirement. It was therefore considered to be a job where one could convert four years of calm garden rest into bank savings. Room, board, service—everything was just about perfect for the *Opperhoofd*; because for the last couple centuries, one *Opperhoofd* after the other had had plenty of idle time to spend making his position as pleasant as possible. New arrivals acquired the property of their predecessors—so that, after two hundred years, room, board, and the sundry comforts of life were more or less completely fulfilled. Because in Japan the position of the father was always passed to the son, the same Japanese families served the *Opperhoofd* for a dozen generations and thus were allied to the *Opperhoofd*'s little court. They had control over household affairs in the broadest sense and skill in the preparation and serving of victuals such as one would otherwise only rarely encounter in the best European cooks and waiters. For someone who was not already too addicted to the amusements of the tumultuous world, there was no reason to spurn the post of *Opperhoofd*. It was indeed quite tolerable for men who had struggled through the years of youth to be in a spacious, comfortable house in the healthiest spot in the world, without any of the concerns of the outside world, with a good table, encircled by servants, like absolute monarchs sitting on their thrones for four straight years. It is true, however, that there was a dark side to all this. In those days, a European woman could never set foot on Decima; so if an appointed *Opperhoofd* were married, he had to leave his wife at home. Nor were any male Japanese allowed to remain on Decima at night either, not even the servants of the *Opperhoofd*. But he was not without service from sunset to sunrise because the Japanese authorities,

---

10. Literally, "chief." The head of the factory.

to shed a little light into the dark of loneliness, allowed servant women[11] on Decima, both day and night. Most *Opperhoofden* made use of these munificent arrangements more or less appropriately, to the best of their understanding. A few, however, sometimes interpreted the unlimited freedom in too Eastern a fashion.

Decima, as it stood before—that is, as a small walled island a few hundred paces in circumference, closed off from the world, with an *Opperhoofd* and a few assistants—vanished from the earth with the opening of the Japanese ports. It is really too bad that the European states did not join together to create, in different corners of the earth, a half-dozen Decimas modeled on the original. Such arrangements would make a pleasant refuge for pretenders to the throne and fallen bigwigs who now and again throw free countries into commotion. Such people, shut up in their Decimas with a half-dozen servants, would be perfectly harmless; they could write their manifestos and proclamations openly and to their hearts' content, without causing any sort of wickedness, other than perhaps causing a passing crow to fear for its life.

Ostensibly, one would think that six or eight Hollanders, surrounded by ever-green forests on their small yet pleasant island in a beautiful bay, where closure to the world also meant that the cares of the world did not intrude—would find their unencumbered lives heaven on earth. And this was, in fact, the case when the *Opperhoofd* was a good-humored, hospitable and jovial man. Then a cheerful, lively tone prevailed among the small society of exiles, and the men feasted several times a week at their host's table which could satisfy the choosiest gastronome, because Japan yields game, vegetables and fruit the likes of which people in Europe could only dream. Moreover, the annual ship from Java supplied their richly compensated host with plentiful stocks of wine and spirits,[12] and the men often enjoyed a full measure of the *Opperhoofd's* free-flowing wine—so much so that late in the evenings, the gloriously drunk and high-spirited assistants would bang on the doors of their nearby houses, waking up the sleeping servants, where they would soon slumber peacefully with the knowledge that on their island there were no neighbor ladies to gossip about their jovial homecomings.

11. This is a veiled reference to prostitutes.

12. While the numbers could vary considerably, a rough estimate is two thousand bottles of wine a year in addition to kegs of arak (a liquor of sugar, rice, and palm sap produced in South and Southeast Asia), gin, beer, and other liquors.

It was very different if the *Opperhoofd* was a cool and dour man, who wished only to use his four years as a piggy bank and therefore limited his hospitality to the narrowest confines. Under such circumstances tiny Decima became a hell of boredom and mutual hate that was doubly oppressive because the men could never avoid each other. For the men did not forget that the *Opperhoofd* stood high and well paid on the officials' ladder while the assistants were like Lilliputians hanging on to the lowest rungs, and could only with relative parsimony make ends meet. Of course there were those among the assistants who wanted to push their way into favor with the little autocrats, and then two factions were created: the *Opperhoofd* with his favorites, and the three or four leftovers. One can understand how awkward this situation must have been, and how pleasant the walk was if both parties were taking a brisk turn around the few hundred paces of Decima after a meal, passing each other every three minutes. Parties and other merriment were not even mentioned until the *Opperhoofd* changed, and only on Sundays were the four or five assistants very solemnly invited by one of the officials to the *Opperhoofd*'s table. Stately in their black jackets, the invitees sat tortured during the tedious meal, partaking in all solemnity of the victuals served, without so much as the seasoning of a kind act or a cheerful word. After the meal, the men remained together for a few more uncompanionable minutes, then took their leave of their cold host after the second cup of tea. Thankful that the obligation was over, each sought his own cabin again; the black jacket rehung on the coat stand for another eight days,[13] and, if an assistant didn't find salvation in immediate sleep, then the rest of the evening was spent grumbling with his neighboring partners in misfortune. They finally separated with the hope that they could sleep far into the day—because upon waking they could only return to grumbling or help each other look over the wall of the warehouse across the way. So they slept, grumbled, ate, walked and gaped through their lives on Decima, where one day was like another and where there was never much news to speak of except the weather, the good or bad humor of the *Opperhoofd*, the catching of a rat, the burning of a meal, or a bit of a squabble with the Japanese serving woman. There was little conflict to speak of in the lives on Decima. Abundant sleep, plentiful food, and several hundred paces in which to exercise daily allowed the body to thrive—unlike most people, who are exhausted through constant effort and worry.

---

13. A week, but counting the rest of that day, which makes eight days.

It has never been tried, but for the sake of science it would certainly be worth the trouble, through the medium of an assistant on Decima, to make a proper reckoning of how long a man can live under the most favorable circumstances. But the gentlemen were replaced every four years; thus can we come to no other conclusion than the certainty that they were seldom or never sick and that they exchanged the pale color they had brought with them from Java for a European bloom. This was due in large part to the healthy climate, but the exceptional circumstances on Decima contributed more than a little to it. If in the middle of the last century a healthy young man of eighteen years had, as a case study, been appointed assistant on Decima for life, then the present question of life expectancy could plausibly be answered. Then we would know how long someone could live in a healthy, temperate climate, receiving just enough money to pay his way—for lodging, simple and nourishing food and no more—and keep him from inherent human weakness; where he could wed according to local custom, but also where, if harmony diminished, he could safeguard against domestic strife by sending his wife away (provided the exchange brings him true happiness). Furthermore, he'd never have to run the gauntlet of our coffeehouses and cafes, would never be jaded by the nocturnal amusements of our big cities. Even if he deludes himself that he is a rake by sleeping past ten, his only exertion would still only be a walk of a few hundred paces around the island a few times a day. His spirit would never be tortured by nagging political or religious questions—and, if this were the case, he would never come to know care, for that side of him cannot surface and cares can't be created from thin air. If a man's situation and near surroundings give him nothing to think about, he consequently doesn't think, so that there are never any intrusive emotions to disrupt the clockwork of life for an instant. I don't see why the lamp of his life would ever be extinguished—not before his body, with all its senses of which nothing was ever demanded, is completely overcome by old age. How long could he last? One or two centuries? We'll never know the answer. The question must be left there, the answer lost forever due to lack of proof and the opening of Decima.

The heedlessness of the lives of those on Decima's hundred paces explains why, in more than two hundred years, it never occurred to an assistant to set word to paper about Japan or, through trusting companionship with Japanese of both sexes, to gain some knowledge of the large, civilized and fertile land that lay outside the walls of the island. He would never bother himself with such matters, and would think even less about learning the native language; if he knew the names of what was drinkable and enjoyable, he had no need for anything further. The little that we did know of Japan, until about twenty years ago when a few ports were opened to international trade, we owe to a few *Opperhoofden*, but especially the doctors[14] who were now and then detached to Decima. Some of these doctors made good use of the time they had on Decima, zealously collecting all they could learn regarding the land and people; on the government; on mineralogical and botanical matters; and on other subjects.[15] Moreover, the doctor was the only one who, through the character of his relations, came into more frequent contact with cultured Japanese in the interior—for though he might not discharge a single pill or powder to his half-dozen compatriots, the remedies of his art were eagerly sought by the Japanese gentry who, through their influence, received permission to visit the European doctor with a small retinue to seek help with their complaints. Our medicine is held in high repute, and since they could not pay with money, they had to settle with gifts or in another manner. Thus the doctor, in satisfying his duty, managed to obtain important information and get drawings, plans, maps, ore and other objects from his distinguished patients or their followers that by one or another secret method escaped the ears and eyes of the *dwarskijker*[16] whose cordon encircled them. Especially, about fifty years ago, Dr. von Siebold[17] excelled at collecting all the worthwhile details concerning Japan, in the days of seclusion. No one did a better job than he of making such scientific investigations of the land and people. The *dwarskijker* triumphed at last over this tireless naturalist,

14. Hendrik Doeff and G. F. Meijlan both published accounts of their time in Japan. Warehouse Master J. F. Overmeer Fisscher also wrote a book.

15. E.g., Engelbert Kaempfer and Carl Pieter Thunberg.

16. In Japanese, *metsuke* 目付. A shogunal official. Sometimes called censors or spies. They had a variety of duties that included investigation of members of the warrior class, inspection of Edo Castle, and fire prevention.

17. Philipp Franz von Siebold (1796–1866) was a German doctor attached to the Dutch factory at Deshima from 1823–1829. He opened a medical school and obtained knowledge about Japan from his many pupils. When Von Siebold left Japan in 1829, a typhoon sunk his ship. Japanese authorities discovered many items that were barred from export among his recovered effects, including maps and military and pornographic prints. Von Siebold was banned for life, but others involved in the affair were imprisoned and executed. While in Europe, Von Siebold published his efforts in *Nippon* (1832–1851), *Flora Japonica* (1835–1840), and *Fauna Japonica* (1842–1850). Changing political circumstances allowed him to return to Japan in 1859 and serve in the Dutch foreign office in Edo in 1861 he but left Japan for the last time later that year.

and the betrayed scholar was banned from the country, to the detriment of science.

It is self-evident that a stay on Decima, with just a small circle of a few people—for the most part of men of unsociable nature—had a significant influence. For example, someone who, while in the bustle of society of Europe, had previously spoken but little, could speak hardly at all anymore after two years on Decima. I myself remember just such an *Opperhoofd* there who, at our first meeting, impressed me as someone who had as good as forgotten how to speak.

About thirty years ago,[18] and thus still in the time of real seclusion, I dropped anchor in the Bay of Nagasaki, near Decima, late in the evening. It was too late to go ashore that evening. I also wanted to delay my landing until the following morning because I wanted to be fresh to meet my compatriots who, having been isolated for so long, had heard absolutely nothing of Europe, the East Indies, the Fatherland or the rest of the world for the past twenty months. I was certain that they would storm me with their questions of the world, and I had therefore made an effort to keep abreast of everything so that their questions were not directed to a blockhead. With the persistence of an assistant teacher who was going up for exams, I had studied all the events bearing on world history in the past months, ferreting out newspapers, magazines and brochures to examine. In order to pump the most important facts into my memory, I created a sort of oral chronicle that I believed would most certainly be welcomed by the isolated exiles on Decima.

After a fortuitously successful sea voyage, fearing no danger because we were anchored as safely in the deep Bay of Nagasaki as in a pond, and surrounded by high mountains, I would under normal circumstances have simply lain my head down and immediately fallen into a tranquil sleep. Weighing heavily on my heart, however, and keeping sleep from my eyes was the prospect of acting as a messenger of salvation to a half-dozen Robinsons[19] who, in just hours, would be hanging on my words as I proclaimed the vicissitudes of the world. I had unfortunately studied too well. The stormy years of 1848 and 1849 had already sped past, and I feared that the many events of those days would escape my memory; I had in a half-wakened state repeated them so many times that my sleep was agitated. My frame of mind was that of a high school

18. 1851; the ship was the *Joän*.
19. Referring to Daniel Defoe's *Robinson Crusoe* (1719).

student of today[20] on the night before final exams—a student whose brain is crammed so full of so many variations of information that he anxiously awaits the moment he can purge his learning in front of the members of the committee and then happily forget half of it. Louis Philippe, De Lamartine, Cavaignac barricades, Ferdinand, Naples, Victor Emmanuel, Cavour, Thorbecke, liberals, radicals, constitutions, Balinese, modernists, orthodox, Louis Buonaparte, schisms, Palmerston, Thiers, Isabella, cardinals, redskins, biology, Garribaldi [sic], revolution— in short, all the news tumbled higgledy-piggledy through my head until finally, while my exhausted spirit fled on the cassock of the Pope from Rome to Gaeta, I fell into a restless sleep.[21]

20. Hogere Burgerschol, a secondary school program in the Netherlands from 1863–1974 lasting about six years. These schools weren't in existence in 1851.

21. **Louis Philippe** (1773–1850). King of France, 1830–1848. He abdicated in face of the February Revolution in 1848 and fled to England. **Alphonse de Lamartine** (1790–1869). Romantic poet, politician and author of *History of the Revolution of 1848* (Boston: Phillips, Sampson & Co., 1849). **Louis Eugene Cavaignac** (1802–1857). A general who stamped out the Workers' Insurrection in Paris in June 1848, using cannon against their barricades. He served as acting head of state until December of that year. **Ferdinand II** (1810–1859). King of Two Sicilies. Accorded a constitution based on the French constitution of 1830 after demonstrations in Naples. Responding to tensions between Ferdinand and the newly elected government, the citizens of Naples also set up barricades, which were smashed by Ferdinand's forces. **Victor Emmanuel II** (1820–1878). Became last king of Piedmont-Sardinia in 1849. In 1861 he became first king of a united Italy. **Count Camillo Benso di Cavour** (1810–1861). Founded an influential newspaper called *The Resurgence* (*Il Risorgemento*) that supported unification and constitutionalism in 1847. He was awarded a government post by Victor Emmanuel II and later became the first prime minister under a unified Italy. **Johan Rudolf Thorbecke** (1798–1872). Drafted revisions to the Dutch constitution in 1848, and became first prime minister in 1849. **Liberalism**. Basis for the revolutions of 1848, which promoted the rights of the individual and free trade. It was the predominant political philosophy of the Netherlands at this time. **Bali**. An independent kingdom but from 1846–1908, the Balinese fought a series of wars that ultimately resulted in their incorporation into the Dutch East Indies, and later Indonesia. The War of Jagaraga was fought from 1848 to 1849 and the War of Kusamba in 1849. **Louis Bonaparte, Napoleon III** (1808–1873). Nephew of Napoleon and Emperor of France, 1852–1870. Won landslide victory in vote for presidency in 1848. **Henry John Temple Palmerston** (1784–1865). Viscount and British foreign secretary who encouraged the revolutionaries of 1848. Had to defend himself from a motion of impeachment in 1848. **Marie-Joseph-Louis-Adolphe Thiers** (1797–1877). Historian and politician. Opposed monarchy. Elected to the constituent assembly in 1848, supported Louis Bonaparte (Napoleon III) until he became too autocratic. Became First President of the Third Republic after the end

Early the next morning several Japanese boats approached from portside, packed with *banjoosten*,[22] *dwarskijkers*, interpreters and all the officials who would bring us ashore under strict police escort. I say *we*, for I was

---

of the empire of Napoleon III in 1871. **Isabella II** (1830–1904). Queen of Spain, 1833–1868. In 1846 the queen married her cousin, Francisco de Asís, and her sister, Luisa Fernanda, married a son of Louis Philippe of France, the Duke de Montpensier. These Spanish marriages, which contravened earlier Anglo-French agreements about the choice of husbands for the two sisters, aroused the anger of England, who feared a Franco-Spanish rapprochement, and caused a temporary severance of the entente between England and France, leading to the liberal uprisings of 1848 and the defeat of Louis Philippe. This is known as the Affair of the Spanish Marriages. **Cardinals**. Under Pope Pius IX (Giovanni Maria Mastai-Ferretti, 1792–1878), pope from 1846 to 1878, a series of insurrections broke out among the papal states due to the unwillingness of his predecessor, Gregory XVI, to allow the citizens any political freedom. Street riots broke out in 1848, resulting in a constitution. His prime minister was stabbed and a papal prelate shot at through a window. Finally the pope fled to Gaeta, followed by many of the cardinals. Terror reigned through Rome until 1849, when France restored order and returned the Pope to Rome. **Redskins**. This might refer to the Treaty of Guadalupe Hidalgo of February 1848, which ceded sovereignty of Mexican lands, including California, to the United States; or to the death of George Washington Barnett (1793–1848), member of the Texas House of Representatives in one of the raids by Lipan-Apache Indians in October of that year. **Biology**. In 1848 Carl Theodor Ernst von Siebold established protozoa as the basic phylum of the animal kingdom. Louis Pasteur (1822–1895), in a series of brilliantly conceived and executed experiments, demonstrated the connection between the optical activity of organic molecules and crystalline structure, thus founding stereochemistry. Claude Bernard (1813–1878). Demonstrated the ability of the liver to store sugar in the form of glycogen. His widely read *Introduction à l'étude de la médecine expérimentale* (1865) influenced the literary world as well as scientists. **Giuseppe Garibaldi** (1807–1882). In 1847 Garibaldi offered the apostolic nuncio at Rio de Janeiro Bedini the service of his Italian Legion for the liberation of the peninsula. News of the outbreak of revolution in Palermo in January 1848, and revolutionary agitation elsewhere in Italy, encouraged Garibaldi to lead some sixty members of his legion home. He offered his services to Charles Albert and the Piedmontese, who initiated the first war for the liberation of Italy, but was rebuffed by the Piedmontese. He and his followers crossed into Lombardy, where they offered assistance to the provisional government of Milan. Garibaldi is regarded as the unifier of Italy. **Pope from Rome to Gaeta**. When the Revolution of 1848 overtook Rome, Pope Pius IX was forced to flee the city. He spent November 1848 to September 1849 in Gaeta, a city in central Italy.

22. This is a Dutch corruption of a Japanese official title—probably *bantō* 番頭. Also called *bangashira*, this was actually the head of the *banshū* 番衆. These members of the warrior class were attendants with a variety of duties that included security.

accompanied by a major of artillery who was ailing. I had been entrusted by the war department on Java to travel with him until he had recovered.[23]

We landed on Decima, and after a half-dozen *dwarskijkers* anxiously inspected the seal on the lock on the water gate and found it to be in order, the *opperbanjoost*[24] at last gave the word to open it.[25] The colossal black door creaked on its hinges and, encircled with guards as if we were state criminals, we walked into Decima. Before us lay a broad street, lined on both sides by warehouses, that cut through the length of the island and the few houses of the Dutch personnel. It was raining fairly hard then, and not a single trace of life could be detected. In the forefront of the street, on the right side, was the residence of the *Opperhoofd*.[26] Arriving there, our guards, after many bows and courtesies, took their leave and left us unguarded in front of the door.

"What the deuce!" said the Major, a tall thin man, whose ailment had made his disposition somewhat irritable. "Where are our compatriots, have they all died off here? I don't see a soul, and I had thought they would rush into our arms when we stepped inside the port."

I also felt disgruntled that no one was to be seen. But it was impossible for me to believe in such indifference, that not a single one of our long-separated compatriots could be bothered to get up from his sofa to shake the hand of his newly arrived countrymen.

"Wait just a minute Major," I said as I rang the bell on the *Opperhoofd*'s residence. "You will soon witness something completely different. All the personnel have certainly gathered here at the *Opperhoofd*'s to welcome us together, rather than on the street, where their embraces would make a spectacle in the presence of the Japanese guards."

A servant opened the door and led us inside a parlor.

"*Opperhoofd*," he said in fairly good Dutch, bowing deeply and sucking on his tongue in the Japanese manner, "is still upstairs, but will be with the gentlemen shortly."

---

23. After trouble with rowdy sailors and smuggling, after the mid-seventeenth century usually only the captain was allowed ashore. The major was named F. S. van Maanen. NFJ 1643, Ingekomen Stukken, No. 65, 12 May 1851. According to the ship's muster roll, he appears to have been aged 40, but this part of the page is badly damaged from insects and water. NFJ 1755.

24. Upper, or senior *banjoost*.

25. There were only two gates to the island of Deshima, the Watergate and the Landgate.

26. F. C. Rose, *Opperhoofd* from 1851 to 1854.

There we stood; we looked around the room, and although the Major was about a head taller than me and half my width, his legs no thicker than my rolled-up umbrella, I still thought it advisable as a safety measure to place him a small step to my right rear to prevent him from turning the first meeting upside-down. Near the half-opened door to the room lay the broad staircase leading upstairs. We waited, expecting to hear at any minute the thumping of school being let out, as our rejoicing compatriots came down together to bid us welcome. But it stayed quiet, and the silence made the wait seem endlessly long. There was something pathetic about our position—we were in mysterious Japan under strict guard, without a single noise outside or a single footstep in the distance; there were no servants coming or going, no doors slamming . . . it was as if all sound had disappeared from the earth. The Major, normally inclined to grumble continually, did not now venture a whisper. He just snuffled and coughed now and then almost inaudibly into his pocket-handkerchief.

"It is the silence before the storm," I thought to myself. If the gentlemen soon came storming down the stairs like an avalanche, then their backslaps and speeches would make this place sound very different. Maybe they had even written a poem to welcome us. Didn't Camoës write his glowing *The Lusiads*[27] three centuries ago, when the island of Macao was secluded from the world? Certainly then couldn't my countrymen on Decima also air their feelings in a rhyming welcome?

"Sh!" hissed the Major, bending forward toward me. "I hear something on the stairs."

I listened attentively and heard someone slowly and softly coming down the stairs. It could be a *dwarskijker* who had come to peep through the crack in the door. "Sh, Sh," I whispered back.

But I was mistaken: slowly the door to the room opened and an elderly gentleman in a long dressing gown and slippers stood before us.

---

27. Luís de Camões (1524?–1580). Portuguese poet who served as a soldier on Portuguese vessels for five years to commute a jail sentence given for wounding one of the king's men in a brawl. He was then imprisoned for what were deemed offensive poems, and another three years' service in the Southern Armada to China was added to his sentence. The epic poem *The Lusiads* is his most well-known work. It glorifies Vasco da Gama. The title means Lusitania, or Portugal. It was started in Goa and finished in Macau, supposedly while living in a cave. On the way back to Goa he was shipwrecked in Cambodia and ostensibly swam with one hand and carried the manuscript in the other. It was printed in 1572.

"Good day, gentlemen," said the *Opperhoofd*, because that is who it was, very calm and composed, speaking in a tone such as if he had met us at the club just half an hour before.

"Good day *Opperhoofd*" said the Major and I together. I hastened to introduce us.

He acknowledged this information with a dignified nod, and spoke after a moment of thought: "I wish the gentlemen welcome."

We thanked him with a slight bow, and then there followed a moment of tension while the *Opperhoofd* looked at the wallpaper on the wall, as if he was looking for a fly there, or an object from which he could draw support.

"What the devil?" I thought, chilled by the ice-cold reception. If the *Opperhoofd* did not ask me for the latest news of the world, then I would also not tell him anything of it: if he wasn't curious, so much the better for him. If the man has forgotten how to speak, I will keep my silence, and hide my light under a bushel basket until asked.

After a moment of painful silence, the *Opperhoofd*'s eyes fortuitously fell on the window where the rain pattered against the glass: that brought relief.

"You gentlemen have been unlucky with the weather," he said slowly. People complain constantly about the changes in the weather, but what would they talk about if the weather never changed? For us at least, this subject was most welcome, and the Major, who until now had kept silent, grasped with pleasure the opportunity to grumble about something. He would not say much for the moment, only that whenever he went somewhere it would always rain; in place of all the lamentations about long droughts that one so often hears, people would be better off sending for him; for it appeared that he brought rain and wind everywhere. He'd had enough of this weather in these last years, and disliked people who always said "It is beautiful weather"—those beautiful-weather proclaimers were satisfied with a little sunshine, but he was thankful for the days the sun burned from the heavens, as well as the other days spotted by damp from the clouds. He'd never brought good weather anywhere in the world, and he certainly wouldn't find it here in Japan either: it was no matter to him if the world was upheld by miserable weather, it was still a miserable business. . . .

The *Opperhoofd*, who perhaps had not heard such a long oration in a year, listened with surprise to this extreme volubility, and could immediately discern from the continuing flow of words from the Major that he still had much to get off his chest.

"Well," continued the Major, "people do not need to look just to the weather. We will have about four months time to talk. So now we should talk about other matters, such as what a fine mess the world is in today. I wouldn't much care about it, if it weren't for the fact that I stand to lose my Indies pension. They let me contribute for almost twenty years, although I would rather have the long life than get a big payoff. If all goes as it should, then the doctors, who said that my health is no good and sent me here, will have to repay my twenty-year contribution to the pension fund. If they do not make me better, then they will have to find some other way to show their skill, and . . ."

Heaven only knows how long the Major would have continued on if the *Opperhoofd* had not staunched the stream of grumbling with the remark: "I hope, Major, that your health will improve here; you can lodge with me. A servant will show you to your room."

He then clapped his hands together, whereupon a servant entered who, after receiving the necessary orders from his master, entreated, with many bows, for the Major to follow him. When I was alone with the *Opperhoofd*, he continued, "You must know, Captain, that you are provided with a free house here. Diagonally across from here, where the door is open, is the Captain's House. It would be my pleasure to see you as a guest at my table until your household is put in order."

With a short word of thanks for the hospitality, I considered our first meeting finished. With my valise in hand and my world history stuck in my craw, I crossed the street and stepped, discouraged, into my prospective home. It looked quite decent and consisted of three wallpapered rooms and a kitchen, all without a stick of furniture. I would have to supply it all myself. Disappointed by the cool reception, depressed by the dead silence that prevailed overall and the heavy, dark sky from which the rain fell down in streams, I sat dejectedly on the planked floor of the largest room, my back against the wall, in the state of mind of one who has been abandoned alone in a cave or even entombed in a crypt.

"Where is everyone?" I thought to myself. "Within a few hundred paces of my periphery, there should be a quintet of my countrymen who, for more than a year, awake or asleep, have known nothing of the world or their fatherland. Have these men no heart, no feelings, no desire to know what new companionship has arrived among them, no need to shake the hand of one who has come from afar and can tell them the news, no desire to see a face or a voice other than the same six faces and voices they've been looking at and listening to for the whole year long? It is even more unbelievable that they just found out that I was here, for the thirteen salute shots that I let loose when I dropped anchor yesterday must have shaken their houses. How will I endure the next four months!

I will get homesick in the middle of these beautiful green mountains. For what other prospects are there than the company of an *Opperhoofd* who is unsociable—who has almost forgotten how to speak and could only wring twenty words from his throat with difficulty in a quarter of an hour—with a Major who grumbles, with assistants who appear to be slumbering, and with a doctor who doesn't make house calls? No! I would rather be in the open sea among my shipmates: there prevails, at least . . ."

There was a knock on the door.

"Come in," I called crossly. It will be an assistant or the doctor, I thought. It is good that he's finding me in this mood; then he can tell the others how their coolness has put me out of humor. But no one came in; instead, there was another unobtrusive knock on the door.

"Come in," I called anew, now in a tone as if I was giving a command to strike the topsail from the afterdeck during a squall.

But still no one came in and, after waiting a moment, I peevishly sprung up and hastily pulled open the interior door myself to catch the knocker ashamed and disarmed with the knob in his hand. A strongly built, dark Japanese kneeled before me, as meek as a lamb, holding a large box over his head indicating by signs that I should take it. No sooner was the box in my hands then the bringer stood up and bowed backwards out the door.

In our day, men in circumstances such as I found myself would assume that the mysterious arrival of a closed box meant, if not a foundling, then certainly a packet of dynamite or a torpedo, because thirty years ago people were not as civilized as they are now. But without the least suspicion, I put the box on the ground and slipped off the lid. As soon as I did, a delicious cake smell rose up to me. The contents appeared after I lifted up a clean white piece of paper with "Gift from the Compradors" written on it in good decorative Dutch letters. A fragrant cake called a Moscow Cake,[28] light as feather, was packed neatly in the box. On top, in the middle of an artfully applied embossed wreath of sugar flowers, stood the inscription "Welcome!" written in large sugar letters. I must confess that "welcome" dissolved my melancholic feelings a good deal. But just as I was ready to sample this treat, there was again a knock at the door.

No sooner had I called, "Come in," than a neatly clad Japanese stepped into the room. After some bows and courtesies—which a well-bred European gentleman could not have bettered—he introduced himself as one of the compradors, supplier of all that I might need. I should mention

---

28. A Madera (sponge) cake with currants.

here that in these times the compradors were partners in an association of some Japanese merchants to whom the exclusive right was granted to provide the Hollanders on Decima with whatever they might need. If one wanted some of the victuals that this land yielded—or any carpentry, smithwork, furniture or other craftwork that could be imagined—the Compradors could supply it all quickly, and it was usually of very good quality. The factory members spoke only Dutch, and hardly even that, but it was easy enough to speak of their affairs with them.

I listed for the Comprador what I could come by from shipboard and asked him how much time he needed to procure the missing items in order that my rooms and kitchen might be made reasonably usable as soon as possible.

"About two hours," said the man, and I gave him leave to depart. His many bows strengthened my opinion that here I was among the most courteous people in the world.

The rain had lifted, the sun was coming out again, and from whatever window I looked out I saw, over the low wall that encircled Decima, the most beautiful views of forested mountains and cultivated fields. The rippling blue waters of the bay with her hundreds of fishermen's boats, in the middle of which my ship lay quietly at anchor like a peaceful Leviathan, and the bright colors of the flag of our fatherland snapping cheerfully in the wind.

"To devil with all homesickness," I thought to myself as I stood admiring God's magnificent creation outside my window, "will I feel abandoned in this paradise? Will I let the indifference of others leave me embittered instead of feeling gratitude for the fact that, after a dangerous journey, I can live safely for several months in this beautiful land? Why should I, encircled by so much, find myself insufficient and without the strength to steer my own path with good grace? Let me not be so foolish as to allow those sleepy assistants to trample the flowers in my path: I must learn to appreciate life without their company. Were it otherwise, then I would be like so many who know no *joie de vivre* because they are in the habit of avoiding the pricks of imaginary thorns, where they have, through their own weakness, set foot."

This discovery taught me the truth of my reasoning. I was ashamed that I had for a single instant lost my courage. To completely forget my weakness, I sat cheerfully on the ground with my gift cake on one side and my valise on the other. Did I not have this godlike nature around me, a field flask in my valise, a cake in a box and a friendly comprador to soon bring my household effects?

I set my pocketknife in the wreath of sugar flowers on my Moscow cake, unscrewed the cup of my field flask and filled it with the "*vieux cognac* of Jules Robin,"[29] thinking of the friendly countenance of the Comprador. A ray of sun shone through my window—and, why should I not say it, I was lord of my domain.

It is often said that "a child's hand is quickly filled," but neither do grown men always require treasures to make them happy. For me at least, at that moment a cake, a field flask, a ray of sun and a friendly face made a happy man. Yet my happiness was not complete. For how true it is that the real benefit of the gift is hidden. He who receives a gift wants to show it to others, and if it is edible, even more, wants others to help him eat it. We can take a pleasant stroll on our own in a lovely place; we can all sit by ourselves at the seashore and feel our spirits lift as our eyes roam over that endless space; we can all admire a beautiful woman or a fine painting alone—but he who would rather feast alone is just a miser or a misanthrope.

"Come in," I called, jumping up when there was again a knock at the door. I hastily lay down the piece of cake I had on the tip of my pocketknife, because this meal was a little too undignified to receive a visit. Two Japanese gentlemen with swords in their girdles—and therefore officials—stepped into the room. While bowing in front of me, one of them stated, in halting, stumbling Dutch, that he was the interpreter Saknozio[30] and his companion was his attending *dwarskijker.* An interpreter may never visit a foreigner without such an official. Saknozio brought me the message that the waterport would be opened now that the weather had improved, and that a few *proa*[31] would be sent to unload passengers and the goods ordered from Java by the officials of Decima; so if I wanted anything from shipboard, I just had to give him a note. I hastily wrote a few words in pencil asking that a few of my crew be sent with my furniture, lamps, a few cases of wine and beer, et cetera, and while I handed this over to Saknozio, I indicated to him the cake and field flask that stood on the ground.

"Have you perhaps a bit of time to partake something? A piece of cake and a cup of French liquor are, however, all that I can offer you," I said, picking up the field flask and holding it right under his nose. Saknozio's

29. In French in the original: "old cognac by Jules Robin." Founded in 1782, this company is still producing cognac today.

30. Yoshio Sakunojō. He also participated in the translation of the encyclopedia by Noel Chomel.

31. Also *pran* or *prahn.* In Dutch *prauw.* This is a Malaysian boat with a triangular sail and one outrigger.

eyes glittered. "*Dwarskijker*!" I went forward to let him smell too, but Saknozio signaled that his chaperone did not understand any Dutch. "Still," noted Saknozio, smiling, "he is quite a fair taster."

"Then without further ado, I bid you, you Japanese never use chairs, so sit on the ground and give me the pleasure of sharing my meal," and moving forward, we all sat down. Thus I had two completely unexpected guests with me, who did full justice to both the cake and the field flask.

When both gentlemen had partaken with relish of a few slices of cake and few cups of cognac, Saknozio—after first writing down the name "Jules Robin Cognac" in his notebook—indicated that he was pleased to have become acquainted, and that it was time to leave. His companion looked with such woozy eyes at the field flask he had helped empty that, in his present state, he could have betrayed all of Japan. When my new friends departed with many compliments, the *dwarskijker* was so cross-eyed that he tried to depart through the wall, even though the hole of the door was right in front of him.

Well within the promised time, the Comprador brought the goods I'd requested, and in less than a quarter of an hour all of my rooms were laid with mats. The Japanese use thick straw mats as floor coverings, much as we use carpets. Such mats are about three inches thick, six feet long, and four feet wide. All rooms are built to this size, so the mats fit neatly. People never describe a room as being so long or so broad; rather that it is a room of so many mats.[32] When the planked floor is covered and curtains are hung in a house, everything is cozier. Especially in regards to decorating, I had excellent help from the carpenter and a few sailors who had been sent from shipboard with my baggage, household goods and provisions, and in a few hours my abode was fairly in order. The Comprador had, with my newly arrived Japanese cook, already stocked the kitchen. The sailors, with sweaty faces, were polishing the tables and chairs and finishing up the last of their work, when a servant of the *Opperhoofd* arrived to notify me that it was time to come to the table. After dressing hastily, I stepped out the front door to cross the street and nearly ran right into three gentlemen, all ruddy young men in summer suits of an extremely old-fashioned cut.

"The assistants, certainly!"[33] I cheerfully called out in a hearty tone. "Gentlemen! I am truly delighted to see you," and I shook the outstretched hands all around.

---

32. *Tatami* 畳. This is still true today. However, there are regional variations as to mat size, and special sizes for apartment buildings.

33. One was J. A. G. Bassle. The other two are unidentified.

"Welcome to Decima, Captain," they all rang out. "Thank you, thank you," I said, my excitement rekindled, as I reached out again here and there to shake hands.

There followed then a moment of introduction, and a few polite questions. After the shock of the first meeting had subsided, the oldest assistant remarked, "We wanted to welcome you this morning but it was raining so hard. Besides, we must still make sure to get enough rest, for when the government cargo is unloaded from your ship, we will be busy enough."

"Last night I had just fallen asleep, when I was woken up at eleven o'clock by your cannon shots; thereafter I had such a restless night, that I had barely turned over once by eight this morning," said another.

"Me too," chimed in the third. "We all thought that it would be foolishness to walk through the rain since we would see good weather before long."

"I'm sorry," I answered, "that I disturbed you gentlemen. In any case I hope to pass a few pleasant months among you."

"Pleasant?" said one of them shrugging his shoulders. "For us it is never pleasant when a ship is here. Then we must spend three hours every day at a desk with the warehouse master."

The warehouse master was an official who, upon the arrival of a ship, was entrusted with the storage and delivery of the government cargo to the Japanese; during the associated work and administration, which on Decima was called "the busy time," he was aided by his subordinates, the assistants.[34] He always arrived from Java on the Japan voyage, and returned that way; he was also now my passenger, and had already disembarked the previous evening. His house stood ready, already furnished for him.[35]

It was clearly apparent that the assistants normally spent time amongst themselves, and that, having never had a stranger in their company, and after asking some polite questions, were at a loss as to how to continue. Indeed what should they talk about with someone who had not been shut up in Decima for three years? In their eyes I was simply a "new man," who came into the world of their island as an adult, but still knew nothing of the vicissitudes of their lives. They began thus to grumble together about the "busy time" and left me in the meanwhile to look at the starlings in the sky.

---

34. The warehouse keeper was Petrus Johannes Lange. NFJ 1493.

35. In earlier times the warehouse master (*pakhuismeester*) was resident on the island throughout the year.

"Gentlemen," finally feeling impatient with their single-minded conversation, "I must go to dinner . . ."

"Oh," said the good youths, looking surprised, as if I had been unnoticed, or as if a whole new apparition had suddenly fallen out of the sky in front of them.

"Don't let me detain you any further," I continued. "Right now my time is limited, but favor me this evening with some more of your company, so we can then make further acquaintance."

The invitation was accepted, and a moment later I stepped into the *Opperhoofd's* dining room. The table was set but no one was there yet, except the Major, who grumpily paced up and down the room.

"How is it going, Major?" I asked. "Have you settled in? How do you like it here?"

"What can I say to you?" was his reply. "It goes for me here just as it does everywhere: if I am hungry the meal is not ready, and if the meal is ready I am not hungry. The Japanese fellow came to get me, a quarter of an hour ago already, just when I had a healthy appetite. I sped downstairs, I smelled the roast chicken in the hall, and now I walk in here to see empty plates for all this time. Anyone's meal would be spoiled this way, especially if they first had to walk back and forth for a quarter of an hour on Japanese mats. One cannot hear one's own footsteps, so I felt as if I was creeping around like a thief. And these beastly things are so elastic, they throw a person a step further than he had intended; when I just now first walked down into the room, I thought I would rotate on the last step before the wall, and in the turn I launched my head against the wallpaper. You are here before you can hear it!"

There remained no time for me to answer him, because before the Major had completely finished his grumbling, a gentleman of about thirty, clothed neatly in black, stout and ruddy, entered the room bowing, and with both hands gripped mine, shook them and wished me a hearty welcome.[36] He overwhelmed me thereafter with a flood of apologies; he'd had a Japanese prince and his retinue with him all morning and thus had been prevented from coming to see me. With a further torrent of words, he declared he was glad to meet me here, and hoped to hear a lot of news from me, as I had come almost straight out of Europe, because he was burning with impatience to learn what was happening in the world; how was it in the Netherlands, how in France, Germany, etc. etc.

36. Otto Gottlieb Mohnike (1814–1887). He would have been about 37. A naturalist as well as a doctor, he is known for being the first to successfully introduce the smallpox vaccine to Japan. On Deshima from 1848 to 1851.

Meanwhile, the Major stood stock-still, like a pillar of salt, a few steps away from us, and pulled a grim face. His stately military bearing seemed to indicate that he was awaiting the homage that had already been withheld from him too long, for he knew that the doctor was a health officer on detached duty.

"My dear doctor," said I, after first declaring my appreciation for his apologies and my thanks for his welcome, "you will find me perfectly ready to tell you the latest world news. But let me first have the pleasure of introducing you to this gentleman who has accompanied me from Java, Major . . ."

On hearing of a higher military title than his own, the doctor leapt as if he had received an electric shock, letting loose my hand, which he still held in his. As the doctor was a health officer with a lieutenant's rank, the Major stood a few rungs higher. In the heat of the first meeting the lieutenant had thus offended the Major because he had overlooked a field officer who was twice as tall as anyone else. Through a nimble sideways turn, he brought himself a few steps in front of the Major, and put on a military front, whereupon he, as to one superior in rank, gave his compliments and a short apology in a few polite words.

"I am not angry with you doctor! For I am not dressed," sounded the cool voice of the Major—who only called himself "dressed" if he was in uniform—as if out of the mouth of a talking mummy, "or otherwise I would think that you had forgotten the honors in this hole."

The doctor was wise enough to ask at once what the Major's ailments were, expressing curiosity when most men would be increasingly complacent; and with his promise to examine the Major's health another day, he cheered the Major up with the prospect of all the do's and don'ts, the tongue, the pulse and the regimens, and how he would in his turn give the Major the honors of his position.

I sensed the meeting between the Major and the doctor was less than pleasant, because it seemed to me that there was always something to banish the good cheer from Decima. It was apparent that the doctor, who seemed to be a cheerful and talkative man, now, in the presence of a superior just slunk out of the field, sought to fit his words to the gravity of his black coat. A dinner in the company of an *Opperhoofd* who had unlearned speech, a grumbling Major, and an overly dignified doctor was a pleasure that could only be enjoyed by one deaf and dumb. I therefore awaited a dreary meal with little interaction with my fellow diners. It was not for me to disturb the barriers of silent gravity, since I was but a fearful underling stuck between a senior official, a major and a lieutenant. It was a matter of indifference to me how distant these different dignitaries meant to keep each other, for I felt no desire in this out-of-the-way corner of the world to sacrifice my dignity on a well-spread table. The rest of the world is teeming with those who are unhappy slaves to civilized society, who think that wrapping themselves in black clothing topped off with a high hat gives them an aura of respectability, especially if they never express joy in anything more than a smile and their words are wrung so infrequently from their throats as to give the impression that they must first be properly filtered through a pure white scarf. Just like anywhere else, I think that men on Decima could do without such examples of human degradation.

Through a trifle, the relationship between the Major and the doctor happily became much more familiar. While we waited in the dining room, a servant brought around a tray with Madeira and port wine. The Major had already imbibed one before the arrival of the doctor, but now there was a servant going around again and he thought before taking a glass of port wine from the tray, he should first ask permission from the sawbones.

"Doctor, a single glass could certainly do no harm?"

"Why absolutely not, Major!" said the doctor, "nor two, or even three."

"There you are, you know better than all the doctors on Java, who would pester me to death about the bottle," said the Major, and thereby saw the doctor as extremely benevolent, because this pleasure could continue.

"Carry on, Major! I have never yet in my entire practice lost anyone through drinking a good glass of port."

The happy patient was still smacking his lips when our host trod into the dining room with a stately step. After the exchange of a few appropriate courtesies, we sat down at the table. The soup was silently consumed, and one heard nothing but a discordant slurp and the rattling of plates and dishes in the adjoining buffet room. When, thereafter, a servant filled our glasses with venerable old Madeira, the *Opperhoofd* looked around as if he was readying himself to break the silence.

"It is still dry weather." He spoke slowly, looking at us thoughtfully, as if his words were only spoken with careful consideration.

"Oh yes, *Opperhoofd*! The air has been clear since two o'clock this afternoon," said the doctor.

"It was one o'clock, doctor, when the sun came out," remarked the Major and then shot a look at the doctor as if to say: in the future wait until your superior has spoken first.

"Oh really, was it one o'clock, Major?" said the doctor somewhat abashedly.

Now or never, I thought to myself, it is time to break the ice, to unburden myself of my world news. The *Opperhoofd* must have decided to begin this conversation with the weather because it was the latest news on his horizon that he could offer to his guests. Indeed, his interest thereby aroused, he will perhaps ask questions and make remarks and thus his ability to speak, lost through long silence, will return.

"Doctor! You asked me before about the news out of Europe," so I began, "but so much has happened that, in brief, the lessons of '89, put back in the box in the year '15, have come anew upon the people of Europe.[37] It is self-evident that the revolution began in Paris, and from there it spread to nearly all the capital cities of Europe: everywhere blood has flowed, the people have stood up against the autocratic monarchy and long for more freedom in all spheres of life. Louis Philippe has been driven away, King Ferdinand has abdicated, the Pope has fled—in short, the political situation is completely changed. I will tell you all about that later, unless maybe the *Opperhoofd* wishes to know something . . ." and I bowed modestly toward the host to hear his answer.

The *Opperhoofd* had, while I spoke, looked around surprised, as if he thought that a ventriloquist sat hidden behind the wallpaper. But now it was necessary for him to answer, and he spoke after a moment of meditation: "Let us hear just a bit, for I have not had time to see the newspapers that were brought."

Finally the moment had come wherein I could cast my historical ballast overboard to my heart's content! I could not do so without also introducing political principles into the discussion, and from that came the panacea for all silent men to start an argument. In less than five minutes we were divided into conservatives and liberals. At first the *Opperhoofd* issued his own observations and assertions slowly and with difficulty; but what his speech cost him in effort he reclaimed in length and quality as he had to defend his political views against the march of events. From a few precise words, he gradually advanced to whole arguments, and ere we were still on the dessert he was a thoroughly well-spoken host who could be justly called the "great attraction"[38] of our table. He scaled a new mount, as it were; the crush of new ideas had broken through the monotony of an almost completely slumbering

37. The French Revolution took place in 1789. The year 1815 saw the second rise and fall of Napoleon, the Congress of Vienna that formed European politics until World War I, and the establishment of Willem II as a constitutional monarch over the United Kingdom of the Netherlands.

38. In English in original.

spirit, one that was apparently too rich in ability to speak a few shy words. Hence, though he was terse, through exertion he called back language, almost forgotten in the silence, to his memory, and he succeeded so well that longer and longer full sentences came out of him, and it became clearly apparent that he was a man of more than common knowledge and education. The Major, who thought only of himself as long as there was still a dish to be served, making only the occasional cross remark, only became irritated at full strength after he had sent down a glass of burgundy after his pudding. The doctor, who only a few years previously had studied at a German academy, was a fervent advocate of the new ideas, which he conveyed in a heated voice; as for me, I was too happy to be emptying my treasure chest of history not to proceed tirelessly. So life and companionship prevailed at last in what otherwise was the quiet dining room of the *Opperhoofd*; the arrival of new ideas had dealt a death blow to gravity, and the meal—which, at the beginning, appeared as if it would pass so dully—was an outstanding success, not just through the choice food and wine but also through the fruit of it. For the *Opperhoofd*, first shy and silent, had regained his ability to speak to such an extent that he finally dedicated a welcome toast to his compatriots; the Major declared that he had not felt this good in a year; the doctor asserted that this was already the beginning of healing—for which the Major thanked him for his "military camaraderie"—and I had disposed of my world news and, having done so, sowed new thoughts on a field that through the long break had lain fallow, threatening to dry out completely.

A spacious covered terrace, which had a beautiful view of the bay, was attached to the *Opperhoofd*'s residence, and after the meal we moved there to smoke and drink tea in the fresh air. Many pleasant hours did I later spend relaxing in this lovely place; after a sweltering hot day we would collect here in the evening's cool. But this time it was necessary for me to quickly take my leave, as the assistants were waiting for me. The doctor, who walked out with me, declared, when we stood at the front door, his surprise at the drastic change in the *Opperhoofd*'s speaking ability.

"I have been here one year now," he said, "and, though I haven't kept count, I am confident that in the last hour he has spoken more words than he has in the whole past year. I can certainly assure you that he is a very kind and upright man. He represents our country here with honor, as much through his modest and dignified manner of living as through his extensive knowledge; though he does not flaunt it, the Japanese are well aware of it. The educated among them place a high value on dignified behavior and scientific development; hence he is highly esteemed by the local authorities, and if the Governor of Nagasaki asks him a question through an interpreter, he can be assured of a short and thorough answer. The companionship of the young assistants does not tempt him. Thus for three long years he has not spoken more than is necessary, but has absolutely not given offense to others, and I cannot complain about his volubility. I hope the arrival of some new blood and a different environment will make him more convivial. I believe that we are well on our way."

"We must do our best, doctor!" I said. "But now, if I may bid you to return quickly to the gentlemen, for if you leave the *Opperhoofd* alone with the splenetic Major, I fear we will have won nothing."

Later it appeared to me that the *Opperhoofd* had slowly made great strides on the right path, and that, given a little good material, his companionship was worth double. Perhaps after arriving on Decima three years ago, he had soon realized that he was poorly understood and decided it was better to be silent and turn inward, than to trouble himself with all the local bickering and doings that tarred the miniature world around him.

At my quarters I found the assistants already waiting. When they had settled themselves comfortably and I had hastily made a few arrangements to provide a liberal reception, I began to apologize for my long absence. I told them that so many important events had taken place in Europe that their discussion at the *Opperhoofd*'s table had kept us longer than otherwise might have been the case.

"They always have something there in Europe to fiddle about with," said one of them, "but fortunately we have nothing like that here, and their quibbles are no matter to us."

I understood at once that I was dealing with some kind of moon men who lived in their own world. The demands that were made in those days on minor officials in the Indies were not especially great, and so if a youth equipped with the best education a lower school of the day could offer, traveled to the Indies with a few letters of recommendation in his pocket, he could almost certainly find a place at the trough of the Indies. It was frequently the case that such a youth, having spent a few months on Java, was appointed as assistant to Japan, and thus, at a very young age, made his entry into the world of Decima. It was not the place to develop oneself further or to gain some practical experience about the ways of men. Isolated from everything, without letters or messages besides the few that were brought by the ship once a year, before long the youth lost all interest in what happened beyond his island, until at last he forgot, through total deprivation of communication, the whole world that lay outside; it seemed to him as if it were an unreachable planet existing only in his imagination. It was thus preferable for him to create his own world, one that he could walk around in a few minutes, in which he knew not only his fellows and their housekeepers, but also the interpreters and compradors, and even the *dwarskijker*, who now and then spied inside their borders as if their presence posed some danger to the Empire of Japan.*[39]

When a man concentrates his entire mind on a specific branch of knowledge, he has the chance to excel; thus it was that the assistants were

*Once, I caught the assistants in a joke, or rather a bit of fun.

In those days we made, as guests of the *Opperhoofd*, a long trip outside the walls to visit the Japanese gardener Magwitz,[40] who supplied vegetables to Decima and whose house lay in a beautiful spot in the mountains. There we enjoyed a festive meal on a verandah decorated with flowers, and delighted in the most magnificent view. It was the custom, on such occasions, to take all foreigners before their departure to write their name on the walls of the verandah in remembrance.

Ten years later I came on my return trip from Yokohama to Shanghai to spend a few days on Decima, and one of my friends there had the courtesy to invite me to a party in the country. He let me choose where I would like to have it. "To Magwitz's," I said, "the landscape is so beautiful there. I remember it from years ago."

Like that other morning we traveled with a small party, well stocked with provisions obtained en route, and a few hours later we merrily sat down together to a delicious "luncheon" amid the delightful nature around Magwitz's verandah.

"My name must still stand on these walls as I wrote it here ten years ago with Japanese ink," I said, looking around the completely ink-smudged cedar planks which wainscoted the interior of the verandah.

"Let us see if we can find it," everyone exclaimed, "and we can see if you have written it neatly after having a feast."

I also helped to look but could not find it, nor could several others, but three of my friends stood together at attention, peering at one of the ink-stained planks. "Did you also find nothing there?" I asked, inserting my head between the trio. "Nothing, nix, nil," said one of them.

"How," I exclaimed, "can you see nothing? Look there on the plank right in front of your noses, there is indeed my name in thick letters," and I saw it encircled with caricatures and graffiti that testified to the humor of the assistants or their later followers.

"Well, we certainly saw it, but the three of us went to stand in front of it intentionally because we thought you might have gotten annoyed at the silly jokes," remarked one of them.

"It is possible!" I burst out laughing, "that you nearly deprived me of a good moment. This discovery is worth gold to me. One of my friends, a chemist, boasted recently to me that through his scholarship he was able to draw the fat particles from a stockfish; but now I can tell him that I have discovered the wit of an assistant, and that will certainly put my scientific friend to shame."

39. This earlier visit is relayed in *Mijn verblijf in Japan* (Amsterdam: Gebroeders Kraay, 1856), 54–57. This return trip was in 1861.

40. Magwitz is the gardener Magoichi who helped Siebold's assistant Heinrich Burger obtain plant and animal specimens.

so well-versed in their miniature world of Decima and their situation that instead of boring them with my European tales and notions, I deemed it wiser to benefit from their local expertise. Unfamiliar as the assistants were with speaking with others, the conversation did not flow at its best with the arrival of a stranger, and they gave me the impression of dazed men who had just been pulled onto land after drowning. Nevertheless, through some very simple treatment, like the blowing of clouds of tobacco and the administering of a few spoonfuls of brandy with hot water, their life force was soon awakened. With pleasure I came to know that, on their terrain, they were very talkative youths, and I listened attentively to their tales about the small deceptions of the compradors, the cadging of the interpreters, the way of life and foodstuffs—in short, through their companionship, I knew in a few hours as much about Decima, with all of its joys and sorrows, as if I had been their fellow in misfortune all along.

Thereafter I spent four months on Decima, and I remember it readily as far from the least happy time in my life. A sailor is usually restlessly drifting around, sometimes bobbing on the ocean for months at a stretch inside cramped shipboard quarters, constrained to everlasting anxiety and wakefulness, so my quiet stay on Decima was like being an exile in the middle of the most magnificent nature—one that might even be considered a small beneficial respite, like a stay at a spa to recover from an illness. Decima is not an island washed all around by frothy waves as one might think; rather, it is a very small corner of the great city of Nagasaki, connected by a stone bridge over a small canal. In the busy time, when a Dutch ship was there, the small space was pervaded with the loading and unloading of goods, bustle and activity enough. But then it also teemed with all sorts of supervising officials, such as upper and under *banjoosten*, interpreters, *dwarskijkers* and the necessary porters or coolies, a strong race of copper-colored fellows, true athletes, who can with their two hands carry a basket[41] of sugar at a trot to wherever it needed to go. It didn't really take four months to unload and load a ship, and so this time had to be spent according to old practices; most days on Decima passed by without what you would call work. The interpreters, of whom there were once fairly many, had their office—or, as they called it, their "college"—on the island, and on quiet days they were never at a loss with what to do with their empty time; they used it, some more desirably than others, to visit me. They had the less pleasant

41. *Kranjang.* Sugar from the East Indies was shipped in these reed baskets.

quality, which can also be found elsewhere, of storming someone's house, as long as they were received cordially, and staying around as long as there was a drop in the bottle. Yet many were civilized folk, who behaved with the utmost courtesy, though their companionship was pleasanter if they weren't eternally constrained by their shadows, the tiresome *dwarskijkers*. Truly one can safely trust that all the Japanese of the higher and middle classes are well-bred folk, and during my stay on Decima, I was never more surprised than when I encountered a civilized and orderly society in this land with its million inhabitants, which for the past centuries had been separated from the rest of the world. Just as in Europe, one can find on this large yet remote archipelago of the Pacific Ocean, officials for all the branches of administration of the needs of the country; men who, in their manner, were outstanding scholars in the various branches of science; merchants; shopkeepers; all kinds of artisans, burghers and farmers. Agriculture and industry had reached an advanced stage. It was thus a mistake to think that the country in its seclusion had fallen into a state of barbarianism, when in actual fact the Japanese had already had their version of civilization for centuries when Europe was still in its infancy.

To visit the city of Nagasaki adjacent to Decima, or to wander her outskirts, required permission beforehand from the *Opperhoofd* but was almost never refused. Rather, a walk outside their island was attended by so many onerous commitments that the residents of Decima rarely made use of this privilege. One could not set foot outside the island without a Japanese escort, which for a walk usually consisted of a half-dozen interpreters, just as many *dwarskijkers*, and a quartet of *onder-banjoosten* (a sort of police commissar). If that was not cumbrous enough, one especially troublesome drawback was that one had to bring along one's own food and drink for the refreshment of all. No one's pantry, except that of the *Opperhoofd*, was ample enough to provide a "luncheon," prepared and spread out in the European manner, for thirty guests in the mountains for the sake of a walk, especially when one had to take into account the Cossack stomachs of the gentlemen interpreters, *banjoosten* and *dwarskijkers*. The honor of entertainment was thus, as a rule, left to the *Opperhoofd*, and let it be understood that he was quite frugal with his requests to walk outside, because for him the walk was really a very expensive outing. Indeed, he was too hospitable, for it was more than now and then that he took up that burden and entertained us with a festive walking tour in the beautiful environs of Nagasaki, an area that I still recall as the fertile green highlands of the "Rheingau."[42] Before we got that far, however, we had to first traverse through the great city of 60,000 inhabitants—and if one can measure the civilization of a people by their demeanor toward foreigners, then it seemed to me that the Japanese plebs are far more decently behaved than people of their sort in our large cities. Of course, the faces of Europeans with beards and strange clothing excited curiosity, but I never detected the slightest trace of mockery or jeering. On the contrary, people laughed and greeted us kindly, and the only liberty taken was by the occasional joker from the slums who tried to draw our attention to the pretty girls in the crowd.

The city was generally extremely clean, to the extent that the night soil was collected quite meticulously for agricultural use, but it was built against the slope of the mountain, which meant that frequently stairs had to be climbed and several hundred feet of planks crossed just to get to the other side of a street. Decima lay on the bay at the lower end of the city, with the mountain range rising steeply out of the water all around it, without a single flat bank. They had a broad view of the surrounding landscape from the island, so they felt less isolated. Indeed, the wall that encircled the island in those days was quite low, and if one stood a few paces back from it one could see a great distance around, including the nearby but much higher-lying city. Moreover, on Decima they had their own garden with a profusion of shrubs and flowers, so that no matter where they looked, they had the most beautiful view of the bay and the green mountain range. Thus it was not as bleak to be trapped between those walls as one might superficially think.

The presence of a greater number of Europeans during the sojourn of the Dutch ship also greatly increased the conviviality. The pleasant atmosphere between us, the many visits from civilized Japanese, and my interest in everything that surrounded me in this strange land—all of these made the time pass quickly, and it was with regret that I watched the approach of the day of our departure. To be away from the rest of the world for four months is not long enough to become bored if one spends the time in a beautiful land with a healthy climate, in a place so safe that no one even bothers to shut his front door, and at a good table without a single trace of earthly cares. Likewise, lack of money—the dreaded dilemma that ruffles so many tempers elsewhere in the world—was, to all appearances, unknown on Deshima. There was not a single wallet to

---

42. Rhine region. De Coningh is suggesting that they look similar.

be found on the whole island; no one had a penny to toss. Each man was
given, as part of his salary, a line of credit at the college of interpreters,
where the administration was handled, and thus lived according to his
position and ability, unconcerned with loss or ever having to put his
hand in his pocket.[43]

On a certain day before our departure, there was a big sale among
the few European personnel of Decima. In addition to the Major,
the warehouse keeper, the *pachter* of the so-called *kambang* trade,[44]
and the doctor were all departing with me to Java, so that only the
Opperhoofd would remain behind with a trio of assistants.[45] After a
heartfelt farewell, the great waterport was closed behind us, and those
left behind turned with leaden steps back to their homes, to forget and
forsake the world, recalled for but a moment, for yet another year to
live on, quietly and monotonously, in their own circle. As for me, when
the anchor was weighed and we had sailed out of the bay, I cast a last
look full of sympathy on the small corner of exile that I had found so
agreeable; and when, shortly after that, the great sea lay before us and
the green mountains and hills of the beautiful Japanese empire stretched
out behind us as far as the eye could see, I was gripped with a wistful
feeling that came from the knowledge that I might never return to see
this dear land again, with its friendly and civilized people. In those days,
no one could have surmised that in a few years Japan would be forced
to break with the system of isolation that had allowed these civilized
people a wealthy existence without hindrance, and for which they owed
centuries of peace and prosperity. The millions of Japanese were perfectly
satisfied with their position, and the thinking part of the nation knew

43. This system was put in place at the end of the seventeenth century by the Japanese
government, which wanted to control the outflow of precious metals from Japan.
De Coningh is mistaken in claiming that these funds were administered by the
interpreters. Instead, the Nagasaki *kaisho* 会所, an administrative body formed by
the shogunate in 1698, handled most of the day-to-day matters involved in foreign
trade.

44. Normally, *pachter* means renter, leaser, or tenant, but in the context of NHM
trade it meant agent or investor. This *pachter* was A. J. J. de Wolff. He himself had
been an assistant on Deshima from 1840 to 1842. *Kambang* was a word unique to
private (as opposed to official Company) trade in early modern Japan. It originated
early in the seventeenth century, supposedly from the Japanese word *kanban,* or
signboard, referring to the auction postings.

45. Rose was replaced the following year by Jan Hendrik Donker Curtius (1792–1864),
who remained in Japan until 1860, successfully negotiating commercial treaties in
1856 and 1858.

very well that Western peoples, when they set foot in Eastern lands, acted increasingly like an army, demanding absolute opening of the fatherland to strangers—a process that begins with missionaries seeking converts and ends with soldiers writing the laws. So great was their antipathy toward Christian missionaries, of whom they had first learned from the Portuguese three hundred years before, that on Decima a cross could never be displayed in any manner and no book with a cross printed on it was allowed; in my government instructions, I was quite expressly ordered that on festive occasions when my ship was dressed out with flags in the Bay of Nagasaki, any flag with a cross should be omitted. The antipathy for the cross, however, did not at all originate from a hatred of religion, for I have never noticed the slightest trace of fanaticism in them. In matters of faith they were so liberal that they could not discern whether their Dutch friends were Christian, Israelite, Mussulman or freethinker. But they were too well informed of world history not to know that the Christian cross of love has eradicated whole peoples and now signified to all Asian and Polynesian races little better than a blood-drenched symbol of proselytization.

But, for all their self-sufficiency and their care to avoid conflict with the outside world, Japan was not fortunate enough to remain above the comings and goings of the world. The ice was first broken by the Americans who, in 1854, sailed with a fleet into the Bay of Jeddo and, with various threats, were able to compel the opening of the small port of Simoda.[46] After that, the English, French and Russians appeared posthaste with their warships; of course, the Dutch negotiated the same concessions as the others. As a result of such a resolute military display by the mightiest nations of the West, the Japanese government was seized with fear, so that, in a manner of speaking, a treaty was extorted under the muzzles of drawn cannons. So it came to be, after endless negotiations—and very much against the wishes of the educated Japanese, who understood that their might was in danger—the port of Yokohama, in the bay of Edo, was set to be opened to the nationals of the treaty powers on July 4, 1859.

The port of Nagasaki opened a few months earlier, and with that opening the low wall that encircled Deshima fell, the *dwarskijkers* disappeared, and the system of isolation and exile, which our countrymen had endured in this small place since 1639, was ended.[47]

---

46. Shimoda.

47. The Portuguese were expelled in 1639; however, the Dutch did not move on to Deshima until 1641.

Chapter 2

Now we turn back to shipboard on the *Argonaut*, entering the Bay of Jeddo under full sail along the beautiful shores. By the evening of September 4, we dropped anchor in Yokohama.

Yokohama—or properly Jokahama, from *joka* or beautiful, and *hama* or beach—is a name it rightly bears, for it lies in a lovely green plain surrounded at various distances inland by a chain of low, overgrown hills.[1] This formerly insignificant Japanese fishing village lay a few hours distant from the capital, Jeddo,[2] and was intended to become the great port of the future, opened to foreigners in Japan. Located in the middle of the realm, at the edge of a safe bay surrounded by fertile countryside, and not far from the capital, this place satisfied all needs, and so it later came to pass that it soon became a flourishing commercial town. Upon our arrival, there was absolutely no trace of town or city to be discerned, no matter how close we came to the shore to drop anchor. The only preparation made for the arrival of foreigners was a large wooden building that the Japanese called their Interpreters' Office surrounded by a sextet of sheds, the whole encircled with palisades, and further beyond these sheds stood four little sentry boxes, which could best be compared to our waffle stalls. Otherwise, one could see nothing else nearby save for the cultivated fields between the lovely trees of the farmers' and fishermans' houses of the real village of Yokohama.

Scarcely had the sails been furled and I had thanked heaven for our safe arrival in the land of promise, when, from a boat that approached our ship in the darkness that had fallen in the meantime, I clearly heard Dutch spoken. A moment later two compatriots, the only countrymen to have arrived in Yokohama before me, sprang on to the deck to welcome us. No Italian bandits in a traveling show could have appeared more alarming than these two visitors. They sported long beards, wore squashed, broad-brimmed hats and high Californian boots,[3] and were

---

1. Yokohama was, in fact, correct. De Coningh was only partially right. "Yoko" derives from the word for *opposite*, meaning that it was across the bay from Edo.

2. Edo did not officially become the capital until 1868, but it was the largest city and home of the shogun.

3. Knee-high, square-toed, pull-on boots, with the top edge usually cut straight across although occasionally peaked in front to partially cover the knee. Most had pegged soles (wooden pegs to connect the sole to the upper), though the best quality would

armed to the teeth with swords and daggers. They would have given anyone a fright. All the same, they were a pair of peaceable gentlemen from Java who had come here three weeks before to try their luck at trade. We had barely sat in the cabin and readied a Dutch welcome drink, when both of them made a motion which I first took to mean that they wanted to take out their watches; instead, they each pulled a loaded revolver out from their belt and lay it on the table in front of them.

"Thank God!" they said, "here at least we can lay these things to rest," and now I heard, to my alarm and surprise, how things stood in Yokohama.

The Japanese middle and lower classes were well enough disposed toward foreigners, but the *Jakoni*, or sword bearers[4]—what one would call a sort of nobility, constituting a large portion of the populace—would have liked nothing better than to exterminate foreigners to the last man. For the most part, the Princes[5] who ruled the provinces independent of the sovereign, were dead set against the foreigners; they believed that their presence meant that the heart of their nationhood would be trampled on, and that sooner or later their happy fatherland would be submerged in foreign influences. They feared the wellspring of gifts of Western society, the extreme politics and religious hate, and understood that the sorrow that awaited could never be made good through international commerce. This is why they saw the newcomers as interloping poachers who hated their independence. They knew all too well what happened to their neighbor China who had, often through a triviality—such as, for example, not unloading enough opium, or expelling all the zealous missionaries—offended the European gentlemen who then, in order to defend their honor, came with their fleets, bombing what they would with missiles sent from sea to shore. Though the Princes were vassals to the *Keisers*,[6] most were little pleased with the treaties made by the *Keiser*

---

have been sewn ("welted"). Some had hobnails added to the sole for durability. A standard men's work boot, they were called Californian because large numbers were shipped to the west coast after the gold rush. They were more likely to have been produced in New England.

4. *Yakunin* 役人. Government official. De Coningh calls them sword bearers because all members of the military class, from which the *yakunin* were drawn, were permitted to wear swords, while commoners were not except rarely as recognition for services to the government.

5. *Landsheeren*. Literally, Lord. This was the Dutch word used to refer to *daimyo*, warlords who had sworn allegiance to the shogun.

6. *Kaiser*, i.e., the Shogun.

and set out to make the foreigners as uneasy as possible in the hope that
they would, disheartened by fear and lack of safety, depart of their own
accord. Since they dared not, for fear of the consequences, openly attack
the unwelcome visitors and put them to the sword, they tried to achieve
their end through assassination and arson. For this purpose they had
all too many "bravos"[7] at their disposal, who knew how to sneak into the
foreigners' quarter using various disguises. Yokohama was, like all the land
for a distance around the vicinity of Jeddo, directly shogunal territory;
thus the foreigners had only to deal with the *Keiser*'s officials, whose duty
it was to protect them against the princes' vagabonds. Whether they truly
took this duty to heart was the real question: for each time there was
a murder, one or another of the princes' *samurais* would "slip through
the net," as the saying goes. The *Keiser*'s authorities would feign great
indignation at the testimony of the foreign accusers, make all kinds of
apologies, and promise sharp surveillance and forceful investigations—
yet a culprit was never caught. They always cast the blame on a powerful
lord from the interior, a certain Prince Mito,[8] a blood relative of the
Keiser, who bore a fierce hatred toward the foreigners and would compel
them to leave through force if necessary. Yet the *Keiser* was too weak
before the might of Prince Mito and the like-minded princes to respect
the signed treaties.

Upon hearing these warnings from my countrymen, I expressed my
amazement at their assertion that those ashore were never for a minute
certain of their lives. After holding a eulogy over the courteous Japanese
that I knew from the past, I lashed out violently against the roguishness
of the Prince of Mito, who, with his assassins and arsonists, was a disgrace
to his fatherland and better branded a common bandit.

"Don't tilt at windmills," said one of them. "Almost no one trusts
the hostile princes, and not one of them trusts that fire-eater, the Prince
of Mito. Your civilized Japanese are so civilized that they are too smart
for our European diplomats. They know very well that they, on their
archipelago, without their own fleet, could be easily punished for each
murder with a couple warships; thus they need a scapegoat to take all the
blame, who unfortunately has so much power that there is nothing that
the *Keiser* can do about it. We endure it here, so the Japanese tactic is to

7. In English in original. Here meaning assassin.
8. Tokugawa Nariaki (1800–1860), head of the cadet house of Mito, descended
from a brother of Tokugawa Ieyasu. Xenophobic, he advocated the expulsion of
all foreigners. He was placed under house arrest in 1843 for his radical views and
succeeded by his son Tsuruchiyo, but remained powerful.

frighten and discourage us until they finally get what they want, which is that we go back from whence we came. The Japanese authorities do whatever they can to work against trade. Each of us faces disappointment and fear of the bogeyman Prince Mito with his sharp swords; no one feels safe here, so some of us have already left, and others are thinking about going. Things might change if we build here, and the Japanese notice that we stand fast and are serious about a settlement; but for the moment we sit here in a wasps' nest. No Japanese merchants dare approach us for fear of the *dwarskijkers,* the sword of Mito dangles over our heads, and God and our revolvers are the only things in which we can place our trust. We go to bed with the knowledge that we may be chopped up or burned in our own beds. Just the day before yesterday, two Russian officers and two sailors from the fleet who had set out for Jeddo were minced to pieces here, right by the Interpreters' Office.[9] We thought that the Russians would surely take revenge on Jeddo and Kanagawa, which are nearby, yesterday. Especially because their minister Muravieff,[10] the Butcher of Poland, is on board the fleet.[11] But the Russian fleet steamed out of the bay yesterday morning. I heard that the Japanese will build a small Greek Orthodox chapel on the grave of the murder victims and cede the Sakhalin Islands to the Russians.[12] In similar circumstances, the English would have demanded a few thousand "pounds"; the Americans would have bombarded and stipulated a million dollars; the French a delegation for apologies, a salute to their flag and an abundance of

9. He must have meant the week before last. This event occurred on August 25, 1859. Ensign Roman Mofet, the only officer, and two sailors named Sokolov and Korolkov were attacked by an unknown number of armed assailants. Another officer, Ensign Avinov, was in the longboat and was unharmed. Korolkov was wounded but survived by escaping to a nearby shop. Mofet and Sokolov died from their injuries. Money was stolen but the general belief was that the attacks were political.

10. Count Nikolai Nikolavich Muravev Amurski (1809–1881). Spelled variously as Muravieff, Muraviev; Amursky, Amurskii. Governor General of Siberia. The title Count Amurskii was awarded for the Treaty of Aigun in 1854, which gained the left bank of the Amur River for Russia. A number of people have been known as the "Butcher of Poland," but the label is not commonly applied to this man.

11. Muravev was on the frigate *Askold.* There was only one steamer, *Amerika.* The rest of the fleet consisted of four corvettes (*Novik, Voevoda, Rynda,* and *Griden*), one gunboat (*Platsun*), and one clipper (*Dzhigit.*)

12. A mortuary chapel was constructed, which was financed by the Russian officers and midshipmen. The Japanese were merely required to provide a guard in perpetuity. While there were rumors at the time that Russia had demanded Sakhalin, this was not in fact the case.

Dirk de Graeff van Polsbroek. C. T. Assendelft de Coningh did not think
very highly of his efforts as consul. Courtesy of the Scheepvaart Museum.

honors—but the Russians were satisfied with a gilded dome and a large
chunk of land. I can't tell you what we or you are worth if our turn
comes with the Prince of Mito; maybe at least a few official letters, for
we Hollanders only have an assistant from Decima as acting Consul,[13]
while the English, French and Americans are represented here by high
diplomats with their subordinate consular authorities."

13. This was Dirk de Graeff van Polsbroek (1833–1916). He was assigned as Assistant
2nd Class to the factory on Deshima in 1857, and was made acting consul in 1859.
He became consul in 1861 and minister in 1868.

When I recollected the Japanese of just ten years ago, this less than rosy news affected me like one who comes to know a nice family while traveling and later, when asked to their remote country estate, realizes he has ended up in a robber's den. I felt especially discouraged by the thought that we Netherlanders, with our old Japanese claims, were represented among these proud people only by a young man as acting Consul; certainly whatever respect, protection or administration of law accorded us would be inferior to that of the other treaty powers, which had hardened Ministers-resident and their attachés residing in nearby Jeddo. Moreover, their consular authorities had been established in Kanagawa, which faced Yokohama. Evidently those in "patria" had received little notice of the opening of the Japanese ports, and it had been left to the Governor General of the Dutch East Indies to take the necessary measures—and he'd handled the matter as if it were an outpost in the Moluccas. The opening of Nagasaki had brought an end to the government trade, so it was not worth the trouble to send anyone here since the whole matter could be ironed out with a few decisions and without spending a cent.[14] And so the *Opperhoofd* received the title of Commissioner-General;[15] the assistants who were not directly necessary to liquidate the old assets were named as consul or chancellor, and in this manner, without costing a penny, the old trade agency of the East India Company, and later of the Netherlands Indies, became the diplomatic representation of the Kingdom of the Netherlands at a bargain. It is true that, when the *Opperhoofd* was named Commissioner-General, the assistants remained in their modest positions. But immediately after the opening of the ports, the new office-holder dismissed a few of them until further approbation, making acting consuls of them, again under further approbation. Those now-free assistants, who had provisionally resigned in haste in expectation of approbation, had ample opportunity as the first present to shake the most golden fruit from the abruptly ripe tree of trade and put it in their pockets. In the midst of this labor came the Governor General's approbations of the dismissals and appointments; and afterwards the official gazette in The Hague printed the notice that trade in Japan was open and the Netherlanders were invited to take part in it.

Thus had the Netherlands, without fuss or cost to her subjects, at least for all intents and purposes, found a safe and legal position in Japan. Our Commissioner-General did not, like the representatives of other

14. After the collapse of the Dutch East India Company in 1799, trade was carried out by a variety of agencies, ultimately coming under the auspices of the government.

15. This refers to Jan Hendrik Donker Curtius (1813–1879), sent to Japan with this title in 1852.

powers, have his offices in Jeddo, the capital[16] and residence of the *Keisers*, where the treaties were finalized; instead, he remained in Nagasaki where nothing happened. He was therefore a lonely figure, and his residency there had as much consequence as if, e.g., the mayor of Amsterdam lived in Lisbon. But on the other hand, he remained quietly lodged in the comfortable *Opperhoofd's* residence on Decima, where it was impossible to come in direct contact with the shogunal government like his foreign colleagues did, and thus he did not have to rack his brains over the complications between the citizens of his nationality and the Japanese the way the other diplomats did. He sat with all the comforts of life, as safe as if he were nestled in the Bosom of Abraham.[17] Our youthful acting Consul had thus to negotiate in Jeddo next to the envoys Sir Rutherford Alcock for England, M. Duchèsne de Bellecour for France, and General Harris for America—so, when the weight of the Netherlands was laid on the scale, it certainly did not measure up.[18] Our prestige in Japan dwindled all too quickly, pushed aside by other foreign influences.

In such a way were the particulars broadly conveyed, my visitors sharing with me what they knew concerning the current situation of our countrymen in Yokohama. Compatriots, disappointed, left to their fate in a hostile land where they could only count on their fists and revolvers, soon become close, and it was late in the evening before my new friends turned back to the shore, having first readied their weapons and lit their lanterns to protect themselves on the few hundred paces they had to walk from the landing to their dwelling.

The next day I made for the shore, which lay a few minutes' rowing distant, and called on our Consul of the last weeks who had to watch over Dutch interests and the very few of our compatriots in Japan at this time. I found him in a small room in one of the few wooden bungalows in which he held office. However, his residence was in a temple in

16. Although the shogun resided in Edo (Tokyo), the capital was still Kyoto.

17. In other words, paradise.

18. **Sir Rutherford Alcock** (1809–1897). A career diplomat, appointed consul general to Japan in 1858 and made minister plenipotentiary in 1859. Left in 1862, but served in Japan again from 1864–1865. **Gustave Duchesne de Bellecour** (1817–1881). Consul-general in Japan from 1859–1860, promoted to chargé d'affaires from 1860–1862 and ministre plénipotentiaire from 1862–1864. **Townsend Harris** (1804–1878). President of New York Board of Education. Tried to accompany Matthew Perry but was rejected. He served as a diplomat in China but was never a general. Perhaps a mistake for consul-general. Appointed consul-general for Japan in 1855, arrived in 1856, and remained in Japan until 1861.

Kanagawa, a city on the opposite side of the bay.[19] In those days, he conducted trade himself, so I, with a ship and cargo directly out of Europe that, moreover, I had the intention of settling for profit, was only half-welcome as a competitor. Yet he was the man whose cooperation was needed for everything. To his compatriots he was the highest official and their only protector; to the Japanese authorities he, and he alone, was the majesty, the power and the glory. The incoming tradesmen were a kind of Western plebian who were a law unto themselves; but the golden braid on the hat of the Consul was a talisman that allowed him, at any hour of the day, to freely enter, without knocking, and exit the Interpreters' Office and to visit the seat of the Japanese Governor,[20] the representative of the *Keisers*. Needless to say, we were completely dependent on the Consul for everything, for he, and he alone, could make requests and provide support, or not. In those days in Japan many were called, but only one, the man with the gilded cap, was favored. A trading house that had the fortune to count a Consul as one of its members had a capital of enormous credits under its elegant cap, because the sale of ships, machinery, or the like, no matter how sound, were rejected by the Japanese government whenever the Consul did not cooperate. Yet if a Consul offered even one hair of his special protection to such business, then the recommendation from under the braided hat was considered a seal of honesty, and those concerned, hauling in an enormous profit, could laugh up their sleeves because they were so grossly overcompensated.

I had hoped that at my first meeting with the Consul, he could immediately designate a place where I could settle ashore. But he had heard nothing of me and, for the time being, nothing could be decided. In fact, a dispute with the Japanese authorities had arisen immediately after the arrival of the foreign representatives over the arrogant manner in which the Japanese had failed to comply with the treaty. It was stipulated that the harbor of Kanagawa would be opened; yet, upon their arrival, they found that Yokohama had been destined for that purpose, and it was there that the above-mentioned Interpreters' Office and wooden bungalows had been built. These last were intended as the Consuls' residences; as far as the merchants

19. In the 1850s it was common practice for the Japanese government to house foreigners in temples because they were large enough and they tended to be set apart from the population centers.

20. *Bugyō* 奉行, a high government official like a minister or secretary.

were concerned, they could n... board their ships. One must ass... ...uac on the grass not satisfied with the arbitrary ar... the foreign Consuls they called upon the treaty and imn... ...ts of the Japanese, for in Kanagawa. The Japanese did everyth... demanded residence in Yokohama but, when they realized that ...ssible to keep them each Consul received a spacious empty templeg was to be done, wooden bungalows thus became available to the ... abode, and the Five or six people moved into each one, so nat... ...ng merchants. anything but comfortably housed. The reason the Jap... ...se wanted to keep the foreigners away from Kanagawa, they asserted...was that it lay on the main highway to Jeddo so everyone must pass by it to go to the capital, and since princes from the interior with their large retinues went to Jeddo almost every day, it was likely that clashes would occur.

The Foreigner's Settlement in Yokohama, 1859. De Coningh's large compound is roughly in the center. *Gokaikō Yokohama ōezu*, Hashimoto Sadahide. Collection of Waseda University Library.

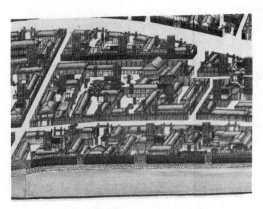

Detail of the Foreigner's Settlement, showing De Coningh's compound. The large yard with animals and elegant two-story building suggest De Coningh was doing quite well.

...sters of the treaty powers—who upon
...personnel had resided in empty temples
...at Yokohama, and held fast to Kanagawa.
...offered me a spot in Kanagawa where I could
...ared not to do anything for me in Yokohama,
...ould soon have to be vacated. He reckoned it better
...the Japanese and the arriving merchants. For the
...ies of the early days, the fact that new foreigners who
...were arriving nearly every day, was a happy circumstance,
...e uninvited guests could both be pressed for a high rent and
also set d firmly in Yokohama. The authorities from the Interpreters'
Office decided to hastily nail together a few dozen wooden bungalows
with matching warehouses on nearby farmland from which the harvest
had been completed; they were strewn chaotically across the uprooted
turnip fields as if they had been shaken out of a box of children's toys.
Yet each bungalow was spoken for long before it was ready because the
foreign merchants, who had keener eyes for their own interests than did
the officials, simply refused to move to Kanagawa, wishing to stay in
Yokohama where the ships could anchor close to the harbor, and was
thus better situated for trade. In Yokohama they could gradually build
their own town on a spacious spot off the main road that was at least
somewhat safe, while those in Kanagawa, a densely populated city,
were certain to secure a trip to eternity. It was thus all very well for the
Consul, who had a strong guard to protect his temple. But in all fairness,
he could hardly require one of his rational countrymen to greet him
with *"ave consules"*[21] in Yokohama, and then immediately send him to
Kanagawa like a gladiator of the Caesars sentenced to death. Insist as he
would, my life was too dear to me to be so rashly deprived of it by Prince
Mito's "bravos." So, thanking the Consul for his offer, I expressed to him
my firm resolve to stay in Yokohama, where I hoped I would be able
to rent one of the planned wooden houses when my turn came. There
were already so many solicitations from all nationalities that the first
place I could get was No. 25 on the list, and in the Consul's opinion it
might take two months to progress to house No. 25 because wheat and
turnips still lay on the ground of the terrain of the new foreign quarter.
However disappointed, I still found it preferable to take a chance at a

---

21. Latin for "Hail Consul." Probably in reference to the apocryphal *Ave Caesar,
morituri salutamus* [Hail Caesar, we who are about to die salute you], which Roman
gladiators were believed to shout to the crowd before battle.

Chapter 2

rented wooden estat…
be hacked to death alon…

In the meantime, I coul… stay alive than to most certainly
that were packed in the *Argona*… months to unload the goods
to be delivered directly from Euro… because they were the first
chance that the market would be flo… port. There was every
thus good business to bring everything to… interval, and it was
But where to stow several hundred chests, … quickly as possible.
port? There were no warehouses—there was ha… nd small, in the
people. Through a fortunate coincidence, one of t… gh shelter for
to the Interpreters' Office was temporarily relinquish… ts belonging
when, a few days later, the cargo had been stored there, … me, and
must press forcefully for a place to stay in the port—how else … ught I
protect my goods from all the potential dangers? To take shelter in one
of the completed wooden bungalows was unthinkable: they were just
like miniature tenements, with few respectable members, most of them
stuffed with rabble, European and American *mauvais sujets*[22] who had
drifted here from China and California, the dissolute fortune hunters
of the day, who, with knives and revolvers, had trekked to the new
golden land, and, untroubled by any judiciary or police, sought to get
rich quick through one swindle or another here. These sorts of people
formed the majority of the civilizer-contingent supplied by America and
England; the few *gentlemen*[23] among these pioneers were, as a rule, agents
of the great trade houses in China, who were ashamed of the gang of
compatriots who made such a sad contrast to the very few Hollanders,
Frenchmen and Germans. In truth, the majority of the perhaps six dozen
foreigners there at the time were a disgrace to Western civilization and
could rightly be called the scum of the white race in their ignoble decay.
Lapsed gentlemen whose main act had played out in the geographic
vicinity of Kamchatka, which had turned them more brutal than the
lowest rabble. Among them could be found persistently drunk doctors,
dissipated lawyers, absconding bankrupts, discharged officers, sottish
ship captains—in short, all kinds of common characters that, just by
the look of them, one would wish sent to the galleys or behind the bars
of a prison. The sight of all these knaves, armed to the teeth, red faces
swollen with brandy and wild beards, inspired in me more revulsion than
Prince Mito with all his bravos. The flow of such folk certainly validated

22. Bad characters.
23. In English in original.

\gners. It was unfortunate that

the hatred the Japanese bo the Interpreters' Office and the
one had to suffer the evil ear the sea, just twenty meters from
A few thousand grove of camellias but otherwise in the
adjoining foreigners the harvest still lay in the field, stood a
the surf, and sha rmhouse. There lived the honorable Josaïmon,
middle of farml his family: wives, sons and daughters. Father
solitary reed-th venerable patriarch, who had barely been noticed
an old farm ers, so his sons had still not experienced the vulgarity
Josaïmon ers ghters had not been exposed to the indelicate glances of
by the f ghters zers from California. He lived isolated from the road that
and his zers cted the foreigners' quarter with the fishing village of Yokohama.
the c

Only a small footpath led through the high grain fields to his house, thereafter coming to a dead end at the seashore.

"It is with great difficulty that I succeeded," said the Consul to me on the day when the last of my goods were warehoused in the Interpreters' Office, "in finding you a lodging as long as you dare to go there. By fortunate exception, the Governor of Kanagawa will permit you to move into the house of Josaïmon, if the man himself allows it, and you will pay him a liberal rent. You know perhaps that it is in a remote spot, so you must look after your own safety. You must keep it well in mind that the *loonings*[24] (bandits) can access the land and water at night with no one the wiser. You can count on the fact that if they know that a *toojing*[25] (foreigner) is living there, you will be their priority—but, in any case, you have the freedom to handle it in accordance with my circular."

"What circular?" I asked.

"Oh, have you not read it yet? I thought to send it around just today. It's there on the table; take a look at it and be so good as to sign off that you've seen it. It is a Dutch translation of the circular that all foreign representatives are sending around today to the citizens of their nationality."

I read in the solemn piece: "experience has shown" and "inasmuch as and pay heed," that the life of a foreigner was never secure, each citizen of the treaty powers was, for this reason, declared authorized to shoot any Japanese who approached them in a suspicious manner at any time of

24. *Rōnin*, 浪人, a masterless samurai.
25. *Tōjin*, 唐人, literally, Chinese person, but often used to mean any kind of foreigner.

the day or night. The postscript was still more droll: "One is reque...
if possible, not to shoot the attacker dead, but only to wound, in ord...
to discover who the principals and their accomplices are."

With firm resolve to shoot someone through the brain or in the
big toe as circumstances required, I signed the circular, which was
immaterial to me. But this trampling of justice greatly grieved me; for,
given the environment in which most of us lived, this circular was a
license to kill extended to a few "British and American subjects" who
imagined themselves inviolable—and of whom England and America
should have been ashamed. This opened the door for every drunken
"settler" with an overactive imagination to shoot down an innocent.
Nothing could have been more dangerous to send out in the world in a
land where tens of thousands carried swords, and none of the foreigners
understood the native language.

I found three old friends I'd known on Decima employed among
the interpreters of the Interpreters' Office—or, in other words, the
"government" in Yokohama. Happy at the prospect of finding a place
to live, I sped to one of them, the first interpreter Sakfsabro,[26] and
asked him to accompany me to the house of the old man Josaïmon
to help conclude the business. Sakfsabro was ready at once, thrusting
both his swords, one short and one long, in his girdle to demonstrate
his status, and so we strode together along the road to Yokohama.
Before long we turned on to the small footpath between the tall stalks
and filed along it until it brought us to Josaïmon's yard. Chickens and
pigs swarmed in the small, enclosed space around the house, and in
the middle was a well with a pole and lever in the air that was used
to raise and lower the bucket, just as one would see in farmyards in
North Brabant.

We stepped, along with a few shrieking chickens, through the open
door of the house which, inside or out, was no different than what
we would have called a large shed. In the middle, on the floorless
hard ground, sat the Josaïmon family at their meal on a spot laid with
mats. I cast off any previous notions I had formed of the patriarchs
Isaac or Jacob with their families that afternoon when I made my first
visit to this Japanese farm family under the wing, so to speak, of my
friend Sakfsabro. There I saw the grizzled Josaïmon, with his wife and

26. Nakayama Sakusaburō (1838?–1868). Eighth generation of the Nakayama
family of interpreters. Acted as one of the interpreters for the Putiatin embassy from
Russia in 1853–1854 and edited an English-Japanese dictionary in Nagasaki before
being dispatched to Kanagawa in 1859.

ncubines,[27] sons and daughters, servants and maids, all kneeling in circle, sitting on their heels, around a chipped collection of pots and pans, eating the fish of the water, the flesh of the animals, and the fruit of the fields. At the sight of Sakfsabro—a *Jakoni* with two swords—they fearfully halted their meal and bowed, resting the upper part of the body on the hands, with the forehead deferentially on the ground. As a tribute of a common sort, this did not make the least impression on my friend, but for me it was like passing a military patrol with a friendly general and feeling flattered by the exhibitions of honor and presented guns. One is tempted to raise his civilian hat to the sentry, trusting that the influence of his friend will extend to him, and no less proud of his companionship; so it was also with me and Sakfsabro. When the circle of foreheads bowed to the earth for his benefit, I saw him with a kind of awe, even though he had been something of a souse on Decima and was known among the sailors as one who liked to drink "a stiff one."

When the good people had lifted their heads again, Sakfsabro began, with the amiable dignity that superiors in Japan are known to exercise toward their inferiors, to inform Josaïmon of the reason for our visit. The old man listened reverentially to his words, but at the beginning I thought I noticed some disappointment on Josaïmon's face, whereby I feared that he would refuse to let his house. Before long, when Sakfsabro's speech, from the few words I understood, apparently turned to money matters, Josaïmon's countenance took on an entirely different expression. However honorable father Josaïmon was, he was too much a farmer to be insensitive to the clink of silver, and it showed me that he, like one often finds among farmers, was, despite his quasi-humility and ignorance, a crafty bird when it came to a pile of silver. From the little that I understood of the negotiations, I noticed that Sakfsabro, as a friend, campaigned strongly for my cause, and that Josaïmon, underneath his reverential bows to the *Jakoni*, was busy in his own way, trying to skin me alive.

It was my preference not to drive these poor buggers from their property for a trifle, and when I understood the sum that Josaïmon meant to ask as monthly rent, I lay down a few extra *itzeboes*[28] so that the business was dispatched in a way that made everyone happy. So pleased was the family Josaïmon with their generous lodger that they

---

27. It is unlikely that these were concubines as taking secondary wives was not commonly practiced outside of the warrior class in Japan. Perhaps they were relatives or servants.

28. *Ichibu*, 一分. A unit of currency, minted in a small rectangular coin.

offered to allow me, if I was so inclined, to move in immediately, for which I thanked the good people quite warmly. Money was still worth something to the Japanese at that time, so my royalty had cost but little. Sakfsabro had bid Josaïmon a monthly rent of 7 *itzeboes*, Josaïmon desired 10, and I finished with an unasked-for 12; that is, a little less than twelve guilders.[29]

It is incredible how quickly my shed was habitable, but then I had incredibly low standards for myself. I stipulated that I be able to move into my house within two days, but only half; Josaïmon could stay for an additional eight days, until he found lodging in the nearby village of Yokohama. I specifically requested that the pigs and fowls not remain in the house with us during these nights, but Josaïmon requested leniency for the chickens for fear of foxes and polecats. There was no ceiling, so one could look directly into the thatch above, and Josaïmon indicated that I would not be bothered if he pushed a few slats across so that about sixty chickens could roost over our heads at night. The companionship of the chickens would not, according to him, annoy me—and, said he, were no more troublesome than the bats and lizards that had their nests in the thick, moldering thatch above us.

There were no handier carpenters or workfolk in the whole world as were in Japan at this time. Moreover, I was promptly helped with everything through the assistance of my old friends, the interpreters. In a few hours the carpenters had laid down a sturdy wood floor in three-fourths of the shed; it took a paperhanger only a few moments to pave the floor with thick mats, and another pair of paperhangers came with a load of draught-screens of about ten feet high and divided the matted room into as many chambers as I desired. Where there wasn't enough light, a square hole was simply sawed into the outside wall, inside of which a window frame, covered with oiled paper, was nailed. On the outside of the frame a board was fitted as a sliding shutter that could be closed with a peg for the night or pushed over the window during wet weather so that the paper panes would not get rained out. After all these preparations, nothing else was lacking but the necessary furnishments, which—as my home stood nearby the beach where as a rule there was little surf—were easily brought by sloop from shipboard. And so I was able to move in, the last piece dragged into my home only two days after I had rented it, and I installed myself for good in the company of the family Josaïmon.

29. Roughly $135 at today's rates.

I had scarcely been busy an hour taking care of a few household affairs when I saw my three friends, the former interpreters from Decima, striding along the footpath to my house with Sakfsabro in the lead. They were paying me a courtesy call to wish me luck with my venture on Japanese soil, and their wishes were even heartier because I had taken care to provide a good reception. Their visit was welcome not just for the sake of our old friendship from years past on Decima, but also because I had samples of all my goods with me that I could show them now, and these aroused their interest more than a little. After presenting each of them a watch with a chain as a gift, I requested their help in drawing the attention of Japanese merchants to my goods. They assured me that they would do so, and they proved to be true to their word: in the next few days, the merchants came to visit my secluded lodging repeatedly and made such substantial purchases that I did outstanding business.

When the necessary refreshments had been consumed, and the friends had looked around the property, they declared their pleasure that I had such relatively good lodgings. I gave credit to Sakfsabro, and at the same time asked him: could I perhaps show my gratitude in some other way?

"To tell you the truth," answered Sakfsabro, "I am at the moment very badly in need of a case of gin; it is necessary to perform my duties. I have been transferred from Nagasaki because the Governor fancied that I am 'very clever' with the English language. Now, in the few weeks since I have been here, I have had to translate the interviews between the English Consul and the Governor daily; the Consul speaks English constantly, and I understand nothing of it. I must translate until he ceases talking, or otherwise I will be punished. When I have a few glasses of gin beforehand, the translation goes very quickly."

While I made arrangements for his gift, I had to laugh to myself at the thought of how well the diplomatic negotiations with the English Consul had ended in the first months when the interpreters still knew no English.

"Do you think I am safe here?" I asked my friends, when they stood before the door ready to depart. The question rose of itself to my lips, when I saw Sakfsabro at full length in his excited state. My friend was a large, heavily built, pockmarked fellow, who now had, thanks to the refreshments he had partaken, a flushed face with bloodshot eyes; with his two swords stuck in his sash, he gave me a clear idea of how a headhunter of the Prince of Mito must look. "Oh, dear Sakfsabro," I thought to myself, "how fortunate it is that we are here in the bright daylight on friendly terms, because if I'd run into you in the darkness, before recognizing you, I would have, in accordance with the Consul's circular, put your lights out before you had time to say, 'Good evening!'"

"Do you think I am safe here?" I repeated, noting that all three of them would have preferred to withhold a straight answer.

"The answer is extremely difficult," answered one of them, the interpreter Tenasabro,[30] who always spoke very bookish Dutch, like a schoolteacher. "A wise man must be cautious so that his life is not cut short. Your goods are quite safe here, but your body is not."

"Just yesterday evening," chimed in Sakfsabro, "at eight o'clock, when it was quite dark, a servant of your near neighbor, Loureiro,[31] agent of a large English house in China, had his head chopped off right in front of his door. He had his master's jacket on; thus the murderers must have mistaken the servant for the master. Since they have not been identified and they did not accomplish their objective, to kill a full-fledged foreigner, they are certainly still wandering around the vicinity, waiting for night to return. You are an easier target for them than Loureiro, as there is nothing near here and . . ."

"Dear friends!" I hastily interrupted, for I was hearing the reading of my death sentence, "a hearty thanks for your visit. Excuse me for now, as I still have much to do." I shook their hands goodbye and went hastily inside, where I threw myself dejectedly in a chair to think over my limited options. My decision was quickly made. My sense of honor rebelled against the idea of a fainthearted retreat to shipboard to spend the night, and, as I was amply provided with weapons and ammunition, I resolved to stay and establish a strong state of defense.

When the men of our civilized society gather a cozy circle of friends together in the evening and speak of perilous situations, one is often amazed at the courage and presence of mind shown in the face of imminent danger. But were we to follow most of those same men to their bedrooms, and see under how many drawn bolts and turned keys they slumbered, then one would be even more amazed at the anxiety which causes the lone peaceful sleeper to protect himself against others. For the hero in the company of others knows that if a single ill-willed person

30. Probably Shioya Tanesaburō; see Yokohama Shiyakusho, *Yokohama shi shiko* (Kyoto: Rinsen shobo 11 v, 1931). Reprint 1985 2 (seiji 2 hen), vol. 5: 492.

31. José Loureiro was the vice-consul for France and an English agent. The murder took place in mid-afternoon in early November, and the servant was a Chinese who had insulted the killer. The murderer was captured and beheaded in 1867. See Joseph Black, *Young Japan* 1 (Oxford: Oxford University Press, 1968), 47–48.

skulks the night streets, the night guard and the police will protect his safety—but he shuts himself away to fortify himself against imaginary thieves and murderers. As soon as night falls, the silence and darkness subdue his courage just as the mercury in a barometer drops when good weather has gone.

When one is completely alone, in an isolated place in a strange land, left to one's own devices, and has been warned by bloody events and the advice of friends to be on the alert, then one cannot rely on third parties to cut in. One must calmly seek council within himself as to how he will handle himself as a man in the hour of danger. Then it is one's foremost duty to "know thyself"; to know whether he will retreat or stand fast to ensure that later, when the sun sets, when his heart sinks to his shoes in the darkness and solitude, through the courage of his convictions, he will dare to stand as resolute as if it were still broad daylight and life was around him.

Dusk had scarcely fallen when Josaïmon and his wives and children returned from their field labor. After partaking of their evening meal by the dim light of an oil lamp, the front door was closed with a wooden peg; the whole family then lay out flat and quietly fell asleep within five minutes. It was only eight o'clock in the evening, but already everything was dead silent all around. Outside one could only hear the soft murmur of the nearby surf—and inside, from the bare earthen floor from which my lodgings were separated by a draught screen, one could hear nothing other than the deep breathing and soft snores from the human nest of the sleeping Josaïmons. After putting my weapons in order, I sat at the table above which I had hung a ship's lantern that could burn the whole night long, to write up my notes for the day. But when I had finished that, it was still too early for me to go to sleep. Even though I had knocked together a bed in the improvised annex that morning, I decided that I would still prefer to seek my rest this night fully clothed on the sofa by the table above which I'd hung a piece of sail as a ceiling so that a dreaming chicken from the slats above would not end up on my head while I slept; the sail also provided some cover from the bats, a couple of which already flapped around. Awakened by the light, they flew timidly around in the space above me as if preparing to take off outside through some hole or another. I still had one more duty to fulfill for myself before going to sleep, one that must never be neglected when strong demands are made on the body and soul. I could call on no waiter to bring me a menu; I could only take my bread and ham out of the tin and dig the modest, banded bottle of Bordeaux out of the straw in the chest in which its makers had buried it.

It is a fact that wine, in whatever circumstances, at least when it is not made by charlatans, has virtues that cannot be denied. Whether it is brought on a silver tray by a waiter in a braided coat in a magnificent banquet hall or uncorked by a wanderer in an isolated hut and poured freely into his glass, wine remains true to its calling and rises above all vanity, maintaining its heartening glow just as well in the flimsy walls of a hovel as in the best room of a stately home. So it was for me too on this somber evening: the Rhine wine was an inspiring refreshment that dispelled all the specters of my doom. I picked up one of the cushions on the sofa, lay two Lafaucheux revolvers[32] and my dagger underneath, and—far be it from me to be governed by fear—I cheerfully flung myself down while mumbling to myself, "Let them come now if they have the heart."

As the light of the lantern slowly dimmed, Japan, with its murderers, disappeared from my waking thoughts, and in gentle slumber my beloved fatherland and its capital came to me. I wandered in a daze through the busy populace, the brightly lit Amsterdam streets: what a life, what a din. The clock tower had already struck midnight, but the crowd grew and I could not work my way out of it; I stood in the middle of a riot. I saw great cobblestones in the hands of a gang of miscreants who, when signaled, flung them at the windows of the houses. What a ruckus! The glass jangled, the houses were crushed, I shuddered awake amidst thousands.

I had been dreaming. But what is that? Good heavens! Am I awake or am I mad? Nearby I could hear a racket that sounded like fifty panes of glass were being smashed. And yet I was awake! Indeed, there on the table stood the bread, the ham, the empty wine bottle, I am here in the hut of Josaïmon . . .

Nay, I had no need to guess any longer: I heard men's voices outside and, right against the outside wall of the hut, a crashing and jangling of iron and steel that shook the ground. I was jolted awake among thousands, but in reality I stood alone, lucidly awake, abandoned in the dead of night against bloodthirsty villains. It goes without saying that,

32. Correctly, Lefaucheux. A non-percussion, internally primed weapon that required a pin fire cartridge. De Coningh probably mentions the type specifically because in 1859 they were cutting edge. The pin fire cartridge was invented in France by Casimir Lefaucheux (1802–1852) and adapted to the revolver in the 1850s by his son Eugene (1820–1871). Although the pin made them fussy to load, they could fire almost as rapidly as a modern revolver. About 12,000 were purchased by the Union during the Civil War.

as soon as I noticed the danger, I sprung up and grabbed my weapons. In the dream I'd shuddered at the dangerous group. But now that I was awake and they came for my life, my blood rushed to my brain and I was filled with a courage born of desperation.

The family of sleeping Josaïmons were awakened by the racket. I saw how they rose, afraid and alert in the half-darkness, stirring against each other, but when they spoke all together, whispering and agitated, I could not understand a word. Indeed I already knew—and now my suspicions were confirmed—that I could not expect a whit of help from these wretches.

"Josaïmon-sang! Josaïmon-sang!"[33] sounded an interrogative voice, as if asking to be let in; and immediately thereafter the clanking iron stamped the ground with renewed force. I heard two or three voices outside that were apparently urging Josaïmon to open the door. The old man gave in and stepped forward immediately to draw the peg that served as a lock.

"Do not open it, damn you!" I roared, springing on him and slinging him to the side. "How dare you, you old scoundrel, sell out and betray me, you despicable hangman's accomplice!" In order to put a fright into him—and to let those outside know I was prepared—I grabbed him by the arm and fired off a revolver shot above his head, whereupon the bullet flew hissing through the roof.

Now arose a moment of fear and confusion where everything went crazy. Old Josaïmon fell on his knees; the women and children screamed; the chickens flew cackling from their slats, each hitting with its wings the thin cord from which my lantern hung, whereupon the light swayed back and forth as if enchanted, casting streaks of lightning over the whole drama. A neck, an arm, a leg—I felt about in the half-darkness, and by each beam of light from the swaying lantern I saw how the lives of the entire family Josaïmon hung on me, while my ears buzzed from their screams. It was evident that they were trying to make me understand something in Japanese. Helpless as I was against the human pack that I sought to keep in check, I saw the old man suddenly slip hastily toward the door, and before I could do anything about it, he shoved it wide open.

"It is over," I thought, while a shudder ran through my limbs. I could do nothing but wait for a pair of scoundrels, with bared swords, to come rushing in. Yet that was not what happened, and I was never in my life so

---

33. Sang = *san*, a gender-neutral honorific suffix commonly attached to names like Mr. or Ms.

taken by surprise after a sudden fright than at that moment, when after so many rumors—in place of murderers flying at me, three peaceful men stepped over the threshold and bowed modestly in front of me. With a lantern in one hand, and an iron staff hung with rings on the top half in the other, one by one they gave me their compliments, and began reasoning with me in Japanese, of which at that time I could understand nothing. Their pantomime however, was as clear to me as glass, for all three of them first pointed at me with a finger, then shut their eyes and opened their mouths wide. When they threw their heads to the side and made a cutting motion with a flat hand across their necks, I completely understood what they meant. And when, immediately afterward, they pointed to me again, and indignantly shook their heads "no," thumped themselves on the breast and stamped the ground with their rattling rods so much that my hearing and vision were strained, I understood, even without Lavater[34] for reference, that these Japanese night watchmen had a gratuity bump on the back of their heads.

One must have nerves of steel when, one moment, you are at the borders of eternity, so to speak, and already feel the nick of the murderous sword across the neck, and five minutes later all is as calm as if nothing had ever happened. It was now evident to me that these people were some sort of night watchmen. I was completely reassured; yet I believe that if I'd had to sign my name at that moment, one would have taken it for the signature of an eighty-year-old. It is peculiar, but the sensation of surprise and happiness inspired in me yet another feeling, one of unfulfilled rage, and I needed to cool it on another human body. Right away, to answer to the cringing courtesy of the night watchmen, I fumbled in my pocket and slipped an *itzeboe* in each of their hands—but at the same time gave them a ringing slap in farewell on their naked brown shoulders, with my flat hand. Thank God! That gave me some relief: my bottled-up anger toward the copper-colored fellows dissipated. They enjoyed the joke, happy from the *itzeboe*, in their eyes blessed with honor and money. They left, bowing out the door with their jingling staffs, thankful and pleased. How relative are honor and riches in this world!

When the watchmen were gone, my compassion for the Josaïmons awoke, for these good people were no less frightened than I was. They

---

34. Refers to Swiss theologian Johann Kasper Lavater's (1741–1801) *Essays on Physiognomy* (1775–1778). Originally published in German and translated into English and French. Went through many editions and was the basis for popularized sciences like phrenology. Here De Coningh is suggesting that he could tell right away that they expected to be paid for their troubles.

had never had such night watchmen at the door. They had spoken with those outside and knew who they were, while I could not understand them. They were just as afraid of me as I was of the murderers! In haste I hunted for a small gift for each of them. As I presented them I clapped Josaïmon and his wife familiarly on the shoulders, stroked the cheeks of their daughters, and we ended with a hearty laugh over the danger we had endured, after which we all lay down to sleep.

Chapter 3

The next day at the Interpreters' Office I complained to the interpreter Sakfsabro about the hellish racket that the night watch had made, and the terror that had resulted.

"I am very sorry about that," said my friend, "but I shall tell you how it came to pass. You know that the night before last one of Loureiro's servants was murdered. Now, this gentleman is an agent of an English house as well as a French consular agent, and his servant had just returned from an errand to an English ship. That is why the English and French ministers are making this murder an English and French affair. They, along with their secretaries, already came here, to the Interpreters' Office, from Jeddo early yesterday morning and demanded to speak to the Governor. Given that the murder victim was in the service of an English house and had just finished an errand to an English ship, the English minister considered the case of such a serious nature that if hefty reparations were not paid immediately, the English fleet from China would appear in Yokohama. And since Mr. Loureiro was a French consular agent, the French minister considered this affair an affront to French honor, so if French demands were not met, then the French General de Montauban,[1] now in China with his army, knew very well what to do in concert with the English admiral to lead the Japanese government to her duty. After these threats they left with their secretaries, to return in twenty-four hours to hear the answer. The Governor, who had never before had to deal with European politics was, after this parlay, more than a little nervous and agitated; for if the affair was not settled, nothing was left for him but to cut his belly.

"Yesterday morning at ten-thirty, the *dwarskijker* reported to the Interpreters' Office that at ten past ten he had settled you into Josaïmon's hut. When we returned yesterday afternoon from our visit to you, we were immediately called to the Governor's office; another *dwarskijker* had already reported that he had seen us go visit you and return. The Governor was still suffering the effects of his interview with the foreign Ministers, so when we responded to his question as to whether or not we had made

---

1. Charles Guillaume Cousin-Montauban, Comte de Palikao (1796–1878). Title bestowed for victory at Pa-li-ch'iao. Fled to Belgium after the overthrow of the Second Empire.

you promise to return to shipboard for the night in the negative, he gave us a thorough reprimand. He hauled us over the coals. Indeed, he thought it would be impossible for a foreigner to make it through the night on the lonesome beach at Josaïmon's, and that tomorrow the Dutch Consul would come for his head, asking for reparations and, backed up by the English and French Ministers, threaten war with Holland too.

"We could not argue with this. Meanwhile, the Governor went and called a *banjoost* of the police and ordered three watchmen, with iron rattling staffs like those used at fires in Jeddo, to watch over your house. Their orders were to awaken you with a great racket at least once to personally ascertain that you remained alive and unharmed. By doing so, no mishap could befall you; and if a declaration of war was made, you would be called as a witness to confirm the truth on behalf of the Interpreters' Office, that the lives of foreigners were protected at night."

I thanked Sakfsabro for his explanation, by which I was completely satisfied. "But," I asked him, "tell me something. The twenty-four hours have elapsed. What settlement have the English and French Ministers received, or has the Governor cut his stomach open?"

"Everything has just now been fortuitously resolved," said Sakfsabro, "for the Governor deliberated over the answer with his council last night, and one of them is very smart. He's a, how do you call it in Dutch, a—, a— twist talker."

"A twist talker?" I asked, puzzled.

"Yes, how do you call that again? Some who is very skillful at twisting affairs with words."

"Maybe you mean a lawyer?" I said.

"Right, exactly, a lawyer. Now, he spoke for the Governor this morning at a meeting about this case. Mr. Loureiro's presence was sought to recount the details of the affair. He related how he had sent his servant on an errand to an English ship and, because it was raining, the servant threw on an old coat. He went on to tell how because of the coat and everything else, assassins had chopped off the servant's head and left shoulder.

"'What was the name of your servant?' asked the lawyer.

"'Tjing-Tjang-la.'

"'Where was he born, in England or France?'

"'In neither, in China.'

"'We don't have a treaty with China,' said the lawyer, 'and your servant was a Chinese. A murdered Chinese doesn't concern us. Thus we will only pay reparations for your coat.'

"'What is your name, if you please?' continued the lawyer.

"'José Loureiro.'

"'Where were you born, in England or France?'

"'In neither, in Portugal.'

"'We have no treaty with Portugal,' said our lawyer, 'and you are a Portuguese. Therefore the Governor must rule that Japan, according to the treaty, has no obligation to pay reparations to France and England for a dead Chinese and a Portuguese coat.'

"On these grounds the business is now resolved, and a great war avoided," concluded Sakfsabro.

I was amazed at the wisdom of the Japanese Solomon. But I could have further reassured Sakfsabro that even without the lawyer, the foreign ministers' bluff would have failed. Just at that moment, and for several months thereafter, England and France had their hands so full in China that all the foreigners, down to the last man, were put in arms and for the time being not a single "blue jacket" or *troupier Francais* could have been spared to avenge us.

Though I knew this, I was wise enough not to tell any Japanese. Haughty England was so powerless in Japan in those days that for eight months long nothing could be spared for the protection of Englishmen but the *Camilla*, an old sailing brig of 12 guns.[2] In the years of 1859 and 1860 I saw the English blush at their weakness compared to other foreigners in Japan, and a blushing Englishman is as rare as a white raven. As for France: in the first frightening months in Yokohama I never saw a single French warship there; all their available expeditionary troops were headed to Peiho[3] under General de Montauban for the mission to Peking. Only once did I ever see French uniforms, specifically a few cavalry officers, including the son of de Montauban, who came over in a private ship to buy horses for the army in China. I would even venture to say that success in the Chinese war of the day[4] was in large part thanks to the benevolence of Japan, even if it had been forced upon them. A thousand horses and an enormous quantity of provisions, supplied by rich and bountiful nearby Japan, were most certainly a vast relief for the "*balle*

---

2. Captained by George Twistleton Colville (1826–1860), and lost in the typhoon of 1860.

3. Now Hai He, 海河.

4. This is the Second Opium War, Arrow War, or Second Chinese War. Although the Treaty of Tianjin was signed in 1858, supposedly ending the hostilities of 1856, in 1859 the British attacked Chinese fortifications on the Peiho, or Hai He River. They were joined by the French in 1860, which resulted in the pillaging of the Summer Palace. Hostilities concluded in 1860.

passé par la gorge"[5] at Palikao[6] during General Montauban's expedition to Peking. England and France, instead of threatening Japan, had at that moment the greatest need for Japan, and because of the adversity their forces suffered in China, preferred to swindle reparations from Japan. I still clearly remember the fear that could be read on the face of every foreigner in Yokohama on the day the tidings came of the defeat that had been suffered by the allied forces at the Taku forts at the mouth of the Peiho. As for America, far too large a storm had begun to brew in its own southern states to worry itself with far Japan, much less make a show of strength. Only once, in a whole year, did an old paddle steam warship, the *Powhatan*, lurch in for a few days, as if to see if all the Yankees were still alive.[7] All the same, the Minister for the "stars and stripes" held his chest high, as did all his officials. Yet when the secretary of their legation, Mr. Heusken, was yanked from his horse and gruesomely murdered, the American Minister could not even consider reinforcing their treaty power with a single warship, and the business was, in the American manner, settled with dollars.[8] Thus, the three great powers with all their threats could impose nothing by force because of their problems elsewhere. That didn't prevent the subjects of these three nationalities from making the necessary boasts, at least in their dealings with the Japanese. An Englishman sounded stately and high-handed: "Britons will soon come to terms with those beggars"; a Frenchman shook his head briskly and exclaimed: "*Mais ces messieurs marchent tout droit à la guerre!*"[9]; and an American snorted crassly through his nose: "They want a good licking."

5. Literally, "bullet through the throat," meaning a bottleneck.

6. Today Baliqiao, a village in Hebei province near Beijing. In 1860 the French and British forces defeated the Chinese army here, which made invasion of Beijing possible.

7. October 3–12, 1859. This ship had been one of Perry's squadron. An account of this voyage can be read in James D. Johnston, *China and Japan: Being a narrative of the cruise of the U.S. steam-frigate Powhatan, in the years 1857, '58, '59, and '60. Including an account of the Japanese embassy to the United States* (Philadelphia: C. Desilver; Baltimore: Cushings & Bailey, 1861).

8. Henry Heusken (properly Henricus Conradus Joannes Heusken), 1832–1861. The assassination occurred on January 16, 1861. Born in Amsterdam, Heusken had emigrated to the United States in 1853. He was popular in the foreign community and his death widely commented upon. His diary was published as Henry Heusken, *Japan Journal 1855–1861*, trans. and ed. by Jeannette C. van der Corput and Robert A. Wilson (New Brunswick, NJ: Rutgers University Press, 1964).

9. "These gentlemen march straight to war."

When I listened to these three blustering great powers, I could not help but think of the prophetic "*débitant de tabac*"[10] of Paris, who had traded under "*liberté, égalité, fraternité*" for the few years of the Second Republic, but with the arrival of December 2,[11] had painted these words on three snuff boxes that he hung on a neat iron rod above his store as an overhanging signboard, with the caption, "*aux trois blagues*."[12]

From the above, one can understand why, in the frightful winter of 1859–1860, about eighty foreigners, mostly English and Americans and otherwise a few French, Germans and Swiss, were left to their fate in Yokohama without any protection. What came for us Dutch in the fall of 1859 was a fairly presentable warship. The *Groningen* was sent to Japan, but unfortunately it was under orders from our Commissioner-General who, in the old manner of the *Opperhoofden*, was very "comfortable" on Decima. As a result, the steamship paraded for months in Nagasaki Bay in front of peaceful Decima, until, finally, when her anchor had practically grown roots, came the cry of distress from our Consul in Yokohama for a warship for our protection. With commendable speed the *Groningen* steamed seawards to show the flag of our fatherland in Yokohama. Knowing that the ship was approaching, we felt our mood revive, and our Dutch hearts reveled in righteous pride because we could put the fears of our unprotected partners in adversity from England, France and America to rest with the comforting words that Holland was watching over them, that within five days the drawn cannons of a Dutch frigate would command Yokohama. Alas! Five, ten, twenty days elapsed, but the protection we so fervently yearned for did not appear. We watched carefully, day after day, until finally, on a fine morning, the news that the *Groningen* had broken her rudder in a storm and returned for repairs to Decima for three months, sank our last hope.

After this small digression to show how unprotected and abandoned we were, we pick up the story after our visit to the Interpreters' Office to complain about the rattling staffs of the night watchmen, back at Josaïmon's hut. It was clear to me that the old man and his family had already had quite enough of the terror the previous night, and that these peaceful people did not feel safe lodging a foreigner. Later in the day,

10. Tobacco merchant.
11. On December 2, 1851, Charles Louis Bonaparte dissolved the parliament, effectively ending the Second Republic.
12. "To three hoaxes."

Josaïmon informed me that he'd found accommodations in a nearby village and thought to move within two days. I should note that day and those that followed, in that first period, were quite cheery with the many Japanese merchants coming to make purchases. I conducted a fair bit of business and had every reason to be satisfied. These merchants were, without exception, very courteous and respectable people, and confirmed the good opinion that I had always had of Japanese civilization, even if some of them were a bit too well endowed with that business acumen people in our country, rightly or wrongly, often attribute to Israelites.

When the day of the Josaïmons' departure came, I was of a mind to get someone I could trust to stay with me because I had no desire to spend nights completely alone in the hut on the beach. The *Argonaut*, like the goods she held, was owned by a few friends and myself. She was destined, if at all possible, to be sold to the Japanese as a sort of warship. She was a very neat, spanking new ship, that delighted a sailor's eye as much as the newest fashion plate would a young woman's. Sleek of form and rigging, she lay in the roadstead at Yokohama, flaunting herself in front of the Interpreters' Office like a coquettish naiad, prettily painted with golden-yellow masts and fluttering pennants; the twelve stout, brightly polished cannon and glittering swivel guns on the poop caught the brilliant rays of sun, like so many enticing glances cast to the Japanese sea authorities who stood gaping on the shore. The ingrates! Enchanted by her beautiful form, they came repeatedly to examine her from up close; they peered through lorgnettes with connoisseurs' eyes, appreciated her beauty and quality, feigning for three months the desire to have her and the willingness to pay gold, but then coldly rejected her because she was only driven by wind and not by coal.

I therefore had the *Argonaut* at my disposal for the first three months. The captain, a venerable old seaman, had already urged me repeatedly to take a couple sailors ashore for my safety. "Good friend!" I said to him when the family Josaïmon had departed, "now I shall follow your council. But one sailor is enough, if he is one of the best. On the journey I always had a high regard for Jan Spuyter, who appeared to me a staunch fellow."

"Jan Spuyter," said the captain, "is a square and resolute chap, that is true; he is always sober and capable. He wouldn't get drunk even if he stood for three days in the big market at Schiedam.[13] I hope to bring him to you myself before evening."

It was about six that evening. I was exhausted by the many Japanese who had visited me during the day. The family Josaïmon had left a few hours

---

13. This Dutch city is known for manufacturing brandy and gin.

before and, now completely alone, I sat on a chair in front of my door to enjoy some rest in the beauty of nature. Twilight slowly fell and with it came silence around me. Here and there stars began to twinkle in the sky, the sharply defined rounds of the hills and forests of the interior melted more and more into the increasing darkness, and were it not for the noise I heard now and then from the verdure in the direction of the so-called foreign quarter, I could have imagined that I was alone in the world. I was already worried that people would forget about me when I heard voices and footsteps approach, and presently the captain stood before me with three armed sailors.

"We got underway early this evening," began the captain, "but we arrived somewhat late. We were held up for a few moments by a commotion in front of Mr. Barber's[14] door. It was hardly even dark when a murderer audaciously broke into his house. Fortunately, Mr. Barber heard the noise and immediately shot his revolver at the rogue. No one knows if he was hit, but he took to his heels so fast his sword and slippers remained lying inside the door. A swarm of *Jakonis* from the Interpreters' Office were on the spot quickly, but of course the bird had flown."

After we spoke another moment over the incident, and I declined the captain's urgent demand to stay the night with his two men, he went back on board his ship. The honest Jan Spuyter commenced his new duties. He looked out into the darkness like a village watchman, with a thick pea coat that served him as blanket and mattress for the night, a leather bandolier over the right shoulder, and an old-fashioned corporal's sword swinging against his legs. When I bade him to go in, he took the tobacco quid out of his mouth and threw it into space out of decency and out of respect for the home he would enter.

The lantern was lit and after Jan stripped off his unnecessary clothing, he began his household labors by straightening up one thing or another, finding where everything was, and figuring out how to cook with Japanese equipment. In the meantime I had made a cold punch ready, and when my servant was done with his duties, I shoved a stool to the table. "Come sit, Jan," I said.

"Oh come now, sir," said Jan abashedly.

"What, come now! Don't stand on ceremony, come sit."

"No, sir," said Jan shaking his head. "I belong in the cabin, and it is not my nature to act the gentleman sitting ashore."

Through repeated urging I finally got so far as to get him to sit down diffidently on the edge of the Indies rattan chair as if he were afraid

14. This was probably James S. Barber. An Englishman originally in the employ of Jardine Matheson, about 1862 he became a partner in the trading company Ross, Barber & Co.

his sailcloth pants would crease, and then, as stiff as if he had a corset on, he looked across the table. After laying pipes and tobacco in front of him and filling his glass with cold punch, to set him thoroughly at ease I insisted he light one and test the punch. I hoped thereby to quickly make him feel at home, and when he blew out the first cloud of smoke he did indeed push himself somewhat further into his chair and took, with the timidity of a young girl, a modest sip from his punch glass.

"Have I used too much lemon?" I asked, because from those few drops he made a face as if what had passed his lips had bitten his tongue.

"Absolutely not, sir! But it is not proper to take a great gulp, and I know how to mind my manners; there I stand among the best."

"You are right, Jan! But we must not trouble with propriety here," I said, and to give credit to his proper behavior, I began to tell him that all along I had, even when on shipboard, noticed that he must come from a respectable family. His eyes glinted with pleasure while I spoke, and when I told him that I had been right to choose him because I could depend on him, he would have, had his sense of decency allowed, grasped my hands with both his tarred ones, for on this muscled chap a word of praise lay heavy.

I had evidently won his trust. "Should something happen, then you can be assured that I will do my part," said Jan in a tone that left me no doubt he was sincere. "My uncle also said that, and he did it too. My father, his brother, was just a shoemaker, and I was thus his nephew, but my uncle could have been a general had he wanted it."

"So, your uncle a General! He was certainly a deserving man then; why did he remain a colonel, what happened?" I asked, interested in getting him to talk.

"I'll tell you that my uncle was really not a colonel either but, and this is now forty or fifty years ago, a quartermaster on board the frigate *Melampus*[15] under Colonel De Man,[16] cruising for Barbary pirates in the Mediterranean Sea."

15. This frigate of forty guns was originally the HMS *Melampus* but was purchased by the Dutch in 1815. It was one of a small squadron under Baron T. F. van de Capellen, who assisted the British under Sir Edward Pellew in the ten-hour bombardment of Algiers on August 27, 1816, to force the release of the British consul and a thousand slaves.

16. Antony Willem de Man (1749–1842). This was the Dutch navy rank *kapitein-ter-zee*, which was equivalent to the US navy rank of captain. In Dutch the proper form of address was *kolonel*.

George Chambers, *The Bombardment of Algiers,* August 27, 1816. Oil on canvas. 1836. A starboard broadside view of the *Melampus* is on the left.

"Aha!" I nodded, curious, and signaled Jan with a meaningful wink to his punch glass, out of which he now, fired up by telling of his famous uncle, took an improperly large gulp, without making a face.

"He was a boss, Colonel De Man, but a regular fellow. He thought well of my uncle, and my uncle also thought well of him. Now, in those times the rogues there on the Barbary Coast—Turks or Arabs, I don't know what people they were—commonly seized all the Christians they could and made them slaves. This Colonel De Man could not allow; he said, 'For my part, they can make all the niggers slaves and whip them to death but they must leave Christian men alone, otherwise I shall clip their claws.'[17] Now there was a sort of boss of the folk on the Barbary Coast that they called Bey,[18] and Colonel De Man thought that one of these fellows had Christian slaves in the city. So he anchored the *Melampus* in front of the city. In order not to cause a stir among those Turkish folk, he sent my uncle the quartermaster and

17. King Willem I abolished slave trade in the Netherlands in 1814, but there was a transition period, during which Jan's story takes place.
18. In Dutch this was defined as the chief in Tunis or Algiers, but was in fact an administrative position in the Ottoman Empire with regional political authority.

two unarmed rowers to shore in a small flat-bottomed boat to find out if there were Christian prisoners there. When they came to land my uncle told the rowers, 'You stay here with the boat; I will mosey along the shore.' With no other weapon than a concealed sheath knife in his trouser pocket, he stepped along to a clump of scruffy people who stood watching in the distance. My uncle spoke their language, for he knew something of French, Spanish, and Portuguese and could speak them interchangeably. As he approached those folk he indicated that he must speak to the man who was more or less the boss over them. Four fellows armed with short pikes took him between them and brought him to a large, foul, square building in the Moorish city. There they pushed him into the door while one said, in almost half Spanish, 'Here you must stay, father,' whereupon the others began to laugh as if to say, 'Now he is snared.'

"My uncle could not endure that laughter. Without the least bit of concern, he looked angrily at the fellows and said in Portuguese, 'If I ever get you on board the *Melampus* before roll call, then I'll make you laugh as the pieces fly off you.' Then he stepped resolutely inside.

"At the end of a great square room, which had other rooms at the sides, their entrances covered in curtains instead of doors, sat a big fat Turk on an old carpet smoking a long pipe, the bowl of which stood on the ground next to him. My uncle saw immediately that this was the Bey, who was more or less the king of the city and the surrounding lands, and went right up to him.

"'Who are you and what do you want?' asked the Bey, looking furiously at my uncle standing before him.

"'I am Quartermaster Spuyter of the *Melampus*, and I give the compliments of Colonel De Man,' said my uncle without batting an eyelid.

"'I return his compliments. Is that all?' growled the Bey.

"'I must know if Christian men are also imprisoned here,' said my uncle, looking him boldly in the eye.

"'Bugger! What business of that is yours!' roared the Bey while drawing his curved Turkish sword to fly at my uncle. Uncle sprung back a step, drew his sheath knife, sprung another step forward, and held the jack-knife under the Bey's nose.

"'Say, what is this? You must not begin any foolishness here, Quartermaster,' said the terrified Bey. He did his best to put on a friendly face, but his brown skin blanched for a moment from fear.

"'Nor you!' said my uncle. 'Put that thing away and be polite.'

"The Bey swore high and low that he held no Christian men prisoner and spoke with my uncle about all sorts of things, just as politely as you here with me.

"'Listen, now I must ask you something,' said the Bey at last. 'You are a quartermaster, so you know quite well that if you don't return before roll call, you will get a taste of the lash,' and he made a motion with his hand as if he was whipping the air.

"'I do my duty as any other, and I understand punishment can be useful sometimes.'

"'With me, you will always be useful. You appear to be a resolute fellow, and thus I appoint you as my general,' pronounced the Bey, laying his hand, each extended finger of which was bejeweled with rings, on Uncle's shoulder.

"Now, a quartermaster is kind of like a corporal, and it made my uncle's head spin to be instantly made general. But uncle had faith in duty and country, and deserting the flag to be a general for the Turks was not something he could decide lightly. He stood thus, thinking for a long while. 'Come now, how about it, won't you be a general?' asked the Bey.

"'No, I will not, it is a *point d'honneur,* as the French say,' said my uncle curtly.

"The Bey took him aside and pulled a green curtain for one of the side rooms through which Uncle saw right into a large room where ten comely Moorish ladies sat around on couches. Uncle looked inside, took off his lacquered hat, and nodded to the ladies, who laughed and giggled as he stood there. He always told us afterwards that he was never in his life as disconcerted as he was in that moment. I myself heard him say that he felt just as ridiculous as they often say in books, and I still remember his exact words when he would tell my father and mother and neighbors of the affair: 'Look!' he'd say, 'I have here on my right arm a foul anchor[19] and on my left arm a flaming heart pierced with two arrows. I would not otherwise like compliments, but right then my heart was so full that I couldn't say a word; I just rolled up the left sleeve of my jacket and let the young women see my left arm so they could know what was going on inside me. And when the Bey said to me: "This is my general's household; do you want it or not?" it was as if all my common sense had fled and I shouted, "Yes! I really want that!" because I was so high on the clouds I felt as drunk as a skunk.'

"No sooner had my uncle said 'Yes' than the Bey gave three taps on a copper cymbal with a drumstick and six Turks with white turbans, called

19. Nautical term for an anchor tangled in its line.

hadjis in the East Indies,[20] came into the room. They circled Uncle and wanted him to shave his head bald; a pair tried to remove his jacket with anchor buttons. 'Get away, scoundrels! What do you want?' he roared, pushing the *hadjis* off him. Then the Bey began to laugh. 'What do they want?' Uncle called out.

"'To make a Turk of you; did you think I would have a Christian general?'

"That brought Uncle to his senses; he instantly regained consciousness. He had been such a good Calvinist all his life that he could recite all the prophets from the Old Testament one after the other as smoothly as the arch of a compass. 'A Dutch boy can never be a Turk!' he shouted, as if he were mad. He gave a pair of *hadjis* such punches with his fists that they tumbled onto the ground; in his haste he also gave the Bey a box on the ear and dashed out the door like a snarling bear. Of the four pikemen who wanted to stop him at the door, two of them got a fist in the eye that knocked them silly and, pursued by the other two, Uncle raced the fourteen-mile trip to the flatboat so quickly his feet hardly touched the ground. Thank God! He arrived at the beach and his rowers sat at the oars. But just as he sprung for the boat, in mid-spring, he received a pike jab from behind through his belly. He heard a crack just behind his back, rolled like a an ox between the seats of the flatboat, roared 'Start rowing!' and knew nothing of what happened after that."

"Good Lord, Jan!" I interrupted him here, "then your uncle came to an unfortunate end."

Jan was so fired up by telling of his uncle that his pipe had gone out and he had drained his glass, which I'd taken care to refill twice, completely empty without noticing. But I listened with pleasure to his artless speech, and I appreciated the pride he and his family had in the honest quartermaster, because if he sometimes blew the trumpet a bit too loudly in the high points, in wider circles, all too little notice is taken of the many examples of the manly loyalty and heroism of the simple seaman or soldier. They get the press but rarely the praise, the duty but rarely the honor; there is no place in written history for their names. It is only the attention of their near relations, who hand these stories down as tradition years after their blood relatives have died, that bring them honor like *Bayard sans peur et sans reproche.*[21]

20. Muslims who had made the pilgrimage to Mecca.

21. "Bayard without fear and without reproach." Seigneur de Bayard, or Pierre Terrail (1473–1524). A French military hero of the Italian campaigns known as the "knight without fear or reproach."

"No, sir!" Jan continued, "that is too hasty, my uncle was not yet dead; he was too tough for that. But he was badly wounded, for the steel of the pike had broken off in his back, and the rest of it had gone right through his stomach. No sooner was the flatboat on board than he was carefully taken charge of and carried to the sickbay. The news spread like fire over the whole frigate: 'Quartermaster Spuyter is badly wounded.' One of the first to visit my uncle's berth with the doctor was the Colonel himself, who as my uncle later told it, was quite shaken.

"'Doctor,' said the colonel, 'see that you save him, for he is the best fellow that the King has in his service. If you see that you can't help him, take care that he has an orderly[22] to help him find comfort in the ever after.'

"But it didn't come to that, for the doctor was a smart fellow who understood the human body. When my uncle first regained consciousness the next morning, he was in terrible pain but felt very relieved. He looked over the end of his berth and saw the doctor sitting by him. 'Doctor,' he asked softly, 'what do you think, has my time come?' 'Not for a long time, Quartermaster!' answered the doctor. 'If you just lie dead-still you will be royally on top again in no time, because I now know for certain that nothing inside you is damaged; there was no unclean matter on the pike when I pulled it out.'

"After three weeks Uncle was completely healed, and when he returned to his duties for the first time he was called to the colonel's quarters. The colonel shook his hand like a friend and poured out two glasses of bitter out of a carafe that stood before him on the table. 'Quartermaster!' began the colonel, 'I clink glasses with you as with a man. I am happy that I kept you safe, and hope that the pennant of the *Melampus* will wave long over your faithful head.'

"'Thank you Colonel!' said my uncle. When he picked up his glass he trembled so much that he fumbled, and in his haste he could not bring it right to his mouth but once he had it in the offing, he threw it back with such a gulp he swallowed it all at once. And the colonel did just the same.

"Uncle clicked his tongue, and the colonel did too.

"'What are you doing, man, why do you smack your lips so?' asked the colonel.

---

22. Dutch *ziekentrooster*. This is normally translated as orderly or medic, but when there was no minister on board, these men also had to perform some religious duties.

"'With your permission, Colonel!' said my uncle, 'you did it too, and it tasted so good to me.'

"'Well, it tasted good to me too,' said the colonel as if he was angry with himself. Irately, he took the carafe and glasses, and threw the whole lot crashing overboard through the porthole.

"I still hear my uncle's own words telling me what the colonel said to him after he did that: 'Quartermaster!' he said to me, laying his hand on my shoulder as if he were my brother. 'Spuyter, old boy, that good taste is wrong. And if you and I wish to stay as we are, working on shipboard, men for Country, King and the *Melampus*, then we must resist that cursed good taste, and never enjoy it again.'

"From that day forward my uncle never again tried any more strong drink, except on August 24, on the occasion of the king's birthday.[23] He was on leave at my father and mother's, after he had returned from the East and received a cross for Palembang. To welcome him, the neighbors had decorated the street, and because it was the King's birthday they came one after the other and from all sides, and my uncle was treated so royally that he had to be brought back by the *kortegaard** that night."

"That was too bad, Jan," I thought I should comment, "but then, I must acknowledge that the temptation was just too great," I added by way of excuse. "And how did it all come out for uncle after that?"

"What can I tell you, sir?" answered Jan. "Instead of ten wives, my uncle never even had one. After all the drifting about he was old before his time, and when he could not go on any more, some bigwigs intervened to get him into an old men's asylum. I never knew him in any other way than in the dress of the old men's home. But he always hung his former attire—his lacquered hat with long ribbons, his blue jacket with anchor buttons and yellow stripes on the sleeves, always neat to show off the polish—above his cot in the dormitory of the asylum. I was his favorite, but he loved children. If he sat on the bench outside the door of the asylum, then all the children in the neighborhood knew the 'quartermaster' was outside. After he told them stories he'd chase the big children to school and let the little ones stay playing until they were taken away by their mothers.

"Although he hoped to become very old because his former colonel, who was much older than he was, still lived in the city near us as a

---

23. This is the birthday of King Willem I, who was born in 1772 and ruled from 1815–1840.

pensioned admiral, my uncle began at last to decline. My father and mother saw that he was not well and one day, after he had been sick for a few days, we got a message from the asylum that the end was near. We went there immediately and when we got to his cot, he lay there pale and wasted in his last moments, but as alert as if he were still in full vigor.

"'Quartermaster!'—for he never wanted to be called anything else, 'Quartermaster, how goes it?' asked my father with tears in his eyes, while my mother and I stood sobbing.

"'The end is near, brother,' he said softly yet clearly, and tried to put his hand on the edge of the cot. My father gripped his hand and pressed it in farewell. Averting his eyes, he made a place for my mother, who now kissed the hand, letting her tears fall on it. When I drew near she placed Uncle's hand on my head. 'Yes Jantje![24] I still know you well,' I heard him say. Running his cold fingers through my hair, he told me to take care of my parents, because in old age, the bread of charity was harder to eat than sea biscuit. Finally he could say no more, and when he said 'God bless you,' my mother lay his hand back under the blanket. Having made his farewells, my uncle rallied a bit and began to discuss with my father what he still needed taken care of. He bequeathed all his things to us; if he was buried, he wished for a Dutch flag over his coffin; father must go thank the gentlemen of the asylum for their care; and I must be sent to the admiral to say, 'The Quartermaster has gone under the sail.' When my uncle had disposed of all that, he said, in a weak voice certainly, but with surprising presence: 'Now I believe I can go on to eternal rest. I have done three good things in the world: I have always loved God and Country, and earned the trust of Neptune.'

"After that he spoke no more; he lay still, and a half hour later he had departed.

"It all went as my uncle had ordered. On the day of the funeral his coffin with a Dutch flag over it was carried to the Karthuizer Cemetery[25] by twelve old men. I followed close behind the coffin, with my hand in my father's. At the gateway of the cemetery waited a tall old man, bowed and curved by the years, with long gray hair, who joined us without a word. The old man was clearly moved and walked with us to the grave as if he were one of the family. When the coffin was lowered

---

24. Diminutive for Jan.

25. Located in Amsterdam, but no longer in existence. A monastery in the fifteenth and sixteenth centuries, today it is a playground.

into the grave, my father took the shovel that was thrust into the sand that had been dug up next to it, and threw, in the old manner, three scoops of earth on the coffin.

"'Good friend! May I also have the shovel for a moment?' asked the old gentleman, affably. He took it, and threw earth upon the coffin as my father had done. Then father could no longer contain himself: 'Sir,' he sobbed, 'May I know who you are? The quartermaster was my brother, and I must thank you for the last honor you have given him.'

"'Master Spuyter,' said the old gentleman, shaking his hand, 'I was Colonel De Man on the Barbary Coast, and now I am the last man from the *Melampus*.'"

I thanked Jan for his explanation of the failed generalship of his kinsman. If I couldn't help but think that the legend of this man's fate had been somewhat embellished, I trusted that the same family blood of the uncle flowed through the veins of his steadfast nephew; and that, with Jan by my side, the night would go by so calmly it would seem as if there were no Japanese murderers in the world. As for the night watchmen with their rattling staffs, I never saw a trace of them again after that first night, probably because one night patrol by the Interpreters' Office was considered sufficient to protect the foreigners.

Chapter 4

A few days later, we both would have preferred a nighttime fright, because all the night watches in the world could not protect us, and we took flight as quickly as the late quartermaster did when he was pursued by the pikemen of the Bey.

—It was unseasonably mild during the days; the evenings, especially, were almost oppressive and dead calm, the kind we associate with the brewing of a storm. Normally, after the light was lit, I had administrative affairs to update, while Jan, as he would say, "stowed the property and cleaned up the galley debris." Door and windows, all was bolted tight; the weapons lay, ready to grab, on the table, for on these evenings, as ever, we followed Cromwell's orders to his army, "pray to God and keep your powder dry!"[1] like a sacred watchword. I had again offered my rattan chair to my faithful servant, to whom I willingly listened, and when he sat quietly, he acknowledged his thanks for the "gentleman's life," as he called it, that he presently enjoyed, and immersed himself in deep philosophical reflections on our present situation. "It is all too true, sir!" he said. "If there were no murders here, then things would really, by my way of thinking, be perfect. But at sea, what do you have there? You always have to deal with nature; storms, high sea, the pull of currents, reefs, all things that one can do nothing about. But on the shore, one has literally no need of nature. So long as the people take care that the chimney continues to smoke and everyone does their work, then nature makes no difference, none, nil, nix."

Without entirely agreeing, I had to grant him that here we did not have to examine every cloud, never had to run the pump to keep from sinking into the ground, and had no need to measure out the charts so we didn't burst by running into some reef in the night. —"Hello!" I interrupted myself, "what have we here now?"

The lantern began wobbling by itself, slowly moving off the table, and we had imperceptibly been lifted off our chairs.

"What the devil!" growled Jan, springing up. "Have they tunneled under this hovel?"

---

1. This well-known quote of Oliver Cromwell actually reads, "Put your trust in God but mind to keep your powder dry." It was often recited to his troops before attacking an enemy across a river.

There was no time to answer. A sort of underground rumbling could be heard, and at the same moment the fire roared, the shack snapped and cracked around us as if it would collapse, and the ground swelled under our feet. Jan, who expected nothing from nature ashore, in the belief that a band of murderers wanted to throw us to the ground of the hut, rose with sword and revolver and shot and stabbed like a lunatic through the cracking outside walls. I hastened toward the front door, which I unbolted with a jerk. Wobbling like a drunk, I looked out and saw, in the moonlight, a great wave like a foaming wall of water thundering up the beach.

"An earthquake!" I shouted. "For God's sake Jan, save yourself, the sea is coming inside."[2]

If ever two men took to their heels in haste, it was the two of us. We rushed through thick and thin in the direction of our fellows in adversity at full speed, as if a troop of Cossacks were on our heels. Not a word was exchanged; only now and then I felt the strong fist of my companion grasp me above the elbow, thrusting me three paces ahead. Only when rattling thunder sounded from a collapsing shed where a cargo of glasswork had just been unpacked, Jan mumbled, panting, "There goes the lot overboard." Before we knew it, perhaps less than three minutes after noticing the first trouble, we stood, dead tired, in an open field amidst fifty foreigners who had just fled their homes. That first moment was a nighttime drama, a Babylonian battle of tongues without one capable of bringing calm. Most appeared to have evacuated by springing directly from their beds. One friend called for his friend; another for his clothing; a third prayed; a fourth swore; until very soon, since the quake had lasted but a moment, good humor over the many droll situations gained the upper hand, whereupon hearty laughter could be heard here and there. When a patrol of on-duty interpreters and officials from the Interpreters' Office appeared in our midst with lanterns and one of the interpreters calmed our disquiet with loud reassurances that the earthquake was "the Japanese way," he was applauded like an outstanding speaker. Each then sought his own abode in the hope that he would find it whole. We also turned back toward our hut, where we found everything in tolerably good order, except that the walls were rather cracked and splintered, such that during the day others would be able to see right through them. The

---

2. October 4. A small tsunami also hit California.

*Colloquial for *corps de garde* [body guard] of the Police Bureau.

next morning we paled again, because the billow of the wave caused by the earthquake had risen so far up the land that we found jellyfish hanging from a thorny hedge that stood right next to the side of the house facing the sea.

It would be tiresome if I digressed at length over all the terrors, mortal dangers and murder attempts to which we were exposed in those first months. It is enough to note here that after the first victims, the four murdered Russians, were buried in a lovely, quiet place, a quarter against the incline of the hills outside Yokohama, the Japanese Government built a small chapel with a gilded dome as demanded by the Russians, and with that the European cemetery was consecrated.[3] And although in this first year the sound climate forestalled serious illness and none of the small number of foreigners died a natural death, nevertheless in short order the new cemetery was the last resting place for many.

As I said above, a great many of the pioneers who settled in Yokohama in the first months were a hodgepodge of the type of fellows never to be seen in Europe, but who thrived in "the far West" of the United States or the pampas of South America. These were the most dangerous, because at the least trifle they would whip out their long knives or revolvers. Another type were those men who could be called the fungi on civilized society: the fallen gentlemen of the world's great cities. They were only dangerous to someone's purse and property. Their sense of honesty was long since dead, while they themselves were alive and kicking, feasting like princes and living day to day at the expense of anyone but themselves. People will rightly ask what led such rabble to a land that had been opened for world trade, these persons who had no goods, no money, no credit; they brought nothing with them but the clothes on their backs. It is true that they never paid for anything and also possessed nothing. But they steamed round the world on credit for the only thing that was left to them: the thirst for gold. They sought gold, and they would find it in Japan. But not by working, digging or mining—no, not by a long shot. Nay, it would just fall in their laps without labor. With just a touch of skill, which for them was merely child's play, they could get their reward at once; with a few hundred dollars they were ready, and it would have been unworthy of such a fortune hunter if he could not find an innocent friend who would lend him this sum within twenty-four hours, although it was a loan for eternity.

3. This was November 19, 1859. A ceremony was held and attended by consuls and foreign residents of Yokohama.

A fact that certainly could not have existed anywhere else in the world since the discovery of America, occurred in Japan as a result of centuries of closure. In the early days of the opening, the gold had a mere third of the value that was conferred on it everywhere else. Thus whoever possessed silver coins could, if he was somewhat dexterous, buy back more than double their value in gold, and that was how the fortune hunters lived. This situation could not really last very long; with each day gold rose against the purchase value, and after two months the last gold piece disappeared out of Japan, and with it most of the fly-by-night fortune hunters, without the time to settle accounts with their dupes.

Let me explain briefly how the gold trade developed and how it was driven. When Japan concluded treaties with the foreign powers, they naturally also had to regulate financial matters between them. It was thus agreed upon with the treaty powers that each nation could import the silver coins of their own nation, which could be exchanged weight for weight, into Japanese silver coins. Thus the Dutchman could come with his guilders, the Frenchman with his five-franc pieces, etc.; but this almost never occurred. From the beginning, the Mexican dollars that also circulated in China were, in practice, the only foreign coin adopted. Before dollars could be used in Japan, one first had to exchange them at the Interpreters' Office for *itzeboes*,[4] long rectangular silver coins, weight for weight in silver, so that for 100 dollars, one would receive 311 *itzeboes*.[*]

In the first six weeks after the opening, it appeared that the foreigners did not yet know that a golden coin, the *kobang*, existed that was worth 4 *itzeboes* and if there were some who knew, they certainly kept the secret. Indeed, the golden *kobang* never came into circulation among us, because the Interpreters' Office strictly watched that gold coins were never brought into Yokohama. Yet, just like everywhere else in the world, there were smugglers in Japan who profited on anything that was forbidden. When these smugglers noticed that the foreigners were very keen on the *kobang*, and how readily they paid one, two, or more *itzeboes* than they could get in their country, they organized themselves into groups who gathered coins from all over the interior to peddle in Yokohama. As simple merchants, sometimes disguised as beggars, they came, pretending to buy or beg in the warehouses of the foreigners, and knew to indicate by signs that they had *kobangs* for sale. Anyone who

---

4. *Ichibu*, 一分, and *koban*, 小判.

[*]The *itzeboe* was thus about ƒ0.83 Dutch cents. —In Japanese currency 4 *itzeboes* = 1 *kobang*.—That's why it was preferred that foreigners didn't buy *kobangs*, for these they had to pay an average of 7 *ichibus*.

had *itzeboes* took the would-be smuggler inside and bought his gold off him—in the first days, for five; thereafter six, seven, and up to nine *itzeboes*. Both parties were satisfied, and no wonder! The smuggler gained a few *itzeboes* on each *kobang*, and the foreigner could count on receiving at least ƒ10 apiece in Shanghai, China, for the *kobangs* were of different qualities and weights.

1856 Mexican Silver Dollar. Restruck Mexican silver coin by PHGCOM http://commons.wikimedia.org/wiki/User:PHGCOM. From http://en. wikipedia.org/wiki/File:Aratame_sanbu_sadame_silver_coin_1859_ Japan.jpg. Available under a Creative Commons http://en.wikipedia. org/wiki/en:Creative_Commons. Attribution-Share Alike 3.0 Unported http://creativecommons.org/licenses/by-sa/3.0/deed.en. Copyright © 2008 PHGCOM http://commons.wikimedia.org/wiki/ User:PHGCOM.

For me, most of the time the gold trade was but a torment of Tantalus.[5] Except for a few thousand Dutch guilders, which were also quickly converted to gold, I possessed nothing to sell but a few hundred chests of goods and a well-fitted ship. If I sold nothing, I had no money to buy gold. The few months in which the gold trade blossomed were soon over, but more than once during this time the smugglers that the others wanted for their gold I welcomed as rescuing friends who should have shown me the door for my lack of *itzeboes*. In retrospect I often lamented that had I

5. Son of Zeus punished for eternity with hunger and thirst by being stuck in a river that drained when he tried to drink it, with fruit on a branch above his head that moved away when he reached for it.

simply departed for Japan with a few hundred thousand rix-dollars[6] that I
could have exchanged for gold within a few months of my arrival instead
of a ship with cargo; I could have departed grateful and satisfied, without
encountering all the miseries that later hung over my head there. To my
only consolation, I had partners in adversity who had come with imported
goods, and certainly not as much reason for regret as a certain esteemed
German merchant from Singapore. He arrived shortly after the opening of
Yokohama in mid-July of 1859, bringing with him twenty chests wherein
twice a hundred thousand Mexican dollars were neatly packed. He'd
intended to buy Japanese products in those first days with this substantial
sum, but when he arrived with his treasure and saw that it could hardly be
housed in a wooden shed, how the Interpreters' Office kept the Japanese
merchants away from the foreigners, and how, on the other hand, not
only his life but also the half a million (as calculated in Dutch guilders)
he had with him were in danger, he presumed, not unjustly, that it would
be irresponsible to stay longer, and decided to leave a country where men
were so unsafe. "*Hier ist nichts zu machen*,"[7] he sighed disappointedly
when he boarded with his dollars, which he shortly thereafter could have
made so fecund. Indeed, the *kobang*-trade arose just a few weeks after his
departure; had he still been in Yokohama and exchanged his dollars for
itzeboes and then again for gold, he could have, as a result, doubled his
hundreds of thousands of dollars twice in two months time.

For me and many others, the gold trade was just an opportunity for
profitable remittance, for the fortune hunters it was lure to leading a
merry life as long as it lasted, but for a few major English houses in China
who possessed the means to exploit this business on a large scale, the gold
trade must have been a source for millions. These houses even had their
own steamships that steamed from Yokohama to Shanghai, China in six
days. These steamships with hundreds of thousands of dollars on board
arrived in Yokohama, where their agents stood ready with the necessary
confederates to change dollars to *itzeboes* as rapidly as possible and at
the same time sniff out smugglers to buy *kobangs* in their place. After
a few days the *kobangs* steamed "full speed" to Shanghai; fourteen days
later, one saw the same steamship return to Yokohama. In two months
time this high-speed maneuver could be repeated several times, and it
is certain that when the gold trade was done, the purses of some of the
English houses in China were swollen with many tons of gold.

6. A two-and-a-half guilder coin.
7. There is nothing to be made here.

People did not think it would fly by so quickly, because a large and expensive staff was required to operate gold trade on a large scale. One could not offer as many dollars for exchange as he wished. Even in the best times, only a few hundred dollars a head was allowed to the subordinates of each of the treaty powers established in Yokohama. Sea officers and ship captains, although not permanent residents, were also permitted to make exchanges. It was thus not possible for the agent of an Anglo-Chinese house to change several hundred thousand dollars into *itzeboes* in a few days alone; he needed help to accomplish this. If all the houses in China sent some of their European clerks to establish mock branches, and all their agents there were put to it, there still would not have been enough exchangers to expedite the business. Then the "charlatans" or gold hunters who, as treaty nationals, had as much right to change money as the best of them, could be thrown into the mix to assist exchanges for considerable compensation. Likewise, the gold hunters were used to trade *itzeboes* for *kobangs*, and because they were exceptionally good at uncovering smugglers, they did good business. Indeed, as much of the silver as of the gold stuck to one or another of their fingers, so that they earned a lot of money without effort. Consequently, such cavalier affluence was generated among many of them that it caused the lives of all the foreigners in Yokohama to become staggeringly expensive.

Everything Japan yielded was, at least in the beginning, exceptionally cheap, especially food. At this time it cost, for example, 15 *itzeboes* for a fat ox, or about ƒ13; usually we bought one together with friends and had it slaughtered on shipboard since the Japanese did not use any ox flesh and thus had no butchers. A sack of potatoes cost ƒ1,20 cts.; a pound of fairly good white sugar ƒ0.20 cts.; a jar of lamp oil ƒ0.15 cts. Game such as hares, pheasants, venison, ducks, chickens, and geese was abundant; a pheasant cost ƒ 0.60 cts., a chicken or duck ƒ0.25 cents. As for vegetables, one could find turnips, carrots, leeks, peas, beans, and so forth, all dirt-cheap; this was particularly true of fruit of all sorts, but especially grapes and oranges in the fall.[8] The enormous quantities of both these fruits were amazing; for a few *tempos*[9] (6 cents) one could buy a whole basketful. But in contrast to these cheap provisions was the fabulous expense for all the necessities a European cannot do without. So for example, one paid ƒ3 for four pieces of washing, ƒ3 for a haircut, ƒ30

8. Mandarin oranges or satsumas (*mikan*).

9. *Tempo-sen*, 天保銭, a copper coin first issued in 1832 and in circulation until it was abolished in 1887.

for a doctor's visit, or f 15 if you went to his house, and f 24 for a pair of shoes. A Chinese cook drew f 60 a month to cook, and those necessary European provisions such as wine, beer, ham, butter, cheese and the like which Japan did not yield, were all terribly expensive. The staggering expense of all that resembled European luxury was the first sad result of the gold trade because many of the scallywags who were well-provided for by it knew no better what to do with their swiftly won gold than to make a big splash. For many, the easily earned money of the early years—first from gold, later with speculation in land, silk and so forth—was too powerful, and one may assume that the desire for luxury that this sparked was the origin of many of the bad practices later found in Japan. At the close of these memoirs I hope to return to this. Suffice it to note here that, at in least that first year, many of the pioneers in wooden houses still maintained honesty, simplicity and good faith, but these virtues were buried by the palaces that were built in their place, and the many later arrivals who basked in regal opulence in Yokohama when in Europe they would not have escaped the righteous arm of the law.

After what I reported above regarding the gold trade, one must not now have too much pity on the Japanese because all their gold coins were exported. They were later smart enough to take back in silver what they had lost in gold through usury to the foreigners.

People say that when Pizarro, the conqueror of Peru, was attacked and defeated through the resistance of his own countrymen, his opponent Gasca struck off his head and, as a bitter vengeance upon the gold-thirsty tyrant, poured molten gold in the mouth of the severed head, whereupon he derisively pronounced, "I satisfy you now with gold, for which you had such a relentless thirst!"[10] Thus we learn from the story of someone who was satisfied with gold after his death. But it was me and the simple sailor by my side who overcame, alive and well, a house that was literally filled to our knees in a mountain of gold. On a dark evening in November, one of the last days we spent in the hut on the seashore, there was a soft knocking on our outer door. The *kobang* trade was then as good as over; thus there were no more smugglers to wait for. But I

10. It was actually Gonzalo Pizarro (1506–1548), lieutenant to brother Franciso Pizarro (1471–1541) in the conquest of Peru, who in 1540 led an expedition down the Amazon in search of the legendary El Dorado. Gonzalo led a moderately successful revolt against the crown caused by the enforcement of the so-called "New Laws" that protected Native Americans. When the Spanish king's new representative, Pedro de la Gasca (1485–1567?), offered amnesty and repealed the laws, his troops deserted him, whereupon he surrendered and was beheaded.

had just a small supply of *itzeboes* in the secret hope that perhaps fortune
in her inscrutable caprice would give us proof of her benevolent wishes
in this late hour. With the necessary caution we went to the front door.
"Who is there?" I asked. "Gold, gold!" sounded the flustered answer.
After Jan had set his lantern on the ground, he placed himself with his
big sword on one side of the sliding door while I carefully shoved it open
a few hand-widths, ready to shove it back with even more strength and
thus pinch the possible invading criminal in between, and then to leave
the matter to be handled entirely by Jan, like the servant with the pirates
in the legend of the "House with the Heads"[11] in Amsterdam. Scarcely
was the door far enough open to allow a man's head or a knave's view
inside, when the glitter of gold dust shone from an extended arm. When
I saw that the fellow was unarmed, I let him in; two of his comrades,
with equally rascally faces, pushed in immediately after him. I slammed
the door shut behind the third, for I was disinclined to snare more than
three of these suspicious gold birds. Jan pointed with his sword, and I
with my revolver, the three men over to our sitting room as we pushed
them before us. To judge by their difficult gait, it appeared that they
were heavily loaded down. Agitated, they looked around fearfully as if
they were afraid they would be taken by surprise, once again showing a
handful of gold dust as if to ask if we wanted to buy it. With burning
eyes we contemplated that glistening stuff, what in hard science is called
"precious metal," and, seized with miserly feelings of greed, I laughed
and nodded covetously to the three rascals. "Yes! Yes! I will buy your
gold!" Intoxicated beyond my own strength, I lay both hands on the
nearest standing bandit and gave him such a shake that he quickly went
tumbling over. As if a specified signal had been given, the three men took
off their outer clothing, and for a moment we saw nothing before us but
a tangled group of Laokoons[12] because their naked bodies were wrapped
from bottom to top with sewn blue cotton snakes filled with gold dust
which, as they unwound them, began to glide down from the weight,

11. *Huis met de hoofden.* This national monument still stands at Keizersgracht 123.
Built in 1622 for wealthy merchant Nicolaas Sohier. Richly ornamented with lions
and gargoyles, it is named for the faces of six gods and goddesses on the façade. There
are many versions of this legend, but the one that is best known is that a maid, left
home alone, discovered that pirates were entering through a hole in the cellar. She
stood by the hole and cut off their heads, one by one, as they entered. The owner
then supposedly had their effigies appended to the house as a warning.
12. A Trojan priest who, with his sons, was strangled by sea snakes sent by the pro-
Greek gods for issuing a warning against accepting the wooden horse.

literally denting the thickly filled floor mats. As much from their fear and obvious agitation as from their anticipation, I was persuaded that these fellows were rogues, and that there was something not proper about their business. But for the moment I had no time to concern myself with that or ask for an explanation; the main thing was to get control of the gold. No sooner had the gold-filled sausages been coiled like cable on the ground, and the fellows had slipped on their outer garments, when a hand went out for money. "How much?" I asked hastily. "Five hundred *itzeboes*" said one of them, who appeared more or less to be the leader, sticking up five fingers. So strong is the desire to haggle in these people that, in spite of my covetousness and agitation over 500 *itzeboes* for 180 kilograms of gold, they would still haggle for 100. "Four hundred, give it up!" spoke the leader so quickly it was as if he begrudged the time it took to haggle, "but quickly, immediately, because if the *Jakoni* catch us, we'll lose our heads." I turned around and grabbed four packets from behind me, each of 100 *itzeboes*; which the fellow practically tore out of my hand, whereupon the trio bolted quickly to the front door and disappeared at top speed into the darkness.

After firmly closing the front door, our first job was to shake empty the gold sausages, and before long we stood in nervous surprise looking over a small gold mountain. — "Jan!" I said excitedly, "what a treasure! But," I continued, as a bitter shaft of doubt shot through my heart, and I clapped my trusty servant on the shoulder: "but Jan?" — "Sir?" said Jan. — "If only it is real gold, Jan?" No matter that the sailor had been my companion for about two months, and that the perilous circumstances in which we had passed this time had, as if of its own accord, brought about an uncommon intimacy between master and servant—he had never for a moment lost the respect in his eyes; indeed, he was indebted to me. Yet when I spoke of my doubts, I noticed a smirk of mocking pity on his weather-beaten face. "What, sir!" he spoke, and reached in to the mountain of gold and held some flat up to the light, "That isn't gold? But I understand completely, it's nerves. That isn't gold?! What is it then, is it lead? Is it silver? Is it copper? No, even a child can easily see that. I'll wager that I have five hundred guilders lying here on my hand." Although naturally I did not set even the least store by his analysis, I still felt the way most people would; as long as the contrary hadn't been proved, it was preferable to believe what I wished for most. — "Well now," I said, "I will accept that it is real gold. But then I still have another reservation: it must certainly be stolen, because these fellows had the most rascally faces that I have ever seen." —But Jan, who was now sitting in the gold, hastened to coat this bitter pill for me. "Why would it be stolen, sir?" he said, "I wouldn't say that. Those fellows must have come out of the mountains of the interior, maybe they are half-savages who know a place in the mountains where gold lays for the grabbing." —Again, I felt, for the sake of my treasure, some inclination to gravitate toward the feelings of my servant. "You are right, Jan!" I answered, "No European has ever been in the interior, so it is possible that the gold there is as abundant as in America, when it was first discovered; maybe there really was such a heap of gold there it could be sufficiently paid for with our four hundred *itzeboes.*" In either case, I understood that the thing was not to speak a word to anyone about our treasure; I pressed this earnestly on Jan. Now, before anything else happened, it was important that the gold was packed up and sent to Shanghai as quickly as possible so we could learn its value.

The next morning we packed the gold into three small chests. In the daylight it appeared to me to be an especially pale color, but I regarded this as a favorable sign. In those times there were three kinds of *kobang,* the best of which was very pale because of its platinum alloy. In Shanghai it brought *f*16—while the least of the lesser, gold-yellow sort was worth just *f*9. With the greatest care the three chests were sent to my correspondents in Shanghai by steamship a few days later, with a cover letter in which I sought to receive report as quickly as possible because the content had been bought as gold dust, and although it was possible that I had been deceived, I anticipated that it really was gold of the most valuable sort. After three weeks of waiting in hope and fear came the following laconic reply: "The metal sent to us is, according to expert examination, bleached antimony[13] that is worth about 20 dollars per picul of 60 kilograms here."[14] I read the disappointing message to my servant and crossly threw the letter on the table because Jan had much at stake, and if the stuff had been pure, he would have done quite well by it. He took it like a man. "It is tiresome that we were deceived by those rogues," he said, "but everything remains the same. When we thought we were sitting on a treasure, we took care not to talk about it with anyone; and now that we know we have been bamboozled, and do not sit on any treasure, we will also be careful not to say a word to anyone."

13. Antimony was frequently used to produce alloys.

14. Or 133 1/3 pounds. This was a weight widely used in China and Southeast Asia, and thus by the Dutch East India Company and Netherlands Trading Society. It was equal to 100 catties. From the Malaysian *pikul,* "the heaviest load a man can carry."

Chapter 5

Seldom has a settlement of Europeans abroad developed as quickly as did that of Yokohama's foreign quarter. Within three months, an entire Japanese city of the many merchants and shopkeepers from Japan's interior, who sought only to take as much from the foreigners as they could, arose on the west side of the Interpreters' Office. On the east side, in the same time, the foreigners' quarter grew from just a few wooden houses to three dozen, with just as many warehouses, and more construction continued daily at a vigorous pace. Everything was, however, rough and ready, constructed of wood, so that one would have to expect the worst if there was a fire. Of paving, sewers, lighting and such things, of course there was no trace. Since the houses were set down without reason on the harvested fields—and since, in the winter in Yokohama it would sometimes rain without pause— it goes without saying that the streets and lanes turned into quagmires, through which one could wade only with difficulty.

Commercial Houses in Yokohama. *Yokohama shōkan shinzu*, Hashimoto Sadahide, 1860. Collection of Waseda University Library.

It was around December 1859 that it was at last my turn to move into a new house. At this time many "settlers" also began a more regulated, social life. Each of us now had his own enclosed plot, upon which stood a fairly comfortable house, storehouse, kitchen, stable, etc., so that one had, at least if one were not too demanding, everything one needed to live and conduct business all together in one place. As far as the table is concerned, as I have noted above, all the stuff for that purpose could be had in such abundance in Japan that one could eat well enough provided one had a good Chinese cook. Such cooks drew ƒ60 a month, and each steamboat from Shanghai brought some, who immediately found places with soberly established foreigners as soon as they stepped ashore. For the most part they were masters in their profession, having learned under the English in China what "dinners" and "suppers" meant to "gentlemen." They could prepare all of these dishes most deliciously. But one had to resolve never to come in the vicinity of the kitchen where such a Chinese cook was at work, or to ask of the origin of the sauces, jellies or other such business, because one would not willingly fast as punishment for one's curiosity.

After I moved to my new house, I too employed such a cook, but when he had plied his art for eight days to my great satisfaction, I lost him for a month through an unforeseen circumstance. Just outside our foreign quarter the Japanese had arranged a large establishment on a great scale that they called Gankiro;[1] which we have in Europe, usually near the most loathsome neighborhood, what we usually call a district of ill-repute. For the Chinese, Gankiro had many attractions and in the evenings, after their work was done, the debauched sons of the Heavenly Kingdom were loyal visitors. My Chinese was also no better than the rest of his compatriots, and had, in that hotbed of lawlessness, misbehaved in some way or another; smashed a few paper windows, and resisted the Japanese police. For his insolent behavior he was arrested and condemned by the Japanese authorities to a one-month prison sentence. They called upon me, as his master, to pay for his board. When, after the passage of a month, the Chinese was released, I received a bill from the Interpreters' Office that read, "Request you to pay 1¾ *itzeboe* (i.e., ƒ1.75 ct) for using one month's board for your servant."

It would perhaps be worth the trouble for public welfare agencies to investigate in what manner the Japanese manage to keep someone alive for a month on ƒ1.75.

The above bill for board is just a small sample of Japanese-Dutch; as a further taste, permit me to follow with a few more letters, in which the meaning is so out-of-hand that I saved them as curiosities.

---

1. This was the best known of the establishments in the Miyozaki red light district. Established by shogunal order in 1859, there were separate sections for Japanese and foreigners. Gankirō was managed by Sashichi and aimed at foreigners. Longer-term mistresses for foreigners could also be contracted through Sashichi. In 1860 there were 36 *yūjo*, or prostitutes, working there.

Thus wrote a friend, asking me for flower seeds:

"To Master Coningh.

I have the honor to write you: if you have the germs, then I wish heartily that you will give me them. They you so friendly and favorably the above make available to me: I send silk work that my wife has made, to you for friendly token. With esteem and trust

Sakano Oei Sio Dsi."

"To Mr. Coningh.

I seek that, if you are not sorry, to give a chest old kloinie (eau de Cologne).

Inomata"[2]

The same Inomata, when he was indisposed:

"To Mr. Coningh.

I seek that a bottle of sourish drink will be given to me, because yesterday night I got diarrhea, I am very thirsty today:

Lemon juice

Red wine   1 bottle each sourish drink.

Luminade

Your servant,

Inomata"

A lover of the hunt wrote:

"To Mr. Coningh.

You remember that last year I bought a sort of hunting rifle, which is so made, that one can load the bullet in its opening on the end of the bottom part, which is fastened with the percussion cap and is detonated through strike down of the cock.

If you now have I will willingly get await your answer.

Your servant,

Junziro."

2. Probably interpreter Inomata Seishichirō.

From the same, shortly before my departure:

"To the valued friend Coningh.

From your letter I have named everything, and commanded my servant rifle and bullet to take with payment.

I wish you to take a very good journey, and to see your happy face again.

Your servant,

Junziro"

A booklover wrote:

"To my valued friend the Honorable Mr. De Coningh.

It is essential to me that your Honor, on this gentleman, who is my best Japanese friend, to see some of your beautiful books, for he presently over the above business is from the high city Edo coming here alone to Yokohama. If your honor fulfills my request, you shall have my great thanks.

Your honor strict gentleman, name me your obedient servant
Tinkuchi[3]

Officer translator in the Government of Kanagawa."

The same "officer translator" on another occasion:

"To my esteemed Mr. D. Coningh.

My friend wants see the dictionary, titled Kunstworden-tolk by Karamer,[4] thus you must trouble to give it.

Tinkuchi."

The following two letters were official summons to appear at the Interpreters' Office, the style of which is no better.

3. Probably Moriyama Takichirō.
4. This was probably J. J. Kramers, *Algemeene kunstwoordentolk, bevattende de vertaling en verklaring van alle vreemde woorden en zegswijzen, die in geschriften van allerlei aard, in de taal der zamenleving, in handel, bedrijf enz. voorkomen, met aanduiding van de uitspraak en den klemtoon dier woorden en naauwkeurige opgave hunner afstamming en vorming* (Gouda: G. B. van Goor). First edition 1847; second edition 1855. It was a dictionary and grammar of technical and specialized terms.

"To Mr. Coningh.
   Please you come, to the Interpreters' Office, to handle some business.
                                        Interpreters' Office Officer"

When I didn't come quickly enough, I received an encore the next day, as follows:

"To Mr. Coningh.
   It is waited that you today, now to bestow by the Interpreters' Office.
                                        Interpreters' Office Officer"

I just observed that when the majority of the long-term foreigners got better quarters, they began to lead a better-regulated and more comfortable life. That more civilized life was only an improvement when compared to what it once was. Most of the various nationalities fraternized fairly often, so that many all-too-spirituous "dinners" and "suppers" were given. Since it was also very easy to keep saddle horses in Japan, large, armed companies rode around the area every day. Most of them remained raw, sordid and savage because . . . there were no women. I have seen a horde of such "gentlemen" of all nationalities, totally removed from the influence of civilized women. Many such white "lords of creation," who inspired in me much greater loathing than the merry-making crowds of the scum of society at our big cities' fairgrounds, were around me in Kanagawa and Yokohama. To give something of an idea of how properly these "gentlemen" knew how to behave, I shall here bring forth the memory of a banquet I attended in those days, given by a Consul in his rooms in a temple in Kanagawa.[5] After consuming the sumptuous meal with much cursing and drinking, the gentlemen, all dressed in black jackets, were rather wound up by dessert. Their language alone would have made a coachman blush, but for these civilized men of the East words alone were not enough; they also had to show by deed that they knew how to amuse themselves. To that end a large tray of raw eggs

5. Although De Coningh has omitted any national identifiers, the French Consul Bellecour is the only one who fits in terms of timing. Harris of the US, Alcock of the UK, and van Polsbroek of the Netherlands were already present. Bellecour arrived in September of 1859. No new treaties were signed until Portugal in August of 1860 and Prussia in January of 1861, when things were already more civilized and women were present.

stood ready on a buffet in the corner for making egg flip⁶—a wonderful
opportunity. One witty guest came up with the idea of planting himself
by this tray and bombarding his friends and countrymen with eggs. In
the blink of an eye, the eggs flew over the banquet dishes and smashed,
splattering on the black coats of the civilized men from the West.
To resist so much fun was beyond the strength of most of his fellow
guests, who now stormed the egg tray and went mad with the contents,
throwing them around wildly. Naturally there followed a protest from
the more sober-minded, which resulted in a quarreling, cursing end to
the official banquet, whereupon the whole company left the Consular
temple in that late evening hour, brawling heavily, to sail together in a
large canopied boat to Yokohama. In front of the temple was a square,
from the middle of which rose a great flagpole where the flag of the
Consul's country had been hoisted for the first time. That was why
we had gathered on this solemn day in our best suits: to celebrate the
dedication of the new flagpole. As I crossed the square amid this messy
jacketed, brawling horde, I once more saw our consular host standing
drowsily in the door watching, then glanced up to the pole where the flag
hoisted for the first time that night hung in the bright moonshine of the
still evening as motionless as an old piece of cloth. Ashamed, I cast my
eyes down in front of the sad bunting, and silently hoped that the secret
of its festive dedication would remain hidden in its folds so that later it
would wave fresh and clear in the morning breeze, the civilized Japanese
never knowing the manner in which their Western visitors had dedicated
the first tall mast from which their flag would flutter, just a stone's throw
from Jeddo.

If the "gentlemen" showed such a lack of manners at this sort of official,
formal-dress meal, one can imagine how they carried on in their day-to-
day affairs. It certainly did not improve Japanese regard for foreigners
when some of them behaved like subjects of the king of Dahomey.⁷ A
street fight, for example, happened now and then, if not more frequently,
between a pair of "gentlemen"—once with almost serious consequences.

On one occasion a certain compatriot found it necessary to respond to
an Englishman who insulted him in his own home by seizing him by the
collar. Both were strong men, and there arose in the Hollander's house a

6. Originated in the eighteenth century by sailors, a flip was beer, spirits, and sugar
that had been heated with a hot iron. In the nineteenth century egg and milk were
added and it became a more genteel drink, essentially like eggnog.

7. Now known as Benin. This kingdom was known for despotism and associated
with the slave trade.

furious fight in which the combatants roundly manhandled each other. Their wrestling sent them tumbling through the thin partitions and sliding paper doors to such an extent that when I came to my countryman's residence, it appeared that the whole house had been broken apart from the inside. The upshot was that the Englishman was thrown out of the house with a bloodied head, so battered and unpresentable that he was not seen for the eight following days. The whole affair, like so many in this world, would have blown over between them if a few weeks later an American, a real Yankee, had not arrived in an evil hour and decided he could still have a little pleasure from the business. He, a doctor on an American steamship, had become acquainted with the Englishman ashore who, still feeling pain here and there following the beating he had received, sought a soothing salve. The American, after learning the cause of his pain, gave him the balm he desired. But he also delivered a second prescription from his American apothecary: to procure satisfaction for himself through a good boxing re-match. At the same time, the kindly doctor took adequate care to trumpet around that it was a shame that an Englishman was unavenged for the beating he had suffered at the hands of a "Dutchman." The result of all this medical meddling was that our Englishman, through some of his compatriots and his doctor, would step into the arena as one highly agitated boxer.

None of us gave the whole affair a second thought because the American's mischief-making did not reach our ears. On a fine afternoon we went horseback riding after the workday with a company of Hollanders around the neighborhood and returned to Yokohama just before nightfall. Everyone had ridden home except Graver, our countryman who had taken in hand Mr. Mob,[8] the Englishman, a few

8. I have been unable to find record of these two. It is probable that they are highly altered pseudonyms because the events related are not complimentary. De Coningh's aliases seem to retain the first and some following letters so Mr. Mob may be Michael Moss, who was caught hunting, which was illegal close to the capital. He resisted police attempts to take his servant, who was carrying the game, and shot a Japanese official. Sentenced to three months in prison and a $1,000 fine, the fine was paid by the foreign community. He served the prison term but he appealed in Hong Kong and won back $2,000 in damages. He tried to sue for $30,000 for the beating he received from the Japanese police and loss of business but was denied. See Michael Moss, *Seizure of Mr. Moss and His Treatment by the Consul General* (London: William Ridgeway, 1863). This same man also was caught liberating a horse; see Fonblanque, *Niphon and Pe-Che-Li*, 81. The only Dutch citizen who was in Yokohama in 1859 whose name began with a "G" that I have been able to find was a merchant named J. A. C. Gerlach.

weeks previous. Graver had dismounted to speak to me about something or another. Our horses were put in the stalls, and we had sat down to talk quietly when a message in English, written in pencil, was delivered for Graver. He took a look inside and, apparently shocked by the contents, extended it to me. I read:

"Mr. Mob is eagerly awaiting Mr. Graver so that he may satisfy a grudge by administering him a sound thrashing in front of the eyes of the English community of Yokohama."

Laughing, I gave the message back to him, because I thought that there was not the remotest possibility that it was earnest, that it must be a prank from some joker. Graver took it very differently, and although disinclined and unprepared to box after returning from his ride, he resigned himself to his fate and asked me to accompany him. With satisfaction I declared myself ready, for I still thought it nothing more than a joke, as did Graver—who, however much he considered the letter to be in earnest, knew all too well what a beating he had given Mr. Mob and so thought Mob would not be in any hurry to exact revenge. That is why he mounted with me, without any preparation, dressed for the horse in winter costume, with a thick pea coat and high riding boots that allowed him to move only with difficulty, like a fully dressed cuirassier of days gone by.[9]

The site where my house stood was, like all of the others, eighty paces long and just as broad, surrounded by a square of fragile plank fence within which were the wooden buildings: a residence, a warehouse; a kitchen, stable and bathhouse were stashed in the corners. Our neighbors' yards were as much alike as one drop of water to another so that the street of our foreign quarter was formed by one long strip of wood fence, above which only the roofs of the houses could be seen here and there rising up from the middle of the square compound. Each resident could keep his yard fairly hard and free from the mud caused by the many winter rains by laying pebbles and gravel from the nearby beach, but if he stepped out of the gate of his fence into the so-called street, he would sink a few feet deeper into the ground. Indeed, the soil of the street, or broad alley, which only months before had been farmland, was churned up day and night by heavily laden hand carts drawn by dozens of stout Japanese, used to transport all the goods to and from the warehouses. The wheels of these handcarts were simple broad serrated disks cut from thick tree

9. A type of cavalry that wore armored breastplates. Not used in the Dutch army after 1841.

trunks. If sunk in the mud to the axle, they could only be put in motion
through brute strength. The deep ruts they made turned the way into
such a morass that if a few people waded through it, one heard the same
peculiar splash as in Holland at the moment a horse comes out of a fjord
in the summer after a wandering ride. My yard lay at the end of the
newly built foreigners' quarter, and the mud stopped by my warehouse;
if one went out the gate of my fence and turned left one would take
a mud bath. But if one went right, after a few steps one stood on a
relatively dry piece of harvested farmland.

As I have just said, I went with Graver, but before we had even gone
out the door, Jan came hastily rushing in. "My heavens, sir!" he cried
out, "What is going on sir? The field by here is full of Englishmen and I
have heard that they have come ready to see the 'Dutchman' get it."

There now appeared to be no doubt that it was serious; in haste I
shared the contents of the message that had been delivered for Graver,
and resolving to remain calm in spite of everything, suggested that we
lay down our revolvers. After all, it was foreseeable that if our nationality
were insulted, we would need to be reined in. One cannot be certain that
self-control will prevail, and to be gripped by the belt by an unguarded
moment of anger could let oneself in for disastrous results. We therefore
gave Jan our weapons for safekeeping with express instructions to stay
within the yard, a charge that he flatly refused to follow; I had to exert all
my authority over him before he at last promised to come later, so that
he would be able to jump in if he judged it necessary. A furious sailor
would only have sown more animosity among the watching pack, and
it was important that this business be kept as much as possible between
two people and a war of nationalities prevented, for in this event we few
Hollanders were badly outnumbered against the many Englishmen.

Graver and I stepped out the house door, followed immediately
thereafter by a whole pack of English and American "charlatans," who
had climbed up my fence and that of my neighbor across the way to
survey the battle as if it were in an amphitheater. Taking no notice of
them, we crossed my yard to the gate in the fence that led to the street.
Graver's way home was left on the muddy street, and apparently the
onlookers feared that he would go there. But we struck out to the right,
walking calmly among the pack, some of who sat above our heads,
having climbed on to the fence, toward the group that stood a few paces
further in a ragged circle in the field. No Spaniard could have shown
more excitement, at the moment the toreador stepped into the arena,
than did these "civilizers of the Japanese"; some "gentlemen" stood ready

to jeer, and the others ready to go for his throat. The circle opened for us, and in the middle stood Mr. Mob in a knit suit, bareheaded, with exposed arms, in the consummate English boxer's costume, waiting for his opponent. In place of some sort of explanation, and without even giving Graver time to undo his heavy outer clothing, the boxer leapt straight at him.

"Mr. Graver!" he said, "you have given me a beating. Now I shall beat you!" At the same moment he gave Graver a thump on the chest that sent him stumbling back a step.

Graver's Dutch answer to the English boxer was a punch to Mob's jaw that audibly jangled his teeth and caused blood to spurt from his nose and mouth. With lightning speed he then grabbed Mob in the middle in order to lift and throw him over at full force; his plan succeeded, but unfortunately his enemy dragged him into the fall, and they both crashed to the ground. Then followed a moment of wrestling, where one, then the other, lay underneath with frantic punches from both sides, but it was evident that Graver could not move as required because of his heavy clothing; the bout was mismatched. At the sight of this unequal struggle, I lost my calm; my blood boiled and, shaking with anger, I threw myself between the fighters.

"That's not fair! Graver can't defend himself like that!" I shouted, blazing with wrath, turning toward the onlookers. "If there is a man among you who is ashamed to see this unequal scandal continue, he will help me pull them apart."

"Yes, yes! You are right, it is not fair; he must first take off his thick clothing!" shouted some of the best disposed, who at the same time rushed forward to help me separate the angry fighters.

When we had both men, panting and bloodied, on their feet again, the fifty English cutthroats were ready to applaud their boxer in what must properly be called hubris, because his battered condition showed all too clearly that he had received his fair share. The few of our compatriots present hastened to press Graver's hand and speak a warm word of encouragement while helping him out of his outer clothing, now doubly heavy with clay and mud. I thought I should not allow this moment of delay to pass unused to put an end to the fight if possible. But the sight of the furious fight, the few punches I had received while coming between friend and enemy, the jeering inciting of the bystanders, some mocking words to the "Dutchmen" that penetrated—all had my Hollander's blood racing so fast that I was hardly master of myself, and a feeling of such courage welled up in me that I would not get out of the way for any army. Blazing with indignation, I turned toward the most civilized of those who had broken from the pack and, with a voice loud enough to drown out the commotion, I expressed my regret that due to the ambush, I had fallen into this company that regardless of nationality, I as a decent man was ashamed of. But now that fate had cast me among them, I would wait to see if anyone had the heart to insult me—or if there were still "gentlemen" present who, like me, understood that the scandal occurring here, before our eyes, did not have to continue.

Many fell in to hold back the fighters who now stood ready for a new assault. In the middle of all the commotion, cursing and clamor, the better disposed might have succeeded in concluding the affair with no further difficulties, had Graver's anger not been newly awakened by an incidental circumstance. Specifically, while both parties stood opposite each other ready to fight, held back by my helpers and myself, an Englishman, a real "snob" stepped out from the crowd with his leather horse- or dog-whip in his hand.

"I say Mob, look here, take my horsewhip to lick that Dutchman!" he said, while he tried to pass the whip to the boxer.

Like an angry tiger Graver tore loose and wrenched it out of the hand of the "snob," smacking it on the ground so that mud spattered about his ears.

"That's a whip for blackguards, not for Dutchmen!" roared Graver, foaming at the mouth, and then he turned toward the boxer. "What! You would thrash me with this whip? I think not! No more with fists; now you will fight the 'Dutchman' with weapons!" and he struck the empty revolver holster that hung at his side.

"That's fine, I'll take that on whenever you want!" replied the Englishman curtly. Apparently he was doing his best to control himself; one could see his naked shoulders shudder while he spoke.

"Tomorrow morning at seven o'clock," cried Graver, and taking the nearest bystander out of the crowd by the arm, he continued, "Captain King,[10] I request you to be my second." The misfortune! In his excitement he had chosen the most bloodthirsty fellow to be found in all of Yokohama.

"I gladly place myself at your disposal, Sir!" said Captain King with a sardonic smile, and it could be seen that he took pleasure in the affair.

---

10. Possibly Captain T. H. King of the *Wanderer,* a schooner of 176 tons and crew of 11 out of Boston. Nephew of Josiah Johnson of the *Fenimore Cooper.* This Captain King arrived in Yokohama on June 30, 1859, and became agent for Heard & Co. in December 1859. *The Wanderer* capsized in this month in a squall, putting King out one thousand dollars, which might explain his impoverished state.

To his honor, Mr. Mob, the boxer, showed that he possessed a high degree of self-control: however much his voice and face amply betrayed what was going on inside him, he preserved the appearance of an imperturbable, ice-cold Englishman. Battered as he was, the muddied tatters of his knit suit hanging from his naked torso, he stepped up to me, and with the same dignity as if he had asked me in a parlor: "Mr. De Coningh, may I request that you kindly stand by my side?"

"Completely at your service, Mr. Mob!" I answered him solemnly.

So now the decision was left to the revolver. The onlookers climbing down from the fence were not dissatisfied, because they had the prospect of seeing a couple of men shoot each other dead the next morning, which for most of them was more piquant than a boxing match.

"Captain King, I await you in an hour at my place," I said to my fellow second while I took Graver under the arm. Then we both stepped between the rows of "Britishers" and "Yankees" into the muddy street to go to his house, heads held high as proud "Dutchmen."

Heaven forbid that I should advocate a duel, which—in a civilized country among civilized men, where one is protected against insult and mishandling by the law, a judiciary, and the police—is simply ridiculous. But if one is left alone in an isolated corner of the world with eighty-odd fortune-seekers of all nationalities, without any trace of order, law or justice except that of the strongest, then that changes everything. And if under such circumstances, the English, who regard the rest of humankind as some sort of pariahs, are the overwhelming majority, then that changes everything even more. Then things are changed so much that any Hollander with some sense of honor will not allow himself to be downtrodden and disdainfully called "Dutchman" by the imperious English; and when he stands, one man before twenty, at the least insult he summons his man before the barrel of his revolver. This is how it was in those days in Yokohama, and whoever could not handle it was not only not respected, but lay himself bare to the most brutal insolence of the biggest and best blackguards.

Where were, one might ask, the consular authorities in such situations? These gentlemen departed in the afternoons to their well-guarded temples in Kanagawa and did not return until the following morning, which in those days meant that they were unreachable during the night.

Needless to say, I had much to discuss with Graver and little time, and it was already completely dark when I sped to my house to wait for Captain King. I intended to bring the wild Indian hunter from Texas into my fold by receiving him with as much dignity and respect as was possible. My house was just like all the others: a small wooden one-story building with a hall down the middle and three rooms on each side. I had it furnished extremely well considering the circumstances. Especially the sitting room, which when brightly lit in the evening was, for Yokohama in those days, a very smart salon, at least in the eyes of someone like Captain King, a fly-by-night type who lodged in heaven only knows what kind of sty, using a chest filled with straw as his bed. To forestall my awaited visitor from clumsily stomping in the open door, I posted Jan in the hallway to serve him properly. My Chinese was told to put on his silk jacket if I called him to serve. I had barely put something on in haste and made my place ready to receive my fellow second when I heard him at the front door.

"Is your master in?" I heard him snarl through his nose like most of his compatriots, when Jan slid open the door that he had knocked upon.

"Yes, Sir!" said Jan, but when the Captain tried to step in unasked, brooking no refusal, Jan stepped in his way, saying, "I beg your pardon, I will first announce you."

The wild captain was not used to so much ceremony when he stepped into the "wigwams" of the Apaches and Seminoles in "the far West"; thus he grumbled somewhat under his breath. But fortunately, Jan did not have far to walk, because he could simply turn around to knock on the paper sliding door of my room, which in a Japanese house represented the inner walls.

"Captain King, Sir!" Jan announced.

"Let him enter," I answered loudly and haughtily, whereupon the modern buccaneer stepped into the room. He was a short, squarely built fellow, who peered wildly out of dark eyes over a heavy, dark wooly beard and mustache. A squat felt hat with a broad rim was set at a slant across his head; a duffle[11] cape lined with sheep's fleece hung over his knitted wool doublet; and the broad belt around his middle was stuffed with long knives and two revolvers. He wore Mexican riding pants, which flared wide at the bottom and were set with buttons to the knees as ornament. He had come by horseback, and had fastened his horse to the front door.

"Hello," he began in a discordant tone, stepping into the room ever so free and easy. "How are you doing there. I have now come so we can discuss the layout a bit because we must make sure they get a good shot at each other."

11. A napped woolen blanket fabric.

I stood to meet him with the dignity and the benevolent smile of a noble receiving a petitioner. As I stepped over to meet him, I directed him with a slight bow to the sofa that stood opposite me in front of the table, saying, "Good evening, Captain King! It is a pleasure to see you. Might I ask you to take a seat?"

Instead of throwing himself, full length, onto the sofa in his muddy riding clothes as I had feared he might, he sat with a "Thank you!" very properly on the edge of the sofa, and even stammered out a few words of courtesy. Thank God! The wild American had been won over. When he sat down instead of lying, I thought I would be able to mold him.

After speaking for a moment about the fight that had occurred, I finally asked: "What, in your opinion, would it be best to do now?"

"Well," answered the American very much through his nose, pensively scratching his beard, "I think we must give the 'gentlemen' a good chance. If we let them shoot their six-shot revolvers at each other from twenty paces, neither of them will have anything to complain about. Therefore your yard here is an excellent place, and whoever gets hit the most, we can immediately carry inside your house."

I had to be careful not to offend the wildman, and remarked only that I found his proposal a little drastic and wished to think it over. Meanwhile, the Chinese came in, dressed in his Sunday best, with tea; but when he stood before the captain with his tray, the Captain stuck his nose into it, and then looking at the Chinese, he asked, "What is that? Tea?" and made a dismissive motion with his hand. But when he turned toward me, he said with the utmost courtesy:

"I only take tea in the mornings, and now that I have the pleasure of being in a 'Dutch house,' perhaps I could now trouble you to allow me the chance to drink a glass of real 'Schiedam.'"[12]

"It's not the least trouble, Sir!" said I, and gave my Chinese a nod to set the tray with the crystal grog set on which stood in the most tasteful manner, a carafe of that most celebrated Dutch product, together with its satellites, the water pitcher and the sugar bowl, in front of my guest. "Have the goodness to help yourself, Sir! It is of the best mark[13] that was ever distilled in Schiedam," I remarked with as much courtesy as I could muster when the tray stood in front of him. Indeed, now that I had bridled his wild nature through captivating dignity, I must now maintain

---

12. Gin.

13. Refers to the maker and line of gin.

it; for when I aired my plan his raw familiarity would come to the surface
again, and then that would be the end of it with the buffalo hunter.

Captain King slowly poured his glass half full and then held it up as
if he were of two minds as to whether he would add water or not. He
appeared to find it better without, and in any case, would first sample a
bit. "Your Dutch gin is as smooth and sweet as milk," he said, smacking
his lips after taking a generous sample. "It would be a shame to tamper
with it," and he took no water.

In the meantime, I had not lost sight of the reason for our meeting,
which was why I, now that we sat together with proper calm, made the
remark that we still had to provide a doctor, who could be no other than
the only one in the place, Dr. Dugger,[14] a terribly seedy scallywag.

"We will have to take him," said Captain King, "since we may call him
a doctor here, but he may as well be a pickpocket. If I was ever the least
bit sick or wounded here, I would rather be taken care of by a Japanese
tanner's apprentice than that filthy Irish."

Dr. Dugger lived close by in the neighborhood, and thus it was not
much trouble to send Jan to him with a message asking if he had a
moment available to come to us. While we waited for his answer, the
American began to calculate which of the fighters had the best chance
the next morning, and on whom he ought to lay his bet. He noticed,
however, that his goal to have me put a handful of dollars on the head of
one or the other was little to my taste, and thus his chance at a windfall
was gone. I went so far as to express my regret over the whole affair with
measured dignity, and assured him that I would do everything possible
to avert the duel since the honor of a countryman was at stake. "And,"
I finally concluded, "I am so revolted by the affair that if one of the
consular authorities could be reached in the night, I would inform him
of it so it would not go forward until I heard from him what to do. But
now I can do nothing to remedy this but consult with you to restrain
everything as much as possible."

Captain King looked at me with wide eyes, and if I had not commanded
him with earnest dignity from the beginning, he would certainly have
erupted; for, had it been up to him, he would most certainly have desired
that the parties shoot each other dead so he could then scalp them. But

---

14. Richard W. Duggan opened Kanagawa hospital in October of 1859. This
Dr. Duggan of Galway is mentioned by Francis Hall for having requested the
cadavers of criminals. John Brooke recounts an incident when he refused to treat a
patient because he had been seen by another doctor but billed him anyway.

now, having laid out my thoughts and spoken of acting in consultation with him, I had found his weak spot.

"In affairs of honor, sir," he said, "Obadjah King is just your man. And now that I see the issue in proper perspective, my first question is: What can be done for honor? Well now, I say, if we could look inside and outside of both 'gentlemen,' we would see that they are both pretty much equally bruised. The honor of one is thus just as good as the other; therefore it would be honorable to have fewer shots. What do you think of two shots for each?"

He had evidently begun to come around; but I still had to put a stop to his excesses.

At this moment Jan came back with the message that Dr. Dugger had been carried into his house dead drunk an hour ago and would not awaken for the first half of the day.

"You heard it, Captain King! Now we do not even have a doctor!" I said, and to drive my point home, I followed with "I trust that a 'gentleman' of your experience knows all too well from your wars with the Indians how helpless the wounded are. This drawback cannot be lightly discounted. I will thus be so free as to offer for your consideration, that one shot each would be sufficient."

"One shot? It is truly too little; we give the 'gentlemen' no chance," said the Captain, "but . . . never mind! Let it be one shot," he allowed after a moment's thought, in the tone of a street hawker who had been bargained down to the last cent.

It was a load off my mind, but now that I had restricted the duel to the narrowest possible boundaries, there still remained the marking of the place in my yard where both parties would meet. We went outside together to confer, lit by Jan with a lantern, and when we had found a suitable place, a stake was beaten into the ground. With scrupulous care, as if afraid he would be off by a millimeter, Captain King took twenty paces from the stake, and standing stock still, invited us to do the same. Followed by Jan, I did as he desired and on the twentieth step I stood directly on his toes.

"All right! You see that the measurement is true," spoke the Captain as he pounded a second stake into the ground. "And now I believe," he continued, going over to his horse that stood stamping by the front door, "that we have taken care of everything; I will now go to Mr. Graver and you shall certainly seek Mr. Mob."

While he untied his horse, I thought to myself that this terrible American really was better than I had expected, and I might have further need of him in the course of this affair so I deemed it expedient to cultivate his timely surge of good nature. "You will not need much time with Mr. Graver, Captain King. May I have the pleasure of seeing you here for supper in an hour?

"I accept your invitation with pleasure," he answered, hopping into the saddle, and horseman and horse disappeared into the darkness.

"Jan, get my horse, quick as the devil! Let me see, it is nine o'clock. Tell the Chinese I will be back at ten o'clock with a 'gentleman,' and that he should prepare a proper supper."

Ten minutes later I sat by Mr. Mob, and one hour later Captain King and I were both back in my house, each conveying the message that our charges were satisfied with the arrangements we had made. Captain King was not one to let a nourishing supper go without doing it full justice, and because the food and the wine were to his taste, he was in an exceptionally good humor. Thereafter he entertained me with his adventures with the Pawnees and Seminoles, of which murders and fires were the warp and weft, and finished, certain that he would please his host, with the assurance that now and then during his enterprises in the far West he sometimes met a Hollander. "That is why," he continued, "I know much about your country. I know that everything has 'dam' on it, like Amsterdam, Rotterdam, Schiedam, and in Indiana I once had a friend who was a Hollander. What the devil was his name again . . . I believe it was Jan Borrendam from Swammerdam. He was scalped by the Iroquois, and then hung! Oh! He was a fine fellow, who was also called John Dam of Borreldam." He left off there, dejectedly shaking his head. Then, as if to brace himself, he took the filled wine glass that stood in front of him, and as he brought it to his lips he spoke, full of admiration, "A fine fellow he was!" and swallowed the contents in one draught as an homage in memory of the scalped Swammerdammer.

This tender spell lasted but a moment for the Indian hunter because with the same hand that had set the empty glass on the table, he grabbed a cold duck leg that sat before him and, with a knife in the other hand, began to peel it with as much diligence as if he were flaying a Seminole. "You see, Sir!" he continued, amidst his work, glancing up at me now and then, "that I know your country and have a place in my heart for your countrymen. That is the reason I was so vexed just now at the boxing match, at the English cad with his whip. By Jove, I thought to myself, if I could raise five hundred dollars, I would certainly hunger for those fellows to brawl tomorrow, and for them to blow out their brains. For you see, Sir! If a man is to make his way through the world, then he must know how to help himself one way or another. If the Indians in my country stay quiet, then I am out of a job and must seek something else that suits my manner of doing business. Yet as a traveling 'gentleman' I cannot bring with me a variety of articles to sell; someone in my position must always manage his business in his brain and what he can carry in his pocket. In California my business lay in the direction determined by digging for gold and assisting friends, and here in Yokohama I have continued my business in the gold sector by exchanging *kobangs* and just as in California I am ready to put my services at the disposal of friends."

Here he was silent for a moment, but I really did not know how to respond. Now that the *kobang*-exchange was done, that only left helping friends. I knew what he meant. I understood all too well through the petition that he tossed out about how he desired to raise an honorarium of five hundred dollars.

"I don't believe," continued the rather disappointed rider of the prairie, "that I can conduct any business in this country. Believe me, Sir, when I say that instead of making money, I have come up short here. So I have, for example, asked my friends Mr. Blowder and Captain Turnip to supper, and if one of my friends does not lend me twenty dollars, I truly don't know what I shall give them to eat."

I could not remain deaf to his outright confession: therefore I thought it advisable to risk twenty dollars before he perhaps went still further.

"Allow me the satisfaction of offering to lend you twenty dollars, Captain King," I said politely, while I laid it with a smile on the table in front of him.

"Thank you, I cannot refuse you," he said, apparently pleased that he had managed again to scrounge up dinner for the following day, "because I would like to be written about in your book. I hope to get along somehow. Indeed, it is astonishing how one learns to make everything right; in the *kobang* time a hundred dollars a day wasn't enough, and now I must get through the next twenty-four hours with this twenty."

For the moment, the modest captain did not desire more than a nourishing meal and twenty dollars in his pocket. He was thus making his farewells when there was some noise at the front door, and we clearly heard several voices in very cultured English, that, when Jan opened the door, demanded to speak to me immediately.

"St,"[15] I said to my guest, "there appear to be visitors. It is after eleven o'clock. What are they after so late at night?"

15. A sound of annoyance.

"Sir!" began Jan, when I called him in after his knock, "Mr. Kesburn,
Mr. Elmstock and Mr. Black,[16] are here and wish the pleasure of speaking
with you," and three real 'gentlemen' who belonged to the *grandezza*[17] of
the foreigners stepped into the room. They were the representatives of the
international trading firms of London and Liverpool, of Shanghai and
Hong Kong, whose signatures were as good as worth a hundred thousand
pounds if they were worth a penny. But even so, in those days they were
housed no better than anyone else in Yokohama. In the bear caps, heavy
duffels, muddy boots and revolvers they wore for this evening expedition,
they looked more like co-conspirators than the pillars of society from the
"city" of London. I had already met these "gentlemen" several times, and
thus was already "introduced," so after the usual greeting, and when they
had taken their places, I presented my guest to them.

"Captain King of Texas," I said, indicating him, and I bowed toward
the buffalo hunter, who apparently was not very pleased with the new
visitors.

The three gentlemen sent an ice-cold, almost invisible nod in the
direction of the Captain, with whom, as it turned out, they were already
very familiar because a few months before he had often been used by, or
lent to, one or another of the men as a hired exchanger and gold hunter.

"I know the gentlemen already from my gold business," said Captain
King to me after he had responded just as coldly to their bows, like
someone with no intention of being pushed around.

It appeared clear to me that the three visitors were little pleased with
their knowledge of, and business relationship with, my guest; therefore I
thought it necessary to inform them how it came to be that this somewhat
disheveled American sat so intimately at my evening meal. "Let me say,
gentlemen," I remarked, "that Captain King took his supper here at my
pleasure because we were chosen to make arrangements for a duel that

16. Probably William Keswick (1834–1912), C. T. Elmstone, and Edward Clarke.
William Keswick was a clerk for Jardine Matheson, coming to Yokohama in 1859.
He moved to Shanghai in 1862, later heading the company. Elmstone had been
captain of the *Joseph Soames,* a 774-ton wooden ship built in 1845. It traveled
between London to Adelaide, Australia, and in 1857 she caught fire, an accident
which was linked to the *Flying Dutchman.* Passengers claimed to have seen the ghost
ship pass before the fire started. Elmstone was sent to Yokohama as agent for Sassoon,
Sons & Co. Edward Clarke was from Dent & Co. He replaced Loureiro as acting
Portuguese consul.
17. Italian for "great," here meaning upper-crust.

will take place between one of my countrymen and Mr. Mob tomorrow morning at seven o'clock, here in my yard, with revolvers."

"That is just what we came to talk about," began Mr. Kesburn. He was still a young gentleman, with thin, reddish sideburns, a somewhat effeminate appearance, and lisping voice; yet a true diplomat who said all that he had to say with an ice-cold, deadened courtesy. During his slow speech, his lily-white hands looked like they strung together his measured words. With a smile on his face, he gave it his saccharine best: "That is just what we came to speak about, Sir! It is a truly tragic affair as well as a very serious matter from a commercial standpoint. Whatever happens here will be read, in two months, in the English newspapers, and such publicity is less than desirable. One would do better to withhold news articles that complain that we are left to our fate here without protection, and call for revenge for the murders that take place now and again here. Confidence in this new port will be so thoroughly shaken that no one in Europe will venture into business with such a precarious establishment. After all the grievances that have already been published, if there are any such men left and they learn that the foreigners here are fighting and shooting each other, then the credit of this place will be utterly destroyed. It is for this reason that we have come to ask for your cooperation in preventing the duel from occurring."

One of the others, a Mr. Black, echoed the words of his friend. He pulled out a written document, remarking that they had prepared the piece together, and that he would take the liberty of reading it. Both duelers were to sign it, and if they did, it would thereby lay the matter to rest. After a solemn introduction, the document explained that, informed by esteemed friends, they were ready to clear up the misunderstanding that had arisen; that they regret this, that they regret that, and after the assurances of the above-mentioned esteemed friends that no one in Yokohama would consider this the slightest wound to their honor, they now through their signatures below, considered the business finished without further conflict.

Captain King furrowed his brow during the reading, as much because he was afraid that the outside chance of a duel would escape him, as because he was being ignored. I thus had to hastily sing his praises because no settlement could come about without his approval; otherwise one could predict that the grossest insults from him and his mates awaited the reconciled fighters. "Gentlemen!" I began after the reading. "It is not possible that you three desire settlement of this affair more than I who, whenever possible, avoids offending anyone. What I mean is that we really should first ask Captain King's opinion, who in matters of this nature could be called a good judge and certainly will know best what he can consent to for the severe insult to Mr. Graver."

The face of the American cleared somewhat, and he deemed it now his turn to say a word: "The credit of this place is a matter of indifference to me," he said. "Mr. Graver was insulted by Mr. Mob, he called him out. It is very simple: if Mr. Mob will now settle this business, let him ask for Mr. Graver's pardon. Then it is entirely possible that he will let him off."

This proposal was not to the taste of the three "gentlemen." That one of their compatriots should ask the pardon of a "Dutchman" was too much for them. Yet it was true that this would be the most just punishment because the entire difficulty arose as a consequence of English notions toward other nationalities. As a result, Mr. Mob had received his first blows. Wasn't that in fact the case?

As I noted earlier, we were among murderers and arsonists, without any protection whatsoever from even a single warship of the treaty powers. We therefore had to guard ourselves during the night for our own safety; and, to that end, all the foreigners able to bear arms had banded together to run patrols each night for two hours in groups of three according to a roster that had been drawn up. The patrol to which Mob belonged was followed by that of Graver, and so it happened that when Mob's two hours were up he came to Graver's bed chamber to wake him. For a countryman, he would certainly have done different, but a "Dutchman" didn't require such a ceremonial awakening, and should jump up immediately as soon as his betters called. "Graver, it is your watch, get up!" he commanded gruffly, standing before the bed. When Graver sleepily grumbled, "Fine!" while yawning and stretching, Mob growled menacingly. "Come on, out now! Or I will throw you out!" Suddenly as fully awake as if water had been thrown over him, Graver sprung out of his bed, and the consequence was that the Englishman was badly manhandled, and thrown out the door. But who is to blame? Surely it was Mob, for his coarseness was the cause of the blows that followed. And the boxing match was also provoked by malice toward Hollanders. "Gentlemen" came to blows everyday—why were spectators invited just in this case? It was for Mob, to see him getting down to business in his boxing costume. The maliciousness with the whip thereafter was caused because the challenge had been made in the first place. How the matter ended and how well I served Mob would depend on the fairness of the steps taken for settlement. The Englishman was in the wrong, so I was firm that he be the one to bow first.

Captain King stood faithfully by. "It is time for me to depart!" he said, standing. "I will not take a step from Mr. Graver, and will make sure that I am with him at seven o'clock here in the yard."

There had to be a decision. The negotiations would surely have foundered on British pride, had not Mr. Elmstock—a robust, jovial Englishman, with a certain engaging bonhomie—intervened. His open, ruddy face was kept in balance by his long, combed-out muttonchop whiskers like a pair of wings on his well-fed, Herculean figure. His cordial, simple tone—really, his whole personality—stood in sharp contrast to that of the effeminate, stiflingly formal, diplomatic Mr. Kesburn, and the somewhat surly, ice-cold Mr. Black. He was an Englishman of the best breeding, such as one often finds there, a solid, good-hearted man who, in the middle of his enormous business, still finds time and opportunity to partake of roast beef and port wine; who said what he meant without much ado; and upon whose word one could depend on like a rock. "Come, come, gentlemen!" Mr. Elmstock began. "Let us not go at each other this way. We are all of the same Anglo-Saxon race, let us not quarrel over nationality; everything will come out well if we acknowledge that Mr. Mob must come around first. I propose that he sign the piece first, then I believe Mr. Graver will be satisfied and not have any objections." Everyone was satisfied then but the American, who hesitated.

"Make no further trouble now, Captain King," continued Mr. Elmstock, "and help us put an end to this affair. We must all help each other here. Today you do me a service, tomorrow I guarantee I will do you another."

Whether the Captain saw in these words the prospect of a new loan or whether he was gratified to put an end to an affair of honor in which he was the deciding factor—whatever the reason, he was all at once very agreeable: "What you say there, Sir!" he said to Mr. Elmstock, "is completely true. If one can do another a service here, than he must not fail to do so. After all, I also find the arrangement between the parties fair, and they must both be satisfied with it. So then, it is now also time that we haul them out of bed to sign the paper."

In the dead of night we all trudged in a procession to Mr. Mob, whom we found half-dozing in his bed. We helped him out of it with difficulty, because he ached all over from the meeting earlier that evening. Through the influence of his countrymen he was immediately prepared to sign whatever was laid in front of him; then we helped him back into bed, covered him up, and left him quietly to further consider the consequences of boxing. Graver, whom we visited next, also dispensed with the necessary wakefulness for lengthy explanations and signed the paper that Captain King held up for him on a plank across his bed, after he had been assured by him that his honor had been satisfied. Each went home with greater peace of mind, but because I awaited spectators in my yard at seven o'clock and had no desire to go into explanations with them, I asked the honest buffalo hunter to put up on a mattress for the night in my house and in the morning give notice to the waiting public that they could withdraw disappointed again.

It was three o'clock in the morning when, exhausted from all this duel trouble, I lay down. I would certainly have slept far into the day from the turmoil and emotion, had I not been awakened at seven o'clock by the shouting outside. The curious spectators had climbed onto the fence of my yard a half hour too early—yet as the time drew near, everything remained dead still. Consequently, impatient shouting began which woke up the sleeping wildman, and he trudged outside.

"Gentlemen!" he cried out to the impatient onlookers, "you can go home again; no duel will take place as the affair has been settled in an honorable manner."

The disappointment was great—so great that the announcement was received with hissing. It was better not to start anything with the irascible Captain, who now loudly declared, with few niceties, that every man in Yokohama had better know that he would rather be damned twenty-five times than give honor short shrift, and whomever of the gentlemen who did not yet know that, he would let him choose between having his throat cut or being shot dead.

None complied with the invitation, and the onlookers slunk away. For the next couple days, fear of the American gun-lover was good insurance. Especially because recently a small American vessel, crewed by six men under an officer, who had come to map Edo Bay was thrown onto the beach, wrecked.[18] While waiting for an opportunity to depart, the officer and his six sailors stayed in a small wooden building. They had, through lack of diversions, begun to quarrel among themselves, and when a couple of them came to blows and did not immediately obey the officer's order to cease, he shot them with a revolver, one of them dead. Since the other was alone with no one to fight, through this American expedient, everything was instantly calm again.[19]

18. Probably the *Fenimore Cooper*, which beached in late August 1859.

19. This was a quarrel between Leonard Ryley, William Medkiff, and Quartermaster Robert Weir on September 4, 1859. The shooting was accidental. According to John M. Brooke, he "found Weir and Medkiff struggling. Separating them and ordering

No more unsettled than a boy who had driven a flock of starlings out of the garden, Captain King stepped back into the house in the best of humor and greeted me with a friendly "good morning." I then invited him to enjoy a handsome breakfast before his departure. He did the meal more than justice and was just as talkative as the previous evening. Yet there was a little something that appeared to bother him. It was that he did not know how, in the absence of business, to get by in Yokohama from one day to the next. His aim was obvious: to get whatever there was to be gotten, and then sound a retreat. As for me, I had no reason to complain about this wild American. I had listened to his tales with pleasure; he had not done me a single discourtesy; and, throughout the affair that had brought him into contact with me, he had behaved loyally toward me. I doubly appreciated his decent ways, just as the chivalry ascribed to Rinaldo Rinaldini[20] set him above the rest.

Before he went he declared to me his intention to visit the three English gentlemen from the previous night, probably for the purpose of obtaining a loan with which to purchase a passage on the first departing steamboat. At any rate, a few days later Captain King had disappeared from the stage, probably to return to the far west to slay Texan and Colorado Indians, until the time and circumstance when, here or there, a new gold country was discovered where he could continue his business.

---

them to stand off drew one of the revolvers to intimidate the men when to my astonishment it went off itself." Weir was hit and died a few days later. Brooke was cleared of any charges. George M. Brooke, ed., *John M. Brooke's Pacific Cruise and Japanese Adventure, 1858–1860* (Honolulu: University of Hawaii Press, 1986), 166.

20. Title character in a popular 1797 novel by Christian August Vulpius (1762–1827). Set in medieval Italy, Rinaldo Rinaldini is a Robin Hood–like robber baron.

Chapter 6

America had shown us what a bunch of wild fortune-hunters like the retreating Captain and his friends it could deliver, but in contrast it was from there that now a lovely apparition emerged in our midst, who in only a few days, turned heads of all the "gentlemen" and became the object of their admiration. Until now, no white woman had ventured to the den of death that was Yokohama. It was almost inevitable that the first to show there, with a cute little revolver and a polished stiletto stuck in her belt, was an American. Most of the foreign "settlers" had not seen a woman dressed in the latest Parisian fashion in the last year, and one can thus understand how the news of her arrival were glad tidings that spread through our foreign quarter. It was no wonder that many people were elated and walking along the street on the day of her arrival, one hardly had the time to say, "Good morning" to a friend before immediately being asked, "have you seen the lady?" And what a lady! Judging by the rumors, she was a young woman of unprecedented beauty, and the rumors appeared to be true. Indeed, while I stood talking to a friend, we turned to a passing ice-cold Englishman with the question of the day; he just turned, sighed "extremely beautiful," looked to the heavens, and then continued on his way.

Think not that the beautiful American was an adventuress. No, she was a proper married young woman come from California with her husband, Mr. Shobber,[1] who had come to Yokohama to establish

---

1. Raphael Schoyer (1800–1865). Emigrated first to Baltimore. In the 1829–1839 Manhattan City Directory, a Raphael Schoyer is listed at 146 Fulton Street as an engraver, and in the 1839–1840 edition at 10 Broad Street as in wine. He is listed in the San Francisco City Directory of 1852 as at 94 Sansome and as being of Rising, Caselli & Company. The next year he is listed at the same address as an independent auctioneer. The exact date of their arrival in Yokohama is unknown but it was probably in early December, 1859. Owner of the newspaper *Japan Express* in 1862. In 1863, he became involved in a battle with Japanese authorities over one of his lots, of which he had apparently acquired several. This one had been subdivided to serve as a boarding house. In this same year he incorporated, forming R. Schoyer & Co. The Japanese wished to acquire the land and Schoyer refused to trade. Despite De Coningh's prediction, he died during a Yokohama council meeting and is buried in Yokohama Cemetery. His wife, Anna, was a painter and taught such Japanese painters as Takahashi Yuichi (1828–1894), and Shimooka Renjō (1823–1914), who is better known as a photographer. She remarried in 1868 in Yokohama to Robert Bruce

himself as an auctioneer. Mr. Shobber was an elderly Israelite gentleman, well past sixty, but still vigorous for his age, who had lost his hair but would live past a hundred before he lost the battle of life. When I saw this incongruous pair for the first time on the afternoon of the day of their arrival, I was surprised by the ease with which the old gentleman, with a smile of pleasure on his face, walked along next to his beautiful young wife.

As soon as the news of the arrival of a young woman had spread, all of the foreign community gathered at the small wooden cottage, a stall really, where the couple had moved in, as might happen when royalty descended. With just as much curiosity as our loiterers, they pressed tirelessly against the oiled paper windows to see something of what they were hiding. Our new fellow citizen, the old gentleman, was perhaps too courteous, because he endured the spectators standing in the mud aimlessly for hours. There was some commotion from inside the sliding door, all eyes fixed upon it; the next moment, the door was pushed open, and standing before us was an old man, straight as a candle, with features just like those men who can be seen without the journey to Yokohama in large numbers in the Hebrew neighborhood of our capital city. After affably greeting the assembled amidst their cheers, he said to them, "Gentlemen! On behalf of Mistress Shobber and also myself, allow me to express our sentiments over your warm reception and interest. Mistress Shobber would like to have done this personally already, but she is still somewhat tired from the trip. This afternoon at three o'clock we hope to take a little walk; if you gentlemen will be kind enough to return then, Mistress Shobber will be very pleased to see you."

After one of those present had thanked him on behalf of everyone, and requested that their "respects" be brought to Mistress Shobber, each went his separate way. But when the clock struck three, every European and American was again faithfully at his post.

The cottage Mr. Shobber had moved into bordered immediately on the Japanese city, which at this time consisted of all kinds of shops built on both sides of a very wide, unpaved street. In the winter, the middle of this street was nothing more than a pool of mud with a hard footpath along the sides, upon which two or three people could walk abreast. All the men of the West gathered along that footpath in

---

Van Valkenburgh (1821–1888), minister plenipotentiary to Japan 1866–1869. Van Valkenburgh returned to the State of Florida and died a state Supreme Court justice, so it is assumed that Anna traveled with him.

anticipation of things to come. Just before the appointed hour the door of Mr. Shobber's house was pushed open, a roomy path was made there, and the "gentlemen," like so many muddy knights, voluntarily left the footpath and stepped backward into the ditch. Then Mr. Schobber appeared, a "*vert gallant*."[2] The old gentleman stepped outside with his tall stovepipe hat at something of a tilt on his head; and then, from under the wide almaviva[3] which hung loose from his limbs, he reached with a bow for the hand of his young wife in order to help her over the low threshold, as if she was being brought on stage. With charming sweetness Mistress Shobber acknowledged the welcoming greetings of her admirers who inflicted them without cheers or catcalls, only through the respectful removal of felt hats and wooly caps; she then took the arm of her husband and began the triumphal procession along the footpath.

She was indeed an enchanting apparition, this young woman who appeared to me to be a Spanish-American *créole* of exceptional beauty. Gracefully, she glided at the side of the old gentleman along the line of foreigners, and the heavenly smile upon her face testified to the truth of the claim that for a beautiful woman respect and esteem is bliss. Nor was Mister Shobber insensitive to the homage shown to her. Looking on with a glow of satisfaction, he lifted the hat from his bald head with a "Thank you gentlemen, much obliged!" repeatedly during the walk among the spectators. What came to mind, as I saw him and his young wife coming toward me from the distance, was old Laban with his beautiful daughter Rachel. I could not continue my reflection because as the wandering pair approached, I only had eyes for the rare beauty that came nearer and nearer. Full of wonder, I saw them slowly glide toward me. With quiet resignation to the Tenth Commandment, I paid my respects to her with a deferential greeting, which was rewarded with a smile from her and a "thank you, Sir!" from him.

After a half hour of walking up and down the footpath, Mr. Shobber thought to bring the production to an end. Before stepping back inside their house, the young woman showed her appreciation for the warm-hearted attention with which she had been received

2. "Green gallant," a reference to Henry IV of France (1553–1610). The archaic French refers to a man who is vigorous for his age. In Henry's case this referred to amorousness.

3. A long, wide mantle slung over the shoulder and fastened with a cord; so called because Count Almaviva in the comic opera *The Marriage of Figaro* by Pierre-Augustin Caron de Beaumarchais (1732–1799) was frequently costumed wearing one.

by waving her hand to all sides and bowing with a charm that gave such delight to all the spectators that an ovation followed, and all hats and caps swayed in the air as if on command. Thereafter each returned home, the roughnecks under the powerful spell of their admiration; those more sensitive were quiet and contemplative, almost despondent, feeling then more than ever, that it was not good for a man to be alone.

So the pioneers of Yokohama received the first woman of Western civilization into their midst. That first flower, whose white color and graceful petals caused many to recall their homeland and what they had left there.

The Japanese, in a second row behind us during the walk, whose country was second to none in the world for beautiful women, had observed with curiosity the newly arrived foreign woman. The small Garibaldi hat[4] with white ostrich feathers; the neat rain clothing from which the most beautiful form emerged, and over which a tasteful velvet cloak was thrown, the wide crinoline, supported by a pair of small, neatly shod feet, which glided swiftly and gracefully forward of their own accord—they admired all this even more than her impeccably charming features. The latter they saw every day in abundance all around them, but unfortunately everything was spoiled by the tottering gait on black lacquered clogs, and close-fitting, droopy nightdresses. Alas! The poor taste. They later made their men look ridiculous by sticking them into European black jackets and setting top hats on their heads, while their beautiful women went unappreciated, allowed to stumble along in their high-heeled wooden clogs and droopy nightgowns. And Europe, which drew to itself all the natural and industrial products of the opened Japanese empire, committed the same folly, introducing the tasteless clothing of Japanese women, which had been an eyesore for perhaps a thousand years, as a novelty of fickle fashion. So you see how quickly things can change: these days one would not look twice at a Japanese walking around Amsterdam in a black suit and high hat while our beauties, with their nightdresses and high heels, could patter to Jeddo without drawing any of the attention or the admiration they valued.

Early the next morning, while I was already busy in my warehouse, I saw the old gentleman with his high hat and almaviva step inside through a door on the other end.

4. A high pillbox hat with braid, styled after one worn by the Italian revolutionary. Also called the Garibaldi pillbox.

"Good morning, sir! How goes it?" began Mr. Shobber, in good Dutch, walking up to me. "I take the liberty of introducing myself to you, and to recommend to you my auctions, if you have some goods to clear out." It was rare for a Netherlander to hear his language from a foreigner, and if he did, it was but a few words. Many English did not even know we had our own language. I was thus more than a little surprised when I was addressed in my mother tongue by this old American as well and as clearly as if he were a countryman.

"Good morning, Mr. Shobber!" I answered. "It is a pleasure to see you. I am quite astonished that you speak my language, and must first ask if you are a compatriot, because you speak Dutch as well as I do."

"That is how it should be," said the old gentleman. "If one is born in Holland, and even more so when you earned your bread for thirty years in the capital on the Joden-Breestraat[5] by trading the bones of Dutch horses and cows.[6]

It was difficult for me to picture Mr. Shobber, who looked just like a baron of old, in his previous position, and I had to call forth all the powers of my imagination before I could envision the gentleman with the stately hat and wide almaviva as formerly a buyer of bones in Amsterdam's Jewish quarter. But now he had been an American citizen for more than twenty years, and, as I later came to know through the integrity of his dealings, one of the worthiest fellow-citizens of Yokohama. He was esteemed by all as a thoroughly righteous, honorable, and scrupulously conscientious man, and he was in the opinion of many a shining example, proud of his untiring efforts to be a millionaire in the New World. No wonder he received the fullest trust of the foreigners and the Japanese. Anyone who had goods which could not be readily disposed of sent them to Mr. Shobber's public auctions, for with his adroit eloquence he had the knack of selling some of the most impossible things in the best interests of his consigners.

A noble act I once observed perfectly characterized the old Dutch-American. I was co-executor in the estate of two murdered countrymen who had left widows in the fatherland.[7] Their goods were set in an empty warehouse of the Interpreters' Office, and Mr. Shobber was invited to

5. Literally, Jewish Broad Street.

6. Bones were used for fertilizer, gelatin, glue, and charcoal, among other uses.

7. This probably refers to the murder of Captain J. Nanning Dekker (aged 40) of the *Christian Louis* and Captain Wessel de Vos (aged 42) of the *Helena Louise*, who were attacked on the main street of Yokohama on the evening of February 25, 1860. (See pages 133–35.) The funeral was held on February 29 at the Yokohama Hotel

inventory and sell them to the public. The old gentleman went to much trouble; the necessary publicity was given to the business, and on the set hour of the auction all foreigners, to the last man, were present. After he addressed the gathering with words to soften all hearts and indicated that he was here to sell, and that joy would be found in the work of charity, he began the auction. Mr. Shobber surpassed himself. With the eloquence of his tribe, he drove all the objects to unheard of prices, and when one finally stuck, then the voice of the old man rang out as he wrote the name of the buyer in his book: "Mr. Johnson,[8] no. 26, God bless you, sir! Thanks for the poor widow, Sir!" So through his skill, for example, a pair of old wading boots, that had already received bids, he drove up sky-high, to over sixty guilders. The lucky buyer of the moldy boots received an extra blessing at the recording of his name: "Happy day for you is this, Sir! You may wear them in health, Sir! God bless you sir, Sir! Thanks for the poor widow, Sir!"

Thanks to Mr. Shobber's troubles, the estate liquidated at fabulous prices. A few days later, after he'd collected the money from buyers left and right through the sweat of his brow, he came to me to settle accounts. After he had counted it out to the last dollar, I asked him for a statement of his expenses, which I thought would amount to a couple hundred dollars. I needed to pay them off at once in order to come to a final settlement. The old gentleman smiled. "Let us not discuss it," he said, "That the property brought so much gives me a great deal of pleasure. I would be ashamed to charge a half cent for costs to the unfortunate widows; thus let that be the end of the matter."

As he had done more than a hundred times during the auction, I thanked him now for the "poor widows." But he desired no thanks; to him it sufficed to have done good, his name remaining unknown even to the parties concerned, because the worthy Israëlite practiced, quietly and without fuss, what we call Christian charity.

So amid the coarse band in Yokohama the greatest human virtues were still practiced by some. One striking example of this was also furnished by Dr. Simmons,[9] an American missionary. The Americans, practical in everything, rightly understood that for a missionary to make inroads

---

and they were buried in the new cemetery. The murderers were never found, but the Japanese government paid 25,000 Mexican dollars in damages to each widow.

8. Possibly Captain Josiah Johnson of the *Fenimore Cooper*.

9. Duane B. Simmons (1834–1889). Minister of the American Dutch Reformed Church. Arrived in Yokohama from New York in November, 1859. Returned to America in 1864. After improving his medical skills, he returned to Japan in 1869

VERBECK, BROWN AND SIMMONS, 1859.

Reverend Dr. Duane Simmons. Simmons is on the far right. Courtesy of the Boston University School of Theology Library.

among foreign folk, nothing could give him greater prestige than to be a doctor of medicine and thus by healing infirmities with his art, he could cloak himself in the nimbus of miracle worker. The doctor-missionary Simmons was a highly modest and thorough man who lived quietly and forgotten in a small house in Kanagawa near the consul's residence. There he kept himself busy studying the Japanese language without anyone interfering, paying no mind to the fact that he was in the middle of an environment where the majority thought only to enrich themselves and have a good time while gaining some advantage in the process. Simply dressed, he walked the streets as if he was in his homeland, unarmed. He came to Yokohama now and then to buy necessities and although he was affable and interested in everyone, always thanking them for all their invitations to meals and parties, he still preferred to tranquilly and serenely go his own way. But he was full of fire for one thing, although it robbed him of most of the time for language study, which was to help his fellow man, whether foreign or Japanese, through his art. Unselfishly, without taking a penning's[10] reward, this apostle of charity

---

as a government doctor and remained until his death in 1889. Known for founding Juzen Hospital in Yokohama and developing a medicine for roundworms.

10. An old coin of small denomination, like a penny or farthing.

roamed around the slums of the Japanese city to cholera cases and lepers, illnesses of all complaints, offering assistance to the hundreds, to whom he was a blessing. We in Yokohama had but one constantly drunk Irish doctor who would not come to the rescue for under forty dollars, which was as good as the ships crews who were deprived of all medical help. Dr. Simmons asked not for dollars but for helpless sufferers, and many times I saw him from the shore during storms and rain, in the distance, in an open boat, wandering from ship to ship to help the sick sailors, regardless of nationality. Of monetary reward there was no question, even among the better off. He only welcomed a small gift of things he had dire need of. I once made him very happy by giving him medicine, of which I had great quantities of in my warehouse, which he could then use for others. In short, I have never met a truer Christian than this skillful, modest doctor-missionary, whose greatest desire was to turn all his powers, all his knowledge and science, free of charge, to the charity of his fellow men, without asking national character, religion, position or skin color. Once, when we were accompanying a murdered foreigner to his last resting place, Dr. Simmons said a prayer for the dead over the grave. The deceased was a Freemason, and when the missionary had pronounced "amen," the brothers present circled the edge of the grave and performed a final brotherly salute to the departed according to the ceremony of their order.[11] Upon returning to the house, Dr. Simmons clapped me on the shoulder. "Why didn't you say anything to me?" he asked, giving me the sign. "Then I would have joined you at the grave in fulfilling the last brotherly duty," because this silent observer of Christ's teachings of love was also a Freemason in the purest and most noble sense.

Let us now return to the worrisome days that we lived through in the winter of 1859–1860, left to ourselves completely unprotected. If a winter in Yokohama, on 36° northern latitude, was not so bitterly cold as ours;[12] if the snow did not lie on the ground for many days; and it froze less, still the winter months were barren and bleak. The

11. This is known as the Grand Honors, which begins with the hands at the sides. The hands are brought up and clapped together just in front of the forehead; the arms are then brought down and placed over the breast, crossing them at the wrists and with the left arm over the right; the series of movements is repeated three times. At a funeral, the salute is referred to as the Silent Grand Honors, as it is done softly and with due reverence.

12. The Netherlands is at 52° 30'.

long nights, the incessant storms and rain flags,[13] and the many dark, misty days made our perilous position doubly frightening. As I recall the first months of 1860 to mind, then I remember as if it were yesterday, the impression made on us by the intimidating rumors of murder, and vividly recall our state of mind as we expected hourly to be put to the sword by those whom we all regarded as outlaws. I, like so many others who lived through those frightening days, found in the end that one can get used to anything and that human character remains essentially the same in all situations. Although naturally no one was indifferent to the danger, the cheerful remained so, the melancholy looked no more somber than usual, the joker kept making his gags, the gourmet kept his appetite, the tippler his thirst; only the weak of heart were almost crazed with fear and made fools of themselves.

Among the many untrustworthy rumors spread among us every now and then by the Translators' Office, there was one that we liked the least of all: namely that the followers of the Prince of Mito would light our wooden city on fire and, in the ensuing confusion, put the foreigners to the sword and throw their bodies into the flames of their own homes. This plan did not seem completely improbable. As I remarked earlier, we had walked nightly three-man patrols since the beginning of winter, and I and the others on watch had prevented this several times, here and there extinguishing a fire set against a wooden fence. Otherwise we never saw a soul all night. But, in spite of our vigilance, one attempt to burn Yokohama down was successful.

It was in the middle of January 1860[14] that one of the houses next to the Japanese city burst into flames during the night, just as the wind gusted over our whole wood-constructed foreigners' city. The first moment of panic sent a shudder through the residents: the "boom bam" of the alarm bell and the cries of the Japanese in the distance; the agitated cries of "fire, fire" from our fellow residents, who hastened to the place of the disaster, thumping an alarm on all the doors and fences; the flames in front of us; the darkness around us—all of this, plus the chance that we could be attacked, was enough to strike terror in the hearts of even the boldest. In view of what might happen, we had previously determined that, in the event of trouble or fire, all foreigners would immediately rush, well-armed, to the place where danger threatened. Within ten minutes, we had gathered about seventy men together, not to extinguish

13. De Coningh is probably referring to red naval pennants used to convey warnings.
14. January 3.

the fire—we thought nothing of that—but to band together in desperate defense so that we would not be helplessly cut down one by one. Not a single warship lay in the roadstead; but with the first outbreak of flames, the captains of the half-dozen merchant ships sent their sloops ashore with as many men as they could spare, so that in a moment we were reinforced by almost six dozen sailors armed with swords and crowbars. As for firearms, we had no lack, for each of us had at least two Lafacheux revolvers[15] and pockets full of ammunition. These circumstances proved to me how handy men were when it came down to their precious lives. We had come together in a jiffy, or as the English say, in less than "no time," as one hundred and thirty men, who would not be thrown into the fire without resistance. It is to this swift "Kriegsbereitschafft,"[16] that we owe the second thoughts of the Prince of Mito's bandits concealed here or there in the darkness. But if the attack was forestalled, their goal to destroy our city with fire and cause us a few hundred thousand dollars of damage was fully achieved.

With incredible speed, one wooden warehouse after another was gripped by flames. Filled with tubs of oil and train,[17] then the main exports to China, there was soon an unapproachable blaze. Although the Governor of Yokohama and his corps of a few thousand Japanese, all in their firefighting costumes, had moved out to extinguish the fire at the first alarm, within a half an hour three large warehouses were aflame and it was clear to see that with Japanese firefighting techniques nothing more would be saved. There were no fire engines; nor was there water either, except the seawater out of the bay, the nearest point of which lay at least a five minute walk distant. Lines of several hundred men were thus formed from the fire to the bay, and seawater was passed from hand to hand in small buckets, until the last man who stood closest by the fire sent it back. However, he could not approach the fire because of the heat, so he had to be content with throwing the water from his bucket as far as he could in the direction of the fire, where it fell a few paces distant, on the ground. But these outposts, like the small band of elite firefighters arrayed in a row who sprayed water on the fire with hand pumps from small water-filled cisterns, had to retreat again and again from the approaching fire. At last, when all was a sea of fire and the one could get no closer

15. See n. 32, p. 55.
16. Battle-readiness.
17. Train oil: whale oil, usually from the right whale as other types were generally called sperm oil.

to the flames than several hundred paces, the Governor of Yokohama gave the order, as the only means to save anything, to break and tear down everything around it, so that the isolated fire would thus burn itself out. So it was that within a few moments whatever threatened to catch fire in the neighborhood had been knocked down and broken by several hundred men. By morning three quarters of our foreigners' quarter was burned down and a value of two million dollars had gone up in smoke. The place, which just a few hours before had still been the center of the mushrooming European trade city, was now nothing more than a large plain with smoldering heaps of rubble where here and there groups roamed to dig under the smoldering beams for clumps of melted dollars.

It is to the credit of the Shogunal authorities and the inland native population of the Japanese quarter that without their vigorous help, not a single splinter would have remained unburned in our foreign quarter. Nevertheless, many of the foreigners were suspicious and cynical that it was not the inhabitants, but rather the Japanese authorities, notwithstanding their assistance in extinguishing the fire, who were not entirely surprised by the arson. This suspicion was defamatory but nevertheless heartfelt. The Japanese knew, from their bloodhounds and *dwarskijkers*, that a band of diehards would try to burn us out and run us off; but it was later revealed that they had secretly readied two pieces of field artillery and a few soldiers in the Interpreters Office in case they were necessary to help us repel an attack.

As for myself, I came out pretty well. Of a small warehouse that I rented far from my house in which a few goods of small value were secured, the next day nothing more than a heap of burned charcoal could be found. But my house and larger warehouse lay on the outside edge of the foreigners' quarter. When the fire moved in that direction I hastened, with the help of twenty sailors, to carry all my valuable goods out of the house and warehouse and well back into the open field in time. But just before it came turn for my house to burn, the decision to tear down was made, stopping it at my front neighbor's house.

The next morning I could already carry my goods back to my warehouse undamaged.

But never will that night, which for us at the outset appeared to have been a night of destruction, be blotted from my memory. We cast our gaze as far was we could see by the light of the flames of our burning city, ready for anything, to see the murderers expected to show up any minute out of the darkness for the battle of life and death. In those moments we were completely indifferent to what burned away behind us because if there was an attack we would have to overcome it or die. There was no thought of flight to, or help from, the peaceful, unarmed Japanese populace of Yokohama. Indeed, had we fled inland in the night, we would have run right into the wolf's jaws, and to get to the pitch dark beach, separated from each other and pursued by angry enemies, where no sloops or rowers were ready for us to flee to the ships—no one would have survived. As for help from our Japanese neighbors, twenty *loonings* would have been sufficient to drive two thousand firefighters pell-mell from the fire.

Fortunately it did not come to that. Perhaps the bandits thought, when they saw everything burning so beautifully, that they had achieved their goal admirably well, and were made happy by the prospect that most foreigners would, in the absence of shelter, sail away the next day, forever leaving their ruins behind. But the outcome was just the opposite because a few months later everything was rebuilt in a much sounder manner than the wooden bunch that had burned down. Having learned from experience, all the new buildings were made as fireproof as possible by plastering them with thick layers of clay and lime. As for shelter, those burned out had the greatest good fortune in that the "Yokohama Hotel," opened just a few days before, had not suffered at all in the fire.

The owner of the "Yokohama Hotel"[18] was the only one who, through disaster, came out nicely on top because he saw his hotel suddenly overflowing with the "gentlemen" who were otherwise at a complete loss. As good as the name "Yokohama Hotel" sounds to the uninitiated, one must not form too high an idea of it as far as the external structure, the apartments, and the furnishings were concerned. The cost of a day's stay was rather more than one would expect, at least double the cost of the most distinguished hotel in the world. Allow me to explain here, how it came to pass that a "hotel" was opened so soon in far Yokohama, and what the original purpose of that building was.

Like all Orientals, the Japanese are a very lusty folk. Lacking contact with Europeans, they did not know our more fastidious customs and supposed their own shortcomings would be found in the foreigners. Thousands of Japanese were mistaken in the notion that the desire Europeans had to visit their country was merely to get to know their women. Many a respectable foreigner who, after a stormy sea voyage, cheerfully landed at the pier in Yokohama to be affronted by the indelicate gestures of some well-mannered Japanese who, by way of welcome, tried

18. In what is presently 70 Yamashita-cho, Naka-ku.

to let him know that he had now reached the paradise for which he had come so far for.

Even the highly courteous Japanese government appeared to labor under this delusion and it is a fact that although at the arrival of the foreigners, nothing more than the Interpreters' Office and four small bungalows were ready, a so-called tea house had already been established, the workforce of which consisted of more than 200 women, sent by order of the government in Jedo. Obviously it was the intent of that very wise government for reasons of state, to pull a real Japanese trick. The thoughtful rulers in Yedo were convinced that the arriving foreigners would concentrate in the teahouses of the Realm, making no attempt to push inland or ask for further concessions—in short, a panacea was found to make the hated strangers harmless. You see, it was the application of the history of Samson and Delilah that fell through rather badly.

The infamous Gankirō brothel. *Yokohama ganki no mikomi no zu,* Utagawa Hiroshige, 1860. Collection of Waseda University Library.

As I said earlier, the Interpreters' Office and the few bungalows stood, in the beginning, close to the beach; the teahouse in question stood a few minutes further inland. It was a wooden building of a few hundred paces long, that I can do no better than to compare to the auxiliary stables for a few cavalry squadrons as are sometimes found in garrisons. In those days the building was about four feet off the ground, barred with latticework such as one might see in a zoological garden, open on the front, but closed at night with sliding shutters. The whole facility was under the supervision and management of the Interpreters' Office. I don't know if men there had ever heard of Samson, but it is certain that in one sense there were always a lot of Delilahs behind the lattice bent on outwitting the passing unsuspecting bearded Samsons from the West. As one might expect, the Japanese authorities, who showed not the least understanding of our European notions of propriety and good behavior, were quite speedily petitioned to clear away this morally offensive establishment. As a result, the quagmire behind the Japanese quarter was filled in and there arose Gankiro, the hotbed of iniquity about which I have already said a word.

When the unfortunate, abject population was brought over to the Gankiro, the long wooden stable became free, and a speculative foreigner[19] sought and received a lease for it from the Interpreters' Office. He began by boarding up the lattice, leaving here and there a window with oiled paper in its place. The floors were swept and new mats laid on the ground, paper screens were set up to make as many compartments as he thought necessary, and enough room was saved to hold a coffee and dining room. He bought himself the only billiard table to be found in the place and whatever else he needed that wasn't too expensive in Yokohama and then hopped on the very first steamboat to Shanghai. He came back with a pitch-black negro, a deserter steward, as "oberkellner,"[20] two Chinese cooks, and as many chests of all kinds of drinks as he could lay his hands on. He needed about six weeks for all these preparations but on the morning of the third day after his return from Shanghai, a trophy of Dutch, American, English and French flags already graced the top of the still-closed entrance. Twenty strong Japanese held steady a gigantic wooden board upon which "Yokohama Hotel" was smeared in white letters the size of a man while it was nailed fast to the planked outer wall. And with the last pound of the hammer, the front door was opened and any "gentleman" who desired to, could step inside. It was a first victory of refined civilization over Japanese immorality, on the very ground where, a few months before had languished the teahouse with its miserable followers. The hospitable doors of the "Yokohama Hotel" opened with European style and relative comfort.

It was not, however, a bargain for the guests. The rooms there were bad but the table was nevertheless very good, thanks to the abundance of greens, game, fish and so forth, and the two Chinese cooks. The accommodations cost as much as ƒ20 a day, not including all the extras

19. A Dutchman named C. J. Huffnagel, who had been captain of the ship *Nassau* and supposedly the fifth Dutchman to arrive after the port opened.
20. Headwaiter.

and drinks, which made everything even more expensive. Some of the prices from the tariff that I remember were a bottle of beer $f3$, a glass of liqueur $f1$, a cup of coffee $f1$, a party of billiards $f3$. The champagne, which cost $f15$ a bottle, was not spared at all, and it often flowed in streams. Many of the lodgers consumed such tremendous amounts, that if, for example, a Dutch assistant teacher with his annual salary in his pocket were to follow their example he would certainly have already been thrown out the door on his third day, in a state of evident insolvency.

It was also in the Yokohama Hotel that the meetings were held; for a society composed largely of English and Americans without meetings is unthinkable. The great fire was naturally a reason to hastily convene a meeting, and by the morning of the following day a circular had been sent around informing of a meeting to be held at seven o'clock that night in the Yokohama Hotel with Mr. Elmstock "in the chair." At that time we did not have a printing press in Yokohama; thus any sort of notification that had to circulate was written on a sheet of paper and brought around from house to house by a servant to be signed after reading.

It was a meeting like so many others, but of this one I want to briefly report to give an idea of the usual goings on. The "Chairman" sat with his committee behind a table on the end of the great bar room of the hotel, and at the fixed hour the "gentlemen" of all the different nationalities came in, one after another. They were a picturesque troop, this band of pioneers, each dressed and armed in his own manner; many wore clothing burnt in the previous night's fire, with a Japanese bearskin or wadded blanket slung across the body and all so savage, at least in appearance, that if an ambitious barber had seen them, he would have done away with himself.

With a bang from a hammer borrowed from the hotel, the chairman opened the meeting.

After an introductory word, the first motion from the "Chairman" was to proffer a memorial of thanks in the name of the foreigners from all nations to the Governor of Yokohama for the help extended during the fire.

Adopted by unanimous vote.

Then followed an argument as to whether it was certain that the fire was maliciously set. But as there was yet no proof of malice, the "Chairman's" second motion followed; to name a commission to investigate the cause of the fire.

Adopted by unanimous vote. This commission had in common with all previous and subsequent commissions that they never produced a report.

Now the "Chairman" began to paint a dark tableau of our dangerous situation. He enumerated the names of our most recently murdered companions; the burning of our city showed us again how dangerous the game was; they were after our very existence; and he pronounced his conviction that their ultimate goal was to run us off and exterminate us from Japanese ground, at least if we didn't leave soon of our own accord. It was also apparent to him that we were mistaken in thinking that our safety was a serious concern for the Interpreters' Office, because for whatever reason, the Shogunal government had not shown the strength to sufficiently protect us. We all knew as well as he did that recently even the American legation secretary, Mr. Heusken, had been murdered in Jedo,[21] and what for us should be considered an especially dangerous sign was the murder of the regent or first minister of the shogun in Jedo[22] of which news had just arrived. He had just been informed that because this high-ranking shogunal councilor was known to be a friend to the foreigners, he was attacked in broad daylight by a large band of murders and killed before his attendants could save him. In the ensuing fight with the Regent's servants, many on both sides were killed, yet not a single murderer was caught. Before they fled, the murderers hacked off the heads of their perished mates and took them so no one could identify them.[23] With such enemies to deal with, opined the chairman, especially because one could not be guarded enough for the nightly surprise attacks, we must take stronger measures for self defense than we had until now. He proposed that we should form a corps of all able-bodied foreigners, and thought that it would be, after deducting a few old people and sufferers of chest- and liver complaints, about sixty men strong.

The proposal was adopted unanimously; now began the bickering over incidental affairs, because it was "after dinner-time" and then the English were, as long as the influence of the copious port wine they had with their meal had not evaporated, drowsy and difficult.

21. See n. 8, chap. 3. De Coningh seems to have jumbled or conflated the chronology of events, as Heusken was not assassinated until January of the following year, which would also explain his placing of the fire in mid- rather than early January.

22. Probably refers to the assassination of Ii Naosuke (1815–1860), who had held the position of *tairō*, or chief minister since 1858. He was assassinated for signing the treaties with Townsend Harris that opened the ports. Again the chronology is off, as this murder occurred on March 24, 1860.

23. Known as the Sakurada-mon Incident for the gate in Edo Palace where it occurred. The attack was carried out by seventeen *rōnin*. According to Rutherford Alcock, one head was carried off as a decoy for that of Ii Naosuke, which was also taken.

Immediately all was ready for the "Chairman" to christen this new militia except for what to name it. All sorts of names were suggested: "Yokohama-volunteers," "Royal volunteers," "Japan sharpshooters," and so forth. A Frenchman proposed "*Chasseurs de la gloire.*"[24] An Englishman thereupon made a passionate plea for the name "Royal volunteers," which the Frenchman, Monsieur Tourniquet,[25] could not agree to, and he asked to speak, although proceedings could only be conducted in the English language.

"Mastaire Chaireman!" began Mr. Tourniquet, a full-blooded Bonapartist, "ze name 'Royal' will not do for French gentelemen, by cause zey are imperial gentelemen. Wattefore would be use for zem, to cry, when zey fight for la gloire: 'Vive l'Empereur!' if zey call zemselves 'Royal volunteers.'" There a few of his countrymen, who stood behind him, did not agree; he turned toward them with a distraught look and said heatedly, "Royal ou Impérial, c'est différent, sapristi! Je ne veux pas être coupé en deux comme volontaire anglais!"[26]

The "Chairman" remarked that because all kinds of nationalities were assembled here, it was better to refrain from "royal" and "imperial." He declared himself for the name "Yokohama Volunteers," which was then, finally, after much discussion, adopted.[27]

Dr. Dugger who, with an annoying drunkards face, had stood watching, now asked for the floor. This drunken Irish quack had served as a medic under General Pellisier in Algeria,[28] or so he claimed. The more he drank, the more he boasted of his friend Pellisier, and the more he, as an Irishman, picked on the English.

"Master Chairman," began Dr. Dugger, hoarsely stammering while nodding, "when my friend General Pellisier stood in front of one hot fire or another in our campaign in Kabylië, he always made a habit of calling for Dr. Dugger. When I came into his tent, he'd begin: 'I am pleased

24. Hunters of glory.
25. Possibly A. Dumarcet.
26. "Royal and imperial are different, for Christ's sake! I do not want to be shot, and doubly not as an English volunteer."
27. John Reddie Black dates this as happening at the house of Edward Clarke on September 24, 1862, after the Namamugi Incident. But Black appears to be wrong, or this was a reorganization. Edward Fontanbanque is vague but suggests they were organized after the assassinations of Dekker and De Vos in February 1860 (p. 101). Francis Hall mentions the Yokohama Volunteers on March 25, 1860.
28. Aimable Jean Jacques Pélissier (1794–1864). Went to Algeria repeatedly, but as general only in 1850. Appointed Governor-General of Algeria in 1860, where he remained until his death.

that you have come Dr. Dugger, tell me just what we should do?' Then
we would deliberate together, and I gave him so much good advice that
in the end we had the whole business under control and Arabians by
the hundred were as good as roasted. I thus have an understanding of
military affairs, and I will give you some good advice. Nothing will come
right of our defense if we don't all have red uniforms. The best soldiers
in the world are the brave Irish in red English jackets and the French in
their red pants, so we must first ensure that each 'gentleman' obtains at
least a red jacket or pair of pants. It is no obstacle that there is no red
worsted in the place because I know that a 'Dutch friend'"—he meant
me—"has several chests of red Moroccan leather in his warehouse. If this
was purchased, sixty red jackets and pants could be made from it. The
English war brig *Camilla*[29] will arrive in the roadstead any day, and if
we asked the commander to send a sergeant of marines ashore for a few
hours a day to drill us, then we'd be ready."

The learned doctor was booed for his brilliant advice, and he made
trouble over that. The chairman asked him to calm down, and then
one of the attendees proposed that the assembly should declare that
Dr. Dugger was drunk and throw him out the door. This proposal had
so much support that without further ado, he was picked up by the head
and legs, and, in spite of his hoarse cries—"Don't manhandle the science!
I am a medical man"—was dropped into the mud outside the door. To
finish the cleanup, another "gentleman" who had repeatedly disturbed
the assembly was also thrown out the door to keep the man of science
company.

After this small distraction, the assembly continued and out of the
sixty useable men, six watches of ten men were formed, each with a
captain at its head. That way everyone had to run a three-hour patrol
every other night. I had the honor of being chosen the commander of
a watch, and as such had to keep order over four Hollanders and two
Germans, all decent men; three American gold diggers from California,
real criminals, drunk and brutal, with sheepskins across their bodies; and
a Sandwich Islander, a deserter from a whaler, a truly dangerous fellow.

After each watch commander had first received a commission and a
list of his troops from the committee, it was about eleven o'clock in the
evening and the meeting ended. By a drawing of lots it fell to me to take
the first watch until three o'clock in the morning. So instead of going

29. HMS *Camilla* under Captain George Twisleton Colville disappeared on
September 9 returning from Hakodate. It was a 549-ton sloop with sixteen guns.

home, with my certificate as captain of the Yokohama Volunteers in my pocket, I stepped outside at the head of my well-armed crew to do the first round.

Oh Rembrandt! If you in your day could have seen our night round file past, in picturesque garb, by the light of a few paper lanterns, silently through the mud against the blizzard, along the ruins of our burned city, then perhaps you would have taken your inspired brush, and presented the world with another masterpiece, a night watch of sorrow and misery in counterpoint to your "Night Watch" of wealth![30]

If one found oneself on a night patrol in Holland, slowly passing through a garrison town, calm and orderly, along a brightly-lit, cobbled street, taking note of the apparently surly men and casting good-natured glances at the serving girls that skipped by from under one's bearskin hat, then duty in such a patrol is not a horrible situation for a soldier. But if one is not a professional soldier, and as a peace-loving man sailed to distant lands with his ship and cargo to trade, the nightly patrol was all the more unpleasant for being unexpected. And if that should happen voluntarily, yes—but really compelled by dangerous conditions, in the middle of an almost Siberian winter, in fierce cold, often in water and mud that came over the knees, against storms, rain and blizzards for hours on end with only short breaks, and all because he has been left unprotected and forgotten by his fatherland, then he becomes embittered. Add to this the need to be constantly alert for surprise attack from every fence and every corner, walking with your finger always on the revolver's trigger; then one will understand that the mood of the patrol, especially the watch from 12 to 3 o'clock, was anything but pleasant.

During the next few weeks the patrols of the Yokohama Volunteers went like clockwork, and many a time suspicious nocturnal wanderers were picked up and delivered to the Japanese watch at the Interpreters' Office. But in spite of the seriousness of our situation and all the miseries of our nightly tours, now and then the patrol was given the opportunity for a joke of some sort or another, and that was fortunate; for as long as a man is in the middle of surrounding danger, he can not suppress the urge to cover even bothersome things with a colorful veneer and get a good laugh out of them, thereby keeping dejection from the door.

When a gruesome murder was committed here in the Residency[31] a few years ago under mysterious circumstances, one could observe how

30. Painted in 1642. In the collection of the Rijksmuseum, Amsterdam.
31. I.e., the Royal seat, or capital, in The Hague.

a whole city could be stricken by panic. If that can occur in a city of a hundred thousand souls, in the middle of a civilized society where people are guarded and protected in every possible way by several Royal Guard regiments, judges and police, then one can understand why the faint-hearted among the handful of unprotected foreigners in the fire- and murder-pit that was Yokohama were increasingly afraid. In some men that fear bordered on insanity, so there were men who were too hopeless to put on the list of "volunteers."

If anything ever reminded me of the "Gevels van de huizen" by our poet Tollens,[32] it was the little house where Monsieur Pétrilleux,[33] a French Swiss, had settled with several chests of watches, goldwork, and especially music boxes and chiming clocks. "Strange!" I thought to myself, when in those pressured days I would sometimes pass by Monsieur Pétrilleux's small home, "How is it still possible that while the others are full of concern, this jolly Swiss is still cheerful? From morning till night he lets his joyful arias play so loudly one can not help but dance when passing by his house and envy the lighthearted resident, who frolics through this fear-filled life to the beat of the music from his music boxes and clocks."

One morning when I again passed his house, I heard such a noisy and chaotic jangling that I immediately stepped inside to see what inspired the spirited man to make such mad music. Behind his house was a long wooden warehouse in which his goods were displayed; when I entered it, I thought my eardrums would burst. A trio of Japanese merchants who had come from Edo to buy music boxes and musical clocks had immediately gotten to work winding up the chimes with the keys that lay next to each music box and clock to hear which had the best sound, so that when I entered more than fifty music boxes and clocks tinkled and chimed together, overwhelming both hearing and sight. And the owner, the supposedly jolly Swiss, had indifferently left them to their own devices. He sat at the end of his storehouse, pale and somber, watching them from a great rattan chair. "Ah! Monsieur Pétrilleux," I called as I laughingly stepped up to him, "quel concert du diable!"[34] Through the noise all around us, he understood only the last word. Jumping up to grip my hand, he shouted into my ear while cold sweat beaded on his forehead: "Le diable! Oui Monsieur, il

32. "Gables of the Houses" by Hendrik Tollens (1780–1856), a very long poem that describes living in a small Dutch town.
33. Probably François Perregaux (1834–1877), from the still extant Swiss watch firm of Girard-Perregaux. François died in Yokohama.
34. "What a devil of a concert!"

nous confisqu'e dans ce maudit pays!"[35] Good Heavens! How I had been deceived by the zest for life that enticed from behind his wooden walls; the daily jolly music was made by curious Japanese who came to wind up his music boxes—while he himself, the supposedly light-hearted man, sat wrestling with mortal fear twenty-four hours of the day.

I succeeded at last in giving him some courage by telling him of the "Yokohama Volunteers," who were always armed the whole night, and whose mission it was to keep the murderers out of our foreign quarter. He therefore went calmly about his business, dealt with his Japanese visitors, and would perhaps have been completely cured had he not received various alarming reports about murder attempts during the course of the day. His house became oppressive to him and while I sat quietly at my afternoon meal, the good Mr. Pétrilleux came bursting in, very agitated, and stood before me, leaning on the table with both hands. He began very nervously, "Sir! You have certainly heard that they are out for us again; that can, that must not, stay that way, something must be done . . . " "My dear Mr. Pétrilleux!" I reasoned with him. "Don't get so wound up over all the intimidating rumors. If we are to be attacked, in God's name I can do nothing about it but help keep the scoundrels at bay. But be calm, it will be alright; laugh a bit." But he who thinks someone on the verge of going mad with fear can be brought to reason with a few encouraging words is sorely mistaken, and I now found that in the case of someone as far gone as Monsieur Pétrilleux, instead of calm, my words provoked resentment. "The matter is too serious to laugh about, Sir!" he said rather angrily. "Something must be done about it. That is your duty and I entrust you with it," and he hurried off, as if I were a sort of fire-eater, who must immediately do a war dance to challenge all Japanese murderers. Desperate to make some headway with this truly piteous man, I invited him to go with me to my neighbor Mr. Elmstock because I saw no chance of calming him down alone. Mr. Elmstock, a very level-headed man, and my battle comrade as fellow captain in the Volunteers, was immediately ready to help me put some heart into the alarmed patient, and the two of us were able to calm him down enough that he walked back to his house between us. When we left him we heartily shook his hand. "Calmez-wous, Monzjeu," said my brother officer, as a last word of encouragement. "Allez dormez, wous êtés gardé par les wolontaires, si les méchang de Japong veut vous couper la tête!"[36]

35. "The devil! Yes sir, he has shanghaied us to this accursed country!"

36. "Be calm! Go rest, you are guarded by the volunteers, who will chop off the heads of the rogues of Japan!" Transcribed in Elmstock's apparently bad French.

Our "*corps de garde*" was in the bar of the Yokohama Hotel nightly, where we went after each round, which took about a half an hour, to rest for fifteen minutes. That night, after the first round at twelve o'clock, my men and I arrived in the lounge with a clatter of weapons to find Monsieur Pétrilleaux lying on his mattress under the billiard table. He had not dared to stay in his house, had left all his valuable goods at home unguarded, and had imagined that nowhere would be safer, at night, than in the midst of the armed forces. Scarcely had we come in when he worked himself from under the billiard table and called at my approach, nervously gripping both my hands, "*Ah Capitaine! Voilà ce que c'est que de monter de la garde!*"[37] and he implored us all in God's name to keep the watch conscientiously. I assured him that he could be at ease about this, and drawing my sword I swung it around, swearing to him to destroy all Japanese murderers. Completely satisfied, he crept back again to his mattress, and we trekked outside to do another round. Then it was proposed that one of us should dress as a Japanese and be brought in as a prisoner; the Sandwich Islander was best suited for this. Upon passing my house, he was appropriately dressed in the clothing of my Japanese houseboy, drawing the headscarf as far as possible over his face. Thus rigged out, he was brought in between bayonets, and when we came to the front of the Yokohama Hotel, we violently shouted and stamped as we pushed open the door with our rifle butts. At this spectacle Monsieur Pétrilleux sprung up and flung his arms around my neck shrieking: "Ah! Mon brave Capitaine, un prisonnier! Un prisonnier!" and then suddenly releasing me he sprung on the false Japanese who he began to punch and kick, with a cry of "le coquin, l'assassin, le brigand!"[38] But when he had just lifted his foot to give "le brigand" a good kick, our Sandwich Islander lost patience, and under all kinds of Japanese soubriquets, he administered a sound thrashing to Pétrilleux until he screamed bloody murder.

With great difficulty we succeeded in separating the angry quasi-Japanese from Pétrilleux, who then fled, howling and screeching, to the most distant corner of the room.

"Monsieur Pétrilleux" I shouted amidst the tumult, "you shall be splendidly revenged this instant," and when I turned to the watch I continued, "bring the blackguard outside, we shall execute him."

With a great deal of resistance and heavy wrestling that made a terrible racket on the plank floor, the Sandwich Islander was shoved out the door,

37. "Ah Captain! It is he who brings up the guard!"
38. "Scoundrel, assassin, brigand!"

and we disappeared with him into the darkness behind the stables of the Yokohama Hotel. Pétrilleux was left to his own devices to wipe his bloodied nose and put his disheveled clothing in order. For a few moments in the darkness noise was made with the weapons, after which a revolver was fired in the air, and then we sped inside to congratulate the respectable Swiss that there was now one less Japanese murderer in the world.

"C'est fini, Monsieur!" I said when I came in and solemnly shook his hand as if I was affected by the death sentence that had just been carried out in front of my eyes. Pétrilleux however, paid no attention. He was much too pleased that one of the murderers, who had made his life so bitter, had been sent to another world. He was so relieved that, in his joy, he proposed that the negro whip up a buffet to entertain the patrol to celebrate fortunately averting danger. There was no reason for us not to be happy with his happiness; we therefore let him disturb the negro who lay snoring under the counter, and while he was shaken awake and the buffet made ready, we made another short round. I only made half the patrol go out for each succeeding interval, and as the night waned we were finally successful in getting Monsieur Pétrilleux to embrace new courage and to laugh. But he never knew who he had to thank for the swollen nose and black eyes that he walked around with for many more days.

But in spite of all our watchfulness, and the patrols with our "volunteers," we could not prevent repeated attempts at murder, especially in the early evening before eight o'clock when the first patrol departed. Certainly most agonizing of all were the incessantly repeated alarming rumors; scarcely a day passed that there was no news told round of enemy plans for the following night. We were certain that should we need help, the Shogunal military watch at the Interpreters' Office could not be counted on, of this I had been all too well satisfied. Once, on a night when an attack was again predicted, out of curiosity I trekked with my company to the Interpreters' Office where, for our so-called protection, a few soldiers were encamped with two field pieces. After we had banged on the gate several times, the door was finally fumbled open by a sleepyhead, who without a single inquiry stepped across the courtyard and lay back down on the mat in his guardhouse. In the dark we almost bumped into the unguarded fieldpieces, which we could have nailed down with ease had we so chosen, and came at last to a door, behind which we saw a nightlight burning in a large room. Stepping inside we found some thirty Japanese soldiers who lay snoring so comfortably on the mats they could not be shaken awake; we satisfied ourselves with taking their rifles, which stood against the wall, and setting them outside the door as a sign of our visit. Highly dissatisfied with this inspection, we went out the gate without disturbing a living soul, and with the certainty that a single headhunter would be sufficient to overcome and slaughter our Japanese protectors.

So it was a true relief for us when one fine day in the month of February 1860, a Russian steam transport warship, newly built in North America and *en route* to the Amur River, dropped anchor at Yokohama. It was not a very heavily armed ship, equipped with but a few pieces, but it stood under military command: besides the commandant and half a dozen officers, there were a hundred and eighty sailors and soldiers on board. All the officers were extremely pleasant fellows who spoke fluent French, and while nothing will ever fly right between the English and the Russians, they demonstrated more partiality to the Hollanders, to whom they showed the utmost hospitality. I also did what I could to welcome them during their stay with us, and frequently had some Russian guests at my table. Thus, just a few days after their arrival, the most friendly relationship sprung up between us which, as we shall see later, had the most outstanding benefit.

About a week after the Russian ship had arrived, I had a few Dutch friends over to dine, one of whom was leaving the next day. It was about seven o'clock in the evening when we sat down at the table for the farewell meal, which meant it had been pitch dark for half an hour. And although I have remarked above that I would not dwell on the many murders that were perpetrated on our small group and will not linger over the graves of pioneers of every nationality whose mutilated bodies rest in the cemetery of Yokohama, I will now, with a few words, bring forth the memory of the violent deaths of two of our countrymen—deaths that awoke not only blazing anger but also deep compassion.

At this time there lay some ten merchant ships in the roadstead, of which two were Dutch, brought by the Captains De Vos and Dekker,[39] both sedate, brave men, the latter an old man; they had just recently arrived and never done a single Japanese the least harm. They still did not know how dangerous Yokohama was after dark, especially if one ventured even just a few paces outside the foreigners' quarter. The fate they met might have been for all of us that night with less rapid action,

39. See n. 7.

but what in particular aroused the general outcry and compassion over these murders was that the slain left behind widows and children. They had only temporarily gone ashore to shop, and were complete strangers to Yokohama who had done nothing deserving harm, dead innocents who were sacrifices in the blood vendetta against the foreigners.

We had barely begun our meal, for which the Chinese cook had done his best on this special occasion, when a tremendous racket arose at the front door. Always on our guard, as one had to be in Yokohama in those days, our first thought was a surprise attack; each hastily gripped the revolver which lay next to him on the table. Suddenly the paper doors that separated the room from the hall were flung open and two compatriots, pale and upset, strode in with drawn swords.

"My God! You sit here!" shouted one, "come with us, quick, with weapons, we have been attacked, two bodies lie already in front of the main street." In less than two seconds we were ready; both of my trusty Japanese servants had lit their paper lanterns in the blink of an eye, and we sped off posthaste, panting silently forward in the pitch dark night, after the two dim lights, through the mud and over the debris from the recently burnt foreign quarter.

I can understand that a battalion of soldiers, wound up by martial music, patriotism, thirst for glory and a sense of honor, strong in their number and full of hope for a splendidly triumphant outcome, might jubilantly storm an enemy. But if, on a dark evening, a peaceful man with a handful of even more peaceful mates, must run to the slaughter, far from his homeland without the slightest hope of victory, through mud and over debris to a scene of butchery, his only consolation found in the thirst for revenge and extracting a high price for his life, then fear and desperate courage surge through the human heart. Only the thought that something might be achieved through determination and unity gives one the strength not to lose spirit.

So we ran in the dark toward the Yokohama Hotel, which had been designated the gathering place in moments of danger. When we passed someone's small wooden house, the blinds were cautiously pushed aside and the resident's lamplight shone outside through the oiled paper doors. Then sounded: "Who is there?" "Friend!" "Stop, I'll go with you!" And so our numbers grew; or otherwise groups like ours called to us and upon the answer "Friend!" they fell in with us, so that after just a few minutes about thirty well-armed men arrived at the gathering place. We were received with cheers by another thirty we found there.

The events called for haste, so now sixty strong we tore to the main street of the Japanese quarter, which bordered the edge of our foreign quarter and began just near the Yokohama Hotel. This main street was more than thirty paces wide; we had proceeded only a short way along it when we encountered the body of Captain De Vos lying in the mud in the middle of the street in a large pool of blood, literally hacked in half through the middle, so that the innards hung out. It was a gruesome sight, the half-hewn body of this spry man to whom, just a few hours before, I had spoken, while he was still full of life and in health. The desire for vengeance instantly extinguished any trace of fear in me. A few armed men and a couple coolies with torches that we had brought from the Yokohama Hotel, stayed with the corpse and we went a few paces further. There we found the unfortunate Dekker lying, so abominably murdered that when the light of the torches fell on the old man's badly mutilated body a shudder of horror went through all those present. A single sword blow had cleft through the back of his head and part of his back; the high black hat that he had worn, sliced as if by a razor, lay next to him. His left hand was chopped off, probably because he had tried to deflect the blow from behind while fleeing, so that his hand had been severed from his body with a single chop. Thirty paces further on we found his severed hand; it thus appeared that after this gruesome mutilation, the old man had sped forward, to the place where the mortal blow was inflicted.

But enough of this barbaric scene of murder, the specter of this somber evening, a bloody clue of what we ourselves might soon expect. There are moments in life the memory of which cannot be erased by time, moments for which the images and conditions that accompanied them encroach so deeply that their impression is not diminished to forgetfulness even after years of the commonplace.

The bodies of the slain were laid side-by-side and covered with a mat brought to us by a friendly Japanese. We, now grown to eighty armed foreigners, set off across the big street with orders to shoot any Japanese who tried to push forward. Hundreds of peaceful citizens from the Japanese city, good simple wretches, such as shopkeepers, small merchants, coolies and other working folk, stood just behind our lines, looking on with their lanterns in hand, and they were obviously as dismayed as we were because their sympathy and indignation were apparent. But behind this innocent crowd could be seen imposing fellows with bandits' faces, followers of lords from the interior, with two long swords in their sashes, scoundrels waiting to strike a blow. I was reminded again this evening how advantageous it was to remain calm and composed, and how dangerous a few hotheads can be for others.[40]

It was then about seven-thirty, which was for many Englishmen too soon after "dinner time" for them to be completely over the influence of the sherry and port that they consumed with their meal, and to be completely capable—or, as we say in Dutch, "nuchter en bekwaam."[41] The sight of blood, the murdered whites, and the red light of the pitch torches made all these men so angry and vengeful that they wanted to storm into the Japanese crowd with their swords and guns, and chop down all that came before them. With the utmost difficulty we held twenty or so of these hotheads back; if they had done as they wished, then many innocents would have fallen, and undoubtedly the band of bandits lurking behind in the dark, who were certainly stronger than we were, would then have pushed forward and put us all to the blade. While we tried to calm the most sober of the hotheads with persuasive speeches and still keep an eye on the double-sworded gang of bandits, we suddenly heard a European command and the orderly pace of a marching detachment of soldiers. In the darkness we saw in the distance a black mass splashing through the mud, and the glitter of Russian gun barrels and bayonets in the dim lantern light was sweeter than the first flowers of May ever were.

At this sudden rescue from our precarious situation, a thunderous "hurray" sounded among us; we made room, the drum was beaten, and the Lieutenant Perlachine, who had lost all the fingers of his left hand at Sebastopol,[42] headed the charge of his troops with bayonets toward the Japanese, who dispersed like chaff in the wind. Gone were the bandits—and to "strike while the iron is hot," so to speak, the Russian Officer did not look at the bodies but instead immediately marched his forty huge and well-disciplined soldiers a few times through the entire Japanese city,

40. According to George Smith, the motive for the attack was revenge: "Captain _____, formerly of the American vessel the _____, on the day preceding the assassination was summoned by a Japanese official to attend at the custom-house respecting some irregular transactions in the course of business. The native officer was peremptorily ordered to quit the room and bear back a defiant reply to his superior officers. He was sent back with another message to the captain, who enraged by this importunity assaulted the custom-house officer, broke his sword and kicked him out of the house." George Smith, *Ten Weeks in Japan* (London: Green, Longman and Roberts, 1861), 257.
41. Level-headed and capable.
42. The Siege of Sebastopol, 1854–1855, the final battle of the Crimean War.

picking up every Japanese that showed his face; if the Japanese had a sword with him, he was shackled and handed over to the Governor of Yokohama.

Thank God! We blessed this Russian commandant of the "*Japonsk*," as the steamship was called, who had sent an armed longboat full of soldiers ashore as soon as he got the message. Had they not been there, I believe we would have been cut to ribbons to the last man that very night.

We now had time to transport the bodies of our unfortunate compatriots to the Yokohama Hotel unmolested. Two days later they were taken from there and buried ceremoniously under the Dutch flag. All the foreign consuls, a detachment of Russians, and a detachment of English soldiers from the war brig *Camilla*, which had arrived in the roadstead that morning, and all the Europeans and Americans were present; not a single citizen of any nationality was missing from the procession. An American missionary[43] read the prayer for the dead over the open graves, a salvo sounded from the Russian guns, and most who had truly and sincerely joined in the last honors to our unfortunate countrymen turned dejectedly back to Yokohama. And I, I stayed to the last; I had known both of the dead quite well and cast a melancholic gaze over the recently turned up earth. I thought of the uncertainty of human life, and the deep mourning over both of these spry men that would be roused in their near relations when the grass had already grown over their graves and they had already rested for months at the edge of the green Japanese mountains.

A sudden scare didn't always end so tragically. And so it was with me, but this time it happened very late in the evening as I sat cozily with a few friends following someone's festive birthday meal.

If I may be permitted to first introduce Mr. Baker,[44] an elderly, distinguished English gentleman, a good-hearted, quiet, decent man, who was in his sixties. Mr. Baker was a great contrast to the many raw customers in Yokohama then. Always dignified, always neatly dressed, friendly to all, venerable and engaging in appearance, he would have been better off as a lord in Parliament than living among the half-feral residents of Yokohama. His civilized manner and affability made him esteemed by all, and Mr. Baker could say that, in spite of the strange

---

43. Possibly Samuel R. Brown (1810–1880), who was of the Dutch Reformed Church. See photo on page 116.

44. Possibly Thomas Baker, who later shot himself. *Japan Daily Mail*, Jan. 6, 1877, p. 7–8.

sort of elements that made up our small society, he did not have a single enemy among them. But Mr. Baker had a heart, and a tender one at that.

Jokesters and gossips such as one finds everywhere had amused themselves by saying that Mr. Baker had an eye on Hannéjamma[45] (which is literally translated as "flower mountain") the beautiful daughter of the Japanese merchant Siroja. Others had embroidered upon this rumor, adding that Mr. Baker had held a Japanese wedding or would soon do so, and that Father Siroja had no less an eye for Mr. Baker's money chest than Mr. Baker had for Siroja's daughter.

No one could believe it until he saw it, and since there had been no prenuptials and no reception held and no newspapers to proclaim it to the world, one had to wait patiently to see what came of things.

We thus sat cheerfully together at eleven o'clock at night, as I've said, when suddenly a cannon shot was fired from the English war brig *Camilla*, which had already been in the roadstead for a few days. Frightened, we all sprang up and grabbed our weapons. But scarcely had we gone outside when the war brig gave the full blast on the flank side, making a hellish noise in the night. What could it be? We could think of no other reason right away than that the city of Kanagawa opposite was being bombarded by the English commander in revenge for another murder. The best thing we could do was to hasten, as swiftly as possible, to the gathering place at the Yokohama Hotel. We had to pass in front of Mr. Baker's house on the way, and just as we got there a "kanga,"[46] or covered palanquin, was carried through the gate of Mr. Baker's yard, accompanied by a number of Japanese men and women with lanterns in hand. A long red piece of cloth hung out from under the palanquin; through the light shining on it, the cloth appeared to be the bloodied clothing of a hapless victim. "Good heavens! They have certainly murdered old Mr. Baker!" rang our battle cry as we surrounded the palanquin, which had been left in the lurch by the fleeing carriers and followers. Hastily and agitatedly the curtains were torn open, our coolies pushed their lanterns forward to light the ghastly spectacle, and we saw . . . the beautiful Hannéjamma, white from fear, in her fire-red bridal gown, as she had been sent by her parents and relations, in the custom of the country, to be wed to Mr. Baker. We all had a hearty laugh, and immediately called back the good folks of the retinue, who now understood from our laughter that they had nothing to fear from us. A few of us took the post of the carriers upon ourselves and

45. This would be Hanayama.
46. *Kago* 籠.

we all went together into Mr. Baker's yard, set the beautiful load carefully in front of his house door, said our farewells through a crack in the door, or otherwise spoke a few words of congratulations to the old gentleman, which were answered with a "thank you, much obliged, gentlemen!" In the Dutch manner of congratulations we shook with both hands those of the old respectable Siroja and his wife, the uncles and aunts of the bride and those of more distant relations. Satisfied and pleased with ourselves, we left Mr. Baker's yard; after all, instead of murder and bloodshed, through this nocturnal expedition we had contributed a stone to the foundation of the world of the future—namely, the brotherhood of nations.

Soon thereafter we heard that the cannon fire was a consequence of a party on board the *Camilla* at which the French and English envoys were present. Over dessert the commander had boasted, and the French envoy wagered against, that in the middle of the night when the whole crew were asleep, they would battle-ready within five minutes of the first alarm.

This trick was executed at once, and ended with the full blast from the battery. We were thus really the dupes of what people called "drunkards fun." But since there were two envoys present, people preferred to call it "official entertainment."[47]

The arrival, shortly thereafter, of the Russian steam warship meant the days of the Yokohama Volunteers were numbered. If their short existence is not so well known to the world as that of the Prussian Free Corps of Schill in the beginning of this century, or as the riflemen of Van Dam and Rookmaker in our country in '30,[48] they had nevertheless faithfully done their duty for several weeks. Still, I can deliver no eulogy for them,

---

47. The evening of March 5, 1860. Edward Barrington de Fonblanque was on board the *Camilla,* dining with Captain Vyse and M. De Bellcour. He says salutes were fired in De Bellecour's honor, and the Russians of the *Japonsk* (*Japonitch*) responded, thinking they were in their honor. In addition, both Japanese and foreigners thought it was in response to the discovery of a murdered corpse, which turned out to be a drunk sailor; see Fonblanque, *Niphon and Pe-Che-Li* (London: Saunders, Otley and Co., 1862), 102–4. Francis Hall only notes the rumor of murder (p. 137).

48. The Freicorps of Ferdinand von Schill (1776–1809), created in 1809 in response to the call of Francis I, the Emperor of Prussia, against Napoleon. Prussia was not at war with France so the actions were independent, thus "Free Corps." The Riflemen of Rookmaker were the Northern Marksmen in the Belgian uprising of 1830. This conflict resulted in the formation of the Belgian state, which seceded from the United Kingdom of the Netherlands. Hendrik Rookmaker (1786–1860), a career soldier, was the Commander of the Marksmen. Like De Coningh, he was born in Arnhem and died in Haarlem, so they may have known each other.

even with the best of intentions, because then I would have to confess that they were destroyed not at the hands of the enemy but through a lack of discipline. It would have been impossible to maintain discipline in the long run anyway, and in the absence of such discipline, most of the Volunteers generally failed to appear for muster. To the honor of the Netherlanders, they always turned up and faithfully persevered the longest. Finally, they too began to feel they would rather throw in the towel than go on watch for sluggards and drunks. They convened a meeting amongst themselves in which more was decided in half an hour than at all the English meetings together. They had, in fact, asked the Dutch Consul to be present at their meetings, and asked him specifically what he could do for their safety. The answer was "absolutely nothing." So we thought to ask him for a written request for help from the Russian warship at anchor in the roadstead. The commandant and officers of this ship, who were our friends and daily guests, wished nothing more than to relieve us of our watch duties, and had stated beforehand that an armed detachment would be sent as soon as the consul made an official request. They held true to their word: from the following evening a patrol of fifteen Russian soldiers walked nightly through our foreign quarter so that we could rest easy again. All the Netherlanders wished Dr. Dugger, with his red leather coats and his drill-sergeant, to the devil. For six weeks after that we were protected and guarded by the Russians; and the English, who could now lay their heads down without a care after their nightly grog, cursed their government that they, as English citizens, must be protected by Russian bayonets. That was a bitter pill to swallow for their "pride."

I do not know if our Government ever gave the Russian commandant and his officers some award for their great service to the Netherlanders in the Far East. If not, it would be a pity if no manner of official appreciation at all was shown for their magnanimous assistance; in any case, it is certain that no citizen could have been better and more effectively protected by a warship of their own nation than we were by these alert Russians, who had perchance encountered us in our sticky situation in Yokohama. For our part, we did what we could to show our gratitude for the assistance rendered. Shortly before their departure, the commandant of the *Japonsk* was presented with a memorial of thanks on behalf of all the Netherlanders; all the officers were invited to the Yokohama Hotel for a banquet for the occasion that, in splendor and variety of dishes and wines, exceeded any yet seen in Japan. There reigned a warm fraternity between Netherlanders and Russians. Many were the toasts made to the success and prosperity of both folk. They were issued at a velocity not equaled since the days when Peter the Great sat with the Amsterdam Burgers.[49]

Shortly after the departure of the *Japonsk*, the Dutch steam corvette *Groningen* arrived in the roadstead. It had been on its way to Yokohama months before but had cut the trip short and turned back to Nagasaki. It was spring; the nights were shorter; we were now adequately protected, everything began to revive, and vigorous efforts were made everywhere to rebuild the burned city on a stronger and more orderly foundation. Since things were calmer for the foreigners than we had ever known, each could improve his business, which understandably had come almost to a standstill during the winter, not only as a result of the prevailing unrest, but also because few Japanese merchants would show themselves among us, fearing that the appearance of collaboration with foreigners would earn the wrath of the *loonings* that roamed the area. With our greater safety everything improved, and another consequence was that married foreigners, who had previously left their wives in China, now brought them over, so that Mistress Shobber no longer remained alone and more women came to adorn the burgeoning Yokohama, by which the wildness of the men was crimped into a more civilized fold.

49. Peter I of Russia (1672–1725) spent the winter season of 1697–1698 working in an East India Company shipyard in Amsterdam and learned about technology, science, and medicine, which he then introduced to Russia.

Chapter 7

Earlier, when I discussed the gold trade, I remarked that the Japanese were later so clever with usury in foreigners' silver as to recover what silver had gone out of the country in gold. See here how willfully they went about this. According to the treaties, each nation could, until July 4, 1860, exchange the silver coins of their nation for an equal weight in Japanese coins at the Interpreters Office. In the beginning this exchange was fairly regulated; one could daily exchange as many dollars for *itzeboes* as what in fairness was needed for trade. So long as the number of foreign merchants remained small, there were enough *itzeboes* available; but when their number increased, exchange was limited to a hundred dollars each per day, and later decreased to twenty. Now, weight for weight, one received 311 *itzeboes* for 100 dollars, or just 62 for 20 dollars, which meant no more wholesale exchanges and the shortage of *itzeboes* that emerged worked greatly to the disadvantage of the dollar.

It was therefore right that the Japanese government, after July 4, 1860, arbitrarily set the worth of the dollar by simply ordering that the Japanese merchants to accept no more than 2 *itzeboes* per dollar. Now the Mexican dollar had a real silver value of f 2.55 Dutch currency, and the *itzeboe* of f 0.82; so for each dollar spent, one lost about 90 cents silver value to the advantage of the shogunal treasury. When, for example, someone without *itzeboes* bought something from a Japanese that cost 200 *itzeboes*, they paid with 100 dollars. The Japanese then exchanged the currency at the mint in Jeddo, receiving 200 *itzeboes* for that 100 dollars, and the mint cast those dollars into 311 *itzeboes*. If one now calculates that in fifteen months at least fifteen million cash dollars were imported for the purchase of export articles, primarily raw silk, than one can understand that the Shogunal treasury fared quite well in this operation. With fairly trustworthy reckoning one may assume that through the gold trade in 1859, roughly 400,000 golden *kobangs* were exported; if the profits thereon were, again roughly, calculated at f 5 a piece, about f 2,000,000 was earned by the foreigners, whereupon in revenge in 1860 and 1861 they were cheated out of f 13,500,000 on their silver.

But, one might naively ask, wouldn't the ministers and consuls of the treaty powers, supported by the commandants of their warships, have had enough force to insist that this swindle of the foreign traders cease immediately? Alas! The crafty Japanese had devised a means to prevent this that was all but infallible. Specifically, in July 1860, before the exchange trade was revoked, all ministers, consuls, and sea officers were invited to continue to exchange 1,000 dollars, or perhaps more, per month. For 1,000 dollars these gentlemen now received 3,200 *itzeboes*; they could immediately change back 2,000 *itzeboes* to 1,000 dollars from the largest and best merchants, and thus enjoyed a quite nice profit of circa *f*1,200 per month. Therefore they found nothing onerous in the dollar question, and remained deadly calm about it, so that these conditions, to their great profit and satisfaction, continued for several years. That this could happen is, alas, a sad truth. This terrible injustice, whereupon a coin in the hand of one is declared a third less in value in the hand of another, which was patiently tolerated for so long, would never have been ended by those who enjoyed the advantage of it. I have been assured that Mr. De Witt,[1] the Dutch Consul-General at this time in Nagasaki, thankfully, abstained from this token of good faith from the Japanese because it reeked of bribery. If this is true, it speaks well to his honor.

The winters in Yokohama are bleak and brutal, and summers are swelteringly hot, especially in August and September, but it is just at this time that there appears, however seldom, sometimes only once in many years, a scene of such horror, that one would think the end has come. Who has never asked the question: What will happen at the end of the world? Will it become uninhabitable to man through slow dehydration, will it perish from heat or cold, through fire, or through water, or will a second deluge of sea and storm destroy everything? When a typhoon rages one would think it is the latter. It is as if all will perish by wind and water. Our fiercest storms would seem but a zephyr when compared with the furious force with which the typhoon slashed the land and whipped the waves across its whole disastrous course.

In the early morning of 9 September, 1860, I was awakened by a thundering roar outside and the vibrating of my house; it was as if I were, house and all, being driven in a speeding express train over a bumpy track. It was the onset of a typhoon. I fearfully awaited the dawn, which arrived late and as if in distress, casting but a feeble glimmer on the ravaged earth; the light of the morning sun could not push through the leaden rain clouds that were swept over us by the hurricane. With a shudder I cast a glance outside, opposite from the side from which the wind came, but could not see even twenty paces distant. It was like one endless waterspout, whistling past with the force and power of escaping

1. J. K. de Wit, consul from 1860 until 1863.

steam. Air and earth were all enveloped in a thick cloud that thundered forward, bending, shaking, and cracking anything that was too strong to pull down. The ground, my whole yard around me, was like a boiling lake caused not so much by the dreadful volume of water streaming from the heavens as the foam and the cresting waves of seawater that swelled in the bay and swept landwards in a horizontal direction. In that foaming water drifted doors, tubs, household goods and all sorts of things; fallen tiles, planks and torn off branches that had been knocked loose with each successive fierce gust were again taken up and dragged further forward. It was as if my servants and I were the only ones in the world in the last hour of her existence.

The hurricane raged with its fiercest strength through the course of the morning. Even though my wooden house was fairly strong and, with just one floor on the street, stood very low to the ground, we did not trust it inside. With my two Japanese servants, I stood in the open door on the leeward side of the house, which was opposite the direction the wind blew. At the slightest snap behind us, we could jump outside, or at least we hoped we would have enough time to do so. At about eleven o'clock conditions became so terrible that we decided to flee—but to where? Because at that moment the weather was so horrible that if all our near neighbors and their houses had come to grief we would not have noticed a thing. What we could hear quite well, despite the roaring of the hurricane, was the terrible crack now and then of collapsing buildings nearby, but where and whose was indiscernible. It did not affect us but served as a warning for us to save ourselves.

In my yard, about eighty paces from my house, I had recently built a warehouse; it had only been two months since it was finished. It was a colossal building, 160 feet long and 100 feet wide—big enough to store an entire ship's cargo, and fireproof. Praised by the English as a model of Dutch thoroughness for its size and sound structure, it had cost several thousand dollars. Should we flee, we would find refuge behind the heavy walls of the leeside of the warehouse. From where we stood, we could see, as if in a haze, the faint outlines of the building where we thought to seek shelter. After hastily packing up this and that of which we might need, we stood ready to hasten through the foaming, driving water, like castaways desperately attempting to grasp hold of the life buoy drifting nearby.

"Wait until I give the signal," I said to my Japanese. "If we move, we all three go at once!"

We stood ready, as in a race, to bolt the hundred paces hand in hand, through the hurricane and foaming water, to reach the promised shelter.

"Not yet!" I bellowed to one of the Japanese, whose left hand I held in my right, and who impatiently had already put his foot forward just as a fierce gust shook the earth. I wanted to wait until the gust passed to choose a moment between the blasts that seemed more manageable.

"Now then, forward!" I shouted just after that, when I thought that the chances were favorable. We sloshed as fast as we could, helped by the storm's wind behind us, through the water, between all kinds of wreckage, in the direction of the large warehouse. There it stood, that sturdy hulk, right by us. We were already halfway—only fifty paces to go and we would be safe—when we were seized from behind by a whirlwind, flung apart, and thrown headfirst into the water. It was like the moment of the Last Judgment. Amid an awful roaring and wailing, the rushing water and the force of the hurricane held us down like an invisible titanic force. A bloodcurdling crack sounded nearby; with a thundering din, the entire section of wall nearest us crashed into the water, momentarily forming a wave that washed over us. The great building that we thought was our salvation had collapsed like a house of cards!

I cannot describe what was going on inside me in that fatal hour, when the gust passed and I saw my establishment destroyed before my eyes. There was no time for me to think deeply about what our fate would have been had we reached our shelter a few minutes before. Men remain men under all circumstances and a disaster that had struck in a few seconds deeply affected my future, and I imagined it was my material ruin. For several weeks now, the warehouse had contained a valuable cargo of more than three casks of gold that had been sent to me from Europe, along with a considerably greater value of raw silk in bales, ready for shipping. Now, defenseless in the midst of the perilous storm, in no state to save our own skins, I saw everything buried under the rubble, exposed to destruction by the torrents of rain and the force of the typhoon.

But the perilous storm roared forth, and it was no time to stand lamenting, because even if I thought I was ruined, I could think only of self-preservation. My only thought was: save who could be saved! Fleeing to the open field, and throwing ourselves down there, was now the only thing left for us.

"Forward, to the plain!" I shouted to my Japanese. All the fencing that had bordered my yard had been blown away in the storm, so we waded as fast as we could over the space, holding overhead a piece of plank or empty basket fished up to protect ourselves from all the wreckage whirling through the air. Reaching some distance in the open field, upon which about a foot of water stood, we threw ourselves on the ground and, protected by a sort of breastwork of the empty baskets we had fished up, waited in this condition for things to run their course.

The mighty gust that had destroyed the warehouse was a sort of "*coup de grace*," before the wind, which had blown out of the Northwestern side of the bay, veered to the Southwest. We had not lain long in our improvised bulwark before the light broke through in the Southwest, and the wind began to blow from this corner; but now, with dry weather, came what the sailors call a "brassy wind." Thus the ground dried quickly, and as soon as it had improved to some extent, we turned back toward our house, which still stood reasonably upright, although it was also very battered and almost none of it had remained dry.

Toward evening the typhoon subsided and before setting, the sun, as if in compassion for the spectacle she had witnessed, cast a ray over badly ravaged Yokohama. More than twenty warehouses were destroyed; not a house remained undamaged; all fences lay blown over; in short, everything was so smashed and battered that a week-long bombardment could not have done as much damage as the hurricane of a few hours. Strangely, many of the best buildings were thrown over, while some wooden warehouses and sheds one watched with distrust in good weather remained standing as if nothing had happened. I thought these observations should not be held back to encourage modern house builders. As my experiences show that just as there are cases when one person breaks a rib after stumbling in the street, while another one tumbles off a roof and goes on his way, unharmed, their houses could withstand a heavy storm by shaking.

The ships in the bay were all driven aground from their anchorages. Fortunately the roadstead in Yokohama is really a bay within a bay, so that they waited out the storm without danger. But in the harbor between the two projecting jetties, was a sad sight; it was so full of the wreckage of all the shattered Japanese boats and small vessels that one could walk across it. I heard nothing of any dead or injured in our foreign quarter; but after such an incident, certainly a number of indigenous folk perished. The English war brig *Camilla*, whose return from Hakodade[2] was expected, should, according to calculations, have been approaching the bay of Jedo on the day of the typhoon. But she remained absent, and nothing more was ever heard of the *Camilla*, or of the two hundred men aboard her.[3]

2. Hakodate.
3. See n. 20, chap. 6.

It sometimes happens that there is fortune within a misfortune, and this was proven for me the next day, when early in the morning we began to clean up the debris from the collapsed warehouse. The long roof, though broken in several places, had fallen horizontally on top of the highly stacked chests, so that much less water had gotten in than I expected. The damage, although considerable, was therefore not so great as it could have been; nevertheless, it was more than enough to assure that the typhoon would remain long in my memory.

Among the many wise maxims we learn in the years of early youth that one must practice in the handwriting lessons at school are some that continue to serve one well in practical life, such as "He who loses money, loses much; he who loses courage loses all." I recalled these few words, which, as a lad, I had copied some hundred times in succession as punishment, as I stood by the wreckage of my worldly goods. Without lamenting too much, we began the task of clearing up the mess with eight-dozen or so Japanese, and to accommodate the greater part of the undamaged goods elsewhere. Before nightfall there was only a large planked floor indicating the spot where an admired, strong warehouse had been knocked down by the typhoon. When it came time to move on, along the principles of the builders of the tower of Babel, another building that was strong enough to safely withstand the next typhoon was put in its place as quickly as possible—thus within a couple weeks a doubly strong new warehouse was erected on the site of the disaster, one reputed to be able to withstand fire and storm. With new courage, valuable European goods were stacked inside; only when the purchase-hungry Japanese were again within the pristine walls, and the clink of their dollars could be heard or their raw silk was dragged in, did the last trace of the typhoon disappear.

For eighteen months I now had slaved and toiled in Japan, and as the folksong says, "I had experienced it all, sorrow and wealth."[4] I had struggled with murder, fire, earthquake and hurricane; trade had prospered and foundered, sometimes giving me joy but more often causing me great concern. Yet amidst all this, there always remained to me one treasure: a strong constitution and a clear mind. I can look back with satisfaction at that fearful time now behind me, because I had been blessed in my labors. From Josaïmon's fishing hut in the obscure village nearby, I was now the head of a major establishment in flourishing Yokohama. In the most fearful and most turbulent days

---

4. Unidentified. "Ik had alles ondergaan, verdriet en weelde."

my strength had all too often fallen short. But no one in Europe of competence and knowledge had the courage to embark to Japan, despite the finest promises, because of the well-known reports of our perilous and uncertain situation. Only after everything had been set in order, and one could count on the safety of his life, could any enthusiasts be found. So at last my replacements arrived from Europe—once the bed had been made and the table set, so to speak.[5] But thereby also came the occasion for me to leave behind Japan with all its joys and sorrows. I shipped out on board the *England*, an old rusty English steamship bound for Shanghai via Nagasaki.[6]

Amid the bustle that reigned on board before the anchor was weighed, I stood leaning over the bulwark, musing, and cast a last glance over the bay where, eighteen months before, only a few wooden huts had lain nestled between the fields and the trees; there now stretched a large city of white plaster buildings. I pondered the many interests that I left behind there, over Yokohama's short past, and lost myself to dreams of what her future would hold.

What I dreamed then of her future never came to pass. A short time of prosperity did follow, but with it unprecedented crass affluence came to the young commercial town. There came to be a number of parvenus, unaccustomed to the sound of dollars, like the legions of Hannibal in affluent Capua of old.[7] With their swiftly earned money they made demands on life that could not be satisfied in the bad days that followed all too quickly. By then prosperity and affluence had become a need, and there followed a period of demoralization in which many put aside all scruples to pursue but one goal: to get their hands on the almighty dollar by any means so the *vie princière*[8] could be continued. It takes strong legs to carry wealth, and during the early years in Japan I saw

5. These were probably his partners. Around this time the firm was known as De Coningh, Carst & Lels. Carst appears to be a J. P. Carst, Jz., of Amsterdam. Lels was Murk Lels (1823–1891), who was born in Amsterdam, started as a sailor, and worked in machine shops and as a bookkeeper.

6. In 1861. This ship was sold later that year to Satsuma province for $120,000. M. Paske-Smith, *Western Barbarians in Japan and Formosa* (Kobe: J. L. Thompson, 1930), 222.

7. Capua was the second largest city in Italy and quite affluent. Hannibal entered Capua in 217 BCE, seated on his last surviving elephant. His legionaries were mercenaries. The Romans put the city under siege in 212 BCE and recaptured it the following year.

8. Princely life.

Panorama view of Yokohama from the Bluff, c. 1861. Photo by W. Saunders. Courtesy of the Scheepvaarts Museum.

more than one tragic example of how wealth and excess can fell her victims just the same as poverty and squalor. During the heyday of trade I knew of young men who came to Japan equipped with breeding, knowledge and civilization; these men would have had a far happier fate with a few hundred guilders in Europe than with thousands of dollars in what was then the golden land. In that world, and in those days, a strong character and self-control had to be at the fore; whoever was weak enough to simply throw away a fortune through the willingness to do with his wealth what so many wantonly did around him was morally and physically lost. The prosperity of the moment destroyed the fine futures of many, and certainly many who lost their wealth and wrecked their health later thought back with bitterness on the disastrous heights to which they had once climbed through the abundance of dollars.

In view of the influence we, the Netherlanders, still maintained in Japan, in those days at least, it was really too bad that our Commissioner-General initially held so obstinately to the old *Opperhoofd* ways of Decima. If, right away in 1859, a skilled Dutch envoy had been headquartered in Jedo along with the English, French and American diplomats, he would certainly have served as the support and font of knowledge for the Japanese government who were totally unfamiliar with international law, European views, conventions and positions. Through knowledge and diplomatic tact, he, as a long-time ally, could have acted as a valuable and dispassionate middleman in the many sometimes ridiculous issues that arose repeatedly with foreign authorities, especially because, in those days, our language was the only one that could be spoken and properly understood, without fear of misunderstanding, by the highest government officials. So it really is a pity that in the first few years the task of maintaining our influence in the Shogunal government fell to the young so-called Consul. Instead of exercising influence, within just a few weeks we were *á la queue*[9] with the others.

The civilized Japanese places a high value on the attributes of steadiness and tranquility in all his actions, and I was always surprised at the dignity and distinction they maintained at all times. The Japanese had for the most part found these valuable qualities in our past *Opperhoofden* and Commissioners–General, and certainly expected us to send a person similarly endowed to Jedo upon the opening of Yokohama in 1859. It is my strong conviction that in the circumstances of the day such a person would have been extremely welcome to the Shogunal cabinet in Jedo.

9. In line.

Indeed, they found themselves in the situation of a patient, repeatedly attacked by shortness of breath, who did not know which regimen was best. Now it is obvious that such a patient would place great trust in the familiar, dispassionate doctor who, soberly dressed in black, closely examines the tongue through his gold-rimmed glasses, and gravely takes a pulse; conversely, he would only grudgingly accept the advice of a young, not-yet graduated, aspiring medic who, with much bluster, came to call in a loose summer suit and great riding boots, and without a single scholarly assessment, recommended pills.

We had thus seen our influence in Japan wane considerably in the first four years, yet we took effective action there one more time. To do so, the wisdom and advice of council was not brought forth; the drawn artillery of our warships would now do the talking. It was then in 1863 that the various murders, the innumerable obstacles that had from the beginning been placed in the way of foreign trade, the shelling of a friendly flag in the Strait of Simonoseki[10]—in short, all the grievances had brought about such a deficit to the balance of the Japaners' account that the treaty powers mutually agreed to administer a combined punitive expedition. So too did the Netherlands join in and that certainly sounded strange to the ears of most people in this country who have been lulled by the legend that we, through our wise policy and more than two centuries of hallowed friendship were, above all others, the chosen people in Japan. Not only was our country mistaken but apparently our Indies Government was even more so, because they had first been entrusted with the policy for Japan affairs, and it was obvious that in their estimation things would continue, full of love and pleasantries, on their own.

Dr. J. van Vloten[11] has said, somewhere in one of his brochures, that the Netherlander is especially devoted to two things: his faith and his purse. I think this learned man, whose pen is just as sharp as his mind, often knows just how to hit the nail on the head. Undoubtedly what he meant by this was that we Netherlanders are difficult if we are asked to pay; but on the other hand, naturally, we jump for joy if we receive money. This national characteristic manifested itself especially after the bombardment of Simonoseki—in which the Netherlands joined England,

10. Shimonoseki.

11. Johannes van Vloten (1818–1883). Historian, critic, free thinker, and prolific writer. A preacher's son with a doctorate in theology. Received international attention for his studies on Spinoza. He advocated a practical humanism. He lived in Haarlem after 1876, and his wife, Elizabeth Gennep, was De Coningh's cousin, so De Coningh probably knew Van Vloten personally.

France and America with a squadron of four ships, and it became known to our people that our quarter of the indemnity imposed on Japan would amount to about two million. Until now only our business and industry had been important in Japan, but now it was popular, indeed people were overjoyed, because the matter had turned out to be an excellent speculation: the ships were already in service there anyway. We joined the bombardment and got two million for it.

Certainly we would expect no less from our navy, which had done her duty well at Simonoseki. But without the two million, this affair would certainly have made much less of an impression.

For a moment, a discordant note sounded softly over the two million. Advised by two skilled lawyers, some two dozen of our top houses in the trade and industrial sectors, which had suffered great losses from the unstable situation in Japan, approached the Government in a most discreet consultation. They argued it was crystal-clear they, and not the State, had suffered damage as a result of all that had happened in Japan and demanded a *small* part of the *great sum* that had been paid by Japan as compensation, not as war booty.

The *beati possedentes*[12] were nevertheless preserved. Our legal council made fair progress several times with a conservative Ministry; the following liberal Ministry adhered to the most conservative principles as far as the two million was concerned. In short, the compensation found a place in the country's great treasure chest, and our industry and trade had to bear their own damages.

Naturally not a soul had a thought for the handful of Spartans who, unprotected, had maintained their Thermopilae[13] in 1859–1860; had they been routed the whole treaty business would have been a waste of time. And the good people of the Netherlands, who, if one hoisted a petard here or there, would willingly remain to look and shout "Beautiful! beautiful!", entertained themselves for a while with thoughts of the two million, sang the tune from *Piet Hein en de zilveren vloot*,[14] called our

12. Blessed possessions.
13. This battle took place in 480 BCE. The Spartans were greatly outnumbered by the Persians but temporarily managed to stave off defeat.
14. *Piet Hein and the Silver Fleet*. Refers to Pieter Pietersen Heyn (November 25, 1577–June 18, 1629). A privateer in the West India Company, in the Eighty Years War he captured enough silver to finance the Dutch army for eight months. The lyrics were written by J. P. Heije and the melody by J. J. Viotta. It went:

Heb je wel gehoord van de zilveren vloot,	Have you heard of the Silver Fleet
De zilveren vloot van Spanje?	The Silver Fleet of Spain

position in Japan a "meddlesome business," and without any further ado let God's water run over God's Acre.

And yet my good, small, dear fatherland went in the wrong direction when, in Japan, it sought its glory in the laurels of battle, vain titles, and ribbons, without showing the least concern for our industry, our trade and our shipping.

They were forgotten, those sources of wealth for many, to stroke the vanity of a few. It was as if they were so intoxicated by the glory of the moment, they forgot the only ends that can justify violence: "after the torch of war, the work is peace." But the latter remained neglected; the commodity "glory" rose but the dollar remained depreciated. So it remained a grave sorrow for many, yet sweet for a few. The days of yore were long gone when the first concern of our fathers to the east of the Cape after Mars had roared, was devoted to the investigation of how the followers of Mercury settled in a new country could serve the wealth of patria.[15] In our day the diplomat still spoke after the cannon.

So our military power steamed from the chastised city back to Yokohama. After Cannae followed Capua;[16] after the racket of the Simonoseki battle came the festive clink of our diplomat's goblets; after the gun smoke had cleared and the destruction was over, the Political Agent indulged, with lively joy, in the most exquisite meals and other sweet pleasures that his hospitable home could create.

A celebratory mood rightly prevailed among our land and sea authorities after attaining this triumph. Yet none of them suffered the pressure under which trade languished for so long by the state of war; none of them were burdened by the gross depreciation of the dollar; on the contrary, the privilege granted to exchange great amounts for the full silver value gave

---

Die had er veel Spaanse matten aan boord,	There were many Spanish sailors on board
En appeltjes van Oranje.	Little Apples from Orange [refers to Dutch Province of Orange]
Piet Hein!, Piet Hein!	Piet Hein!, Piet Hein!,
Piet Hein, zijn naam is klein,	Piet Hein his name is little
Zijn daden benne groot,	His deeds are great
Zijn daden benne groot:	His deeds are great
Hij heeft gewonnen de Zilveren Vloot,	He won the Silver Fleet
die heeft gewonnen, gewonnen de Zilveren Vloot,	He won won the Silver Fleet
die heeft gewonnen de Zilvervloot.	He won the Silver Fleet

15. Mars is the god of war, Mercury a god of trade. A comment on colonialism.
16. Cannae was a major victory for an outnumbered Hannibal in 216 BCE.

them advantages not to be scorned. It thus gives me real pleasure to be able to assert that the campaign to Japan bore delicious fruit for many. On the other hand, it gives me great sorrow that a few of these gentlemen, who held the highest positions on land and at sea in Japan, later gave disadvantageous advice as "official experts" in their memorials on trade as a concession for past war losses, out of the compensation of two million. After all, it is no wonder that the "official experts," based on their own prior experiences, claimed it would have been ridiculous to speak of past damages in Japan! Rather, these "experts" gave the concerned minister the same report as the spies sent to the Promised Land in the time of Moses and Aaron. Indeed, in the Book of Numbers, we are told that the spies returned to the camp of the Israelites, and pointing to the sweet grapes they had plucked in the Promised Land announced their findings to the gathered worthies: "We have come to that land where you sent us, and, indeed, it is one where milk and honey flow, and this is its fruit."*

Of all the endeavors I have just listed and while the combined fleets remained in Yokohama as a show of strength, the representatives of England, France, America and the Netherlands took the opportunity to conclude a dollar-peace with Japan that boiled down to Japan paying an indemnity of three million dollars (about eight million Dutch guilders). Of the two million that was the Netherlands' share, it was calculated that after about three and a half tons of gold was deducted for war costs, there was a nice net profit of sixteen and a half tons of gold. The Japanese were better off paying this compensation; for them it amounted to nothing more than a small portion of the millions they'd "skimmed" from the dollar trade, and through many other means, into their own coffers.

With this agreement, the affair was over. The state received money, the navy gained her laurels, and the political agent received the higher title of Minister-Resident by which he was elevated to "Excellency." Behold our success through the bombardment of Simonoseki.

*So it was in the days of dollar exchange for a Consul, who grabbed at the stream of silver as if he was in the mines of Potosi [Bolivia.] This darling child of fortune was also a lucky duck in getting ranks and titles outside of our Consulate. Three or four other small European states who later signed treaties with Japan, deemed it not worth the trouble to send their own Consul because their citizens had little to do with that country. Our man exchanged his thousand dollars each month as Consul of the Netherlands then he began working with a thousand dollars for each of his darlings: e.g. Switzerland, Portugal, Denmark, Norway or whatever country it was. In short, except for the trouble of tallying, he enjoyed an exchange windfall of 2,000 dollars—say ƒ5,000 or ƒ6,000 a month. Poor Holland! It would cause extreme distress to pay your envoys to London, Paris or Berlin half of what the benevolent goodwill of the Japanese gave to your diplomat, who made good on his titles.

But for all the powder shot, the pointed bullets, and the Bourbon grenades,[17] the new trade we obtained was as good as nothing. There was no reduction of taxes, no freer movement, no opening of more ports, no better currency regulation—nothing of the sort; it was as if the muzzles of the drawn cannons had only been aimed at the Japanese purse. Alas! It seemed that the negotiating diplomats cared only for dollars, and that father Hieronymus van Alphen[18] had sung for them in vain:

What is wealth? What is honor?
A handful of insignificant mud[19]

"Give money!" Those were the terms of peace for the Japanese: "Give dollars, many dollars, three million dollars, because 'that is the question!'"

Nevertheless, all that money and glory was not enough to help Dutch trade, which still suffered under lawlessness. After all, this did not matter to you, as your vanity was stroked by those, such as the *Japan*

17. Bullets used to be round. Elongated bullets were invented in the 1820s but not adopted until mid-century. Bourbon grenades were invented by Charles de Bourbon.

18. Attorney and poet of moral poems for children (1746–1803).

19. De ware rijkdom

Geen geld bekore ons jong gemoed,
Maar heiligheid en deugd.
De wijsheid is het noodigst goed;
Het sieraad van de jeugd.

Wat is toch rijkdom? wat is eer?
Een handvol nietig slijk.
Gods vriend te wezen is veel meer;
Die Jesus lieft, is rijk.

Komt vallen we onzen God te voet
Om deugd en heiligheid:
Zo wordt op aarde ons jong gemoed
Ten hemel voorbereid.

Dan krijgen wij dien besten schat,
Die nimmermeer vergaat.
Dan loopen wij op het deugdenpad,
En schrikken van het kwaad.

[*Proeve van Kleine Gedigten voor Kinderen*, 1779]

Herald—an English newspaper that had come out in Yokohama a few years previous[20]—which repeatedly reported the *faits and gestes*[21] of "His Excellency The Netherland Majesty's Minister in Japan." Nor did it matter to the Netherlanders, good sports that they were, that he now and then drew the attention, which he had coming, of the humorous *Japan Punch*,[22] with its witty drawings depicting their highest authority as braggart "viveur,"[23] and made light at his expense. But their now higher titled head, who had risen, since 1859, from assistant on Decima to his present position, and thus must be an exceptional man, could have, had he so wished, worked earnestly to improve the legal situation of his countrymen in Japan. It is possible that he made remonstrances to our government on these matters, but it is certain that nothing came of it for many years thereafter. He was still acting Consul, but within half a dozen years he accomplished what was so difficult for many: reaching the highest rung on the officials' ladder. He, more than any other, should have known that without legal protections, Japanese trade would be run into the ground.

Here is an example, from the first year after the opening, of our dispensation of justice and how obliquely it was resolved. In 1859 and 1860, there were about twenty-five of us Netherlanders in Yokohama, and now and then small squabbles arose between us, that annoyed the young consul. "You know what," he said at last, "we will make up a list and set up a court." The list was made and posted against the wooden wall of the consular bureau on the public street. On the days court was in session we all gathered there; one person acted as judge for the moment, and another of us sat as defendant. On the many quarrels and disturbances, judgments were pronounced and fines imposed that were never executed or paid. Fortunately Mr. De Witt, our then Commissioner-General on Decima came to know, one way or another, that we in Yokohama were busy sentencing each other to the galleys or the poorhouse, and the result was that one fine day our court was unceremoniously disbanded, with instructions to toss its sentences in the wastebasket.

Unfortunately, nothing better came in its place, because henceforth the outcome of judgments on all questions was left to the consul. Things dragged on in this way for a few years but it must be said that in the

20. Commenced publication in November of 1861 by Albert William Hansard.

21. Accomplishments and tales.

22. Published by Charles Wirgman in Yokohama from 1862 to 1867.

23. Reveler or pleasure-seeker.

days of prosperity things were pretty quiet; it is a truth that men are not quarrelsome when things go well for them, and are, as a rule, honest as long as their money chest remains filled with dollars.

But the golden time, when each could live in his fleshpot of wealth, sped quickly to an end, and by the days when the dollar-peace was concluded, the prosperous years were passed. Yet, surprisingly, the number of Netherlanders established and employed in Japan increased. If there was ever time to take matters forcefully in hand and demand a sound rule of law for our countrymen, it was just after the peace was made because then our treasury was stocked with dollars from Japan. They had cash in hand and need not consider any costs. After all everyone knows: "Wo du nicht bis, Herr Organist."[24] Not even a national government can always make improvements, but in these circumstances the usual official denial that "there as yet were no grounds, and no measures had proved necessary" were not at all applicable.

In my opinion it would have been desirable for the government, which itself urged our traders in the open ports of Japan in 1859 to establish business there or take part in trade with that country by sending our manufactured products there, at the same time to have ensured the legal safety of her subjects. What merchant, what industrialist would dare in the long run to risk dispatching a quantity of goods to a country where there was no other guarantee of the faithful representation of his interests than an unqualified belief in human decency? Who would dare send thousands of dollars for the purchase of silk, tea or other products to a land where a disloyal accountant could, if he decided to reward himself, appropriate it without being troubled by a judiciary or police? Let the people of our day in Europe in a bustling commercial city experiment but once by throwing Themis[25] out the door, conducting all market, trade, and exchange business, all the sacred rights of ownership, outside the protection of the law and left to the honest conscience of civilization. Then one could see how much injustice is lurking in Adam's offspring.

In the beginning, our countrymen in Japan compared favorably to other nationalities. But alas! I know many examples of how some went

24. . . . . du schweigen all flöten. "Where you are, Organist, the flutes are all silent." From the hymn "Herr Jesu Christ mein Fleisch und Blut," by Erdmann Neumeister (1671–1756). Published in 1700 in *Geistliche Cantaten statt einer Kirchen-Music* ("Sacred Cantatas in Place of Liturgical Music"). An expression meaning "Where in the devil are you," but in this case De Coningh is suggesting concerted action is required.

25. Greek Titaness who represents proper procedure or social order.

bad through lack of law and punishment. Certainly the early years of prosperity made luxury a part of life which some, in the days of adversity, had no desire to rein in, preferring to maintain it at the cost of the trust others still had in them. And so Yokohama more than once proved to be a Danaïden[26] vessel, in which all could be thrown in but nothing could be taken out. Many disappeared through the bottom, enriched with silver, sustained by the full enjoyment of life, once honest hearts that had succumbed to past impunity. Men did not go bankrupt there; they played the part of "a grand Seigneur" in life as long as the supply lasted. If it stopped, they would disappear to California or China, often lingering for a short-lived existence as a *mauvais sujet*[27] in the drinking dens of Yokohama.

So there it was; but it need not have been the case if the courts and laws of our nation had curbed their transgressions in time. Was it any wonder that under such conditions those who first eagerly began businesses in Japan would later withdraw, one after the other, often after the most bitter experiences, from the chaos of lawlessness?

Who is to blame? It was the Consuls, young men who had come to Japan as assistants or mercantile employees and therefore, by the nature of their occupations, had never been concerned with the legal concepts of our fatherland. They always sought these functionaries on site, and by so doing could have officers without pay, merely by bestowing a title. We have already proved how strong this tendency to take care of everything through the award of a title was. We have seen how, starting with a title change, in six years an assistant can be made into a Minister. Certainly in this way they saved themselves a lot, because they obtained the representation of a senior official in a distant land by telegraph as it were, and so not a penning disappeared from the country's treasury for travel and moving costs. Yet conversely, we cannot deny a few drawbacks to this arrangement. The ascending functionary could only be known, more or less, through his political writings; otherwise we knew not whether in him slumbered the spirit of a Colbert, or Pombal or Pitt,[28] or if the

26. The fifty daughters of Danos were called Danaïde. Forty-nine of them killed their husbands and in the underworld were made to fill a vessel that leaked and thus would never be filled.

27. Bad character.

28. **Jean Baptiste Colbert** (1619–1683). Minister of finance to Louis XIV of France. Managed to offset the lavish expenditures by the throne. Believed in mercantilism, and formed many policies to maintain a favorable balance of trade known as *Colbertisme*. **Sebestião José de Carvalho e Melo,** Marquis de Pombal (1699–1782).

ideas of the East Asians, which had surrounded him since he became an adult, had the upper hand in his feelings. I propose that this is the great drawback, both literally and figuratively, of a telegraphic promotion.

For half a dozen years the lives of our authorities in Japan were strewn with gold, silver and luxury, but it was very different after 1865, and the consuls appointed since have really had a very difficult task. When the erstwhile celebrated dollar exchange was still going, I don't deceive myself, they did not enjoy a salary, only the honor, yet they had a mission from which many lawyers would have recoiled. At this time Netherlanders in Yokohama were numerous but of various calibers, and the Consul had not only to handle the administration of extremely inferior elements, but also to maintain order among these dregs. Indeed, this was no easy task, because he wielded no judicial authority; I believe he did not have a single complete instruction. Among the good Netherlanders— our peaceful, trading countrymen, who were settled as citizens of their own freeholds and who conducted important business in and outside of Japan—questions frequently came up in matters of trade, exchange, freehold, ownership, and mortgage rights that required the knowledge of a jurist. Then there was notarial business that arose as a matter of course in a European society that existed through its civilization and industry: transfers, wills, deeds from all areas, etc. As for the concerns of those of low caliber—deserted sailors, debauched gentlemen and so forth—these sometimes went so far with their scandals and fights that a police commissioner of our great cities would have reeled from them. On all these matters, the Consul alone had to try and reach compromises without knowledge of the law or judicial authority; thus his position was nothing to be envious of.

No wonder that someone who had to intervene in so many different affairs and issue judgments to the best of his knowledge, sometimes fell short in his legal and notarial expertise. It was therefore a pity that the State did nothing in thirteen years to ensure that its citizens had an adequate legal position according to our laws. Indeed, if the worst happened, one could simply say that the Netherlanders in Japan stood outside the law and were handled at the individual discretion of the Consuls. To my mind, it would have been magnanimous of the State, which in name cared for the administration of its citizens in distant

---

Held a variety of political posts under King Joseph of Portugal, effecting significant changes such as the abolition of slavery and encouraging industry by favoring monopolies. **William Pitt,** First Earl of Chatham (1708–1778). Prime minister who led England to victory during the Seven Years War.

lands, to take the responsibility when an unpaid diligent servant, from whom so much was demanded, lacking instruction, had erred in good faith. If all a State had to do was have its citizens maintain authority and was certain that they would maintain their laws, then it might just as well, along the lines of Gesner[29] with his Swiss, be satisfied with hoisting their consular caps on the Dutch flagpole in Yokohama.

Oh ye, who in the days of surplus, so often bemoaned how little was done for the poor in Java,[30] allow me too a plaint, that not a single penning of the surplus of two million benefited the poor Netherlanders who had no rights in Yokohama! And yet, just as crumbs from the rich man's table revived Lazarus, likewise a small part of the great treasure for a Dutch legal administration in Japan would have gladdened the Netherlanders who yearned for it.

In an open trade port like Yokohama, a prominent merchant appointed as Consul always received proper respect but since he was granted jurisdiction, he should have been granted a well-paid, young and reliable jurist to give help and guidance in legal knowledge, titled, for example, Chancellor. Then, under the chairmanship and secretariat of the Consul and his Chancellor, a consular court could have been composed from our most respectable citizens to adjudicate all our recurring affairs according to our laws. Absent would have been the disloyal bookkeepers, non-paying renters, arbitrary money-changers and any such of the kind of people who, known as "franc-tireurs"[31] of another's purse, always flourished in Yokohama; they could have been summoned to appear before the consular court to be ordered constrained or punished as circumstances demanded. And then too, "last but not least," a steamship 4th class—a "gunboat" as the English call it—should have been stationed in the roadstead, so that it could have served as a "strong arm" to be invoked by the Consul to ensure respect for the court's decisions. Without such a "strong arm," sentences might be passed but no one would heed them. Had they been of the mind to provide some legal oversight in lives of the Netherlanders in Yokohama immediately after the dollar-peace, for many absentees it would have forestalled great

29. Probably refers to Salomon Gessner (1730–1788), a founder of the reformist Helvetic Society, which advanced ideals of political egalitarianism and patriotism.

30. An oblique reference to *Max Havelaar* (1860) by Multatuli, the pen-name for Eduard Douwes Dekker (1820–1887). The semi-autobiographical novel is critical of Dutch administration in the Netherlands Indies.

31. Snipers, but also used to refer to guerilla warfare, and in this case people who operate outside the rules.

losses, and the fear of legal punishment would have kept many good-for-nothings in check, who otherwise made good sport with their absentee dupes.

But above all, "the strong arm" of the Consul should not have been wanting because demoralization had greatly increased from years of wealth and impunity. Inasmuch as I can give a few statistics on the Dutch element, for more than a dozen years in Yokohama, as far as I can recall, it consisted of the following: one part was brave, law abiding men; the rest was people whose honesty was highly questionable, some drunken rabble, and one murderer.

Let us hope that a better legal administration has been established for our countrymen in Japan, and that the sad story that I have had to tell belongs to the past for good.

I have shown above how we quickly lost our influence because of the predilection of our Commissar-Generals for the old Opperhoofd-heaven Decima; how through lawlessness our trade declined and how our squadron at the time returned home after obtaining a booty of two million without letting those in Patria know anything more of our position in Japan or ever showing the flag of our warships there again.

Yet there are many Netherlanders, and many more will still go to that fertile land, with its beautiful natural environment and sound climate, to test their luck in various ventures. So then, the Netherlands should not forget its natives and take care not to alienate them—for now, more than ever, we are casting our lot beyond our Indies Archipelago. For more than two centuries we were the first everywhere; let us now guard against being the last. The world is wide enough, our vigorous young men must go abroad instead of struggling by the hundreds to stay alive by clinging to the posts of their native soil. But—a citizen of a country that possesses naval officers as capable as those of the best maritime power in the world does not have a license for ignorance outside of her colonies.

We must also trust that there will still be a place in modern Japan for many more of our countrymen, and the blame will not rest on us because we, through mistaken policies, are not on friendlier terms. I traveled boldly, for twenty years, as a pioneer in lands that were then unknown. I have written frankly my opinion of how we fell short, so that one may see clearly how, through indifference, we went from the first to the last.

INDEX

Shanghai, xxxi, 29, 77, 78, 83,
  85, 102, 121, 128, 146
Shimonoseki [Simonoseki], xx,
  xxi, xxxii, 149, 150, 151, 152
Shobber, Mr. [Raphael Schoyer],
  108–13
Shobber, Mrs. [Anna Schoyer],
  109–110, 139
silk, xvii, 80, 86, 96, 140, 143,
  145, 155
Simmons, Dr. Duane B., 113,
  114, 115
smugglers, 76, 77, 78, 79, 80
Spuyter, Jan, xxii, 62–65, 68–72,
  73–74, 81–83, 92, 96, 98–102

Tollens, Hendrik, 127
Tourniquet, Monsieur, 124
typhoon, xxxi, xxxii, 10, 59, 141,
  143, 144, 145

Vernede, A., xviii, xix
Vloten, Dr. J. van, xxiii, 149

warehouse, xviii, 8, 10, 14, 22,
  33, 44, 45, 46, 76, 84, 91, 92,

111, 112, 115, 117, 118, 125,
  127, 142, 143, 144, 145
Witt, J. K. de, 141, 154

Yankees, 60, 95
Yokohama, xiv, xvi, xvii, xviii, xix,
  xx, xxi, xxiv, xxv, xxxi, xxxii,
  4, 29, 34, 35, 36, 37, 40, 41,
  42, 43, 44, 45, 46, 47, 49, 51,
  57, 59, 60, 61, 62, 75, 76, 78,
  79, 80, 84, 87, 88, 89, 90, 91,
  94, 95, 96, 101, 102, 13, 106,
  107, 108, 109, 111, 112, 113,
  115, 116, 117, 118, 119, 121,
  122, 127, 131, 132, 135, 138,
  139, 141, 144, 145, 146, 147,
  148, 151, 152, 154, 156, 157,
  158, 159
Yokohama Hotel, 112, 119, 121,
  122, 129, 130, 132, 133, 135,
  136, 138
Yokohama Volunteers, xxxi, 124,
  126, 128, 137
Yoshio Sakunojō [Saknozio], xiii,
  20, 21